The

RHINO
KEEPERS

THE RHINO KEEPERS

Clive & Anton
Walker

JACANA

Note

A percentage of proceeds from the sale of the book will be donated to the Waterberg Museum Foundation's Rhino Programme, which focuses on the re-establishment of the Rhino Museum and its associated education and awareness programme.

First published by Jacana Media (Pty) Ltd
First and second impression 2012

10 Orange Street
Sunnyside
Auckland Park 2092
South Africa
+2711 628 3200
www.jacana.co.za

© Clive & Anton Walker, 2012

All rights reserved.

ISBN 978-1-4314-0423-0

Set in Sabon 10.5/15pt
Job No. 001776
Printed and bound by Ultra Litho
(Pty) Ltd Johannesburg

See a complete list of Jacana titles at
www.jacana.co.za

Dedicated to the memory of
Dale 'Rapula' Parker
and
Blythe Loutit and Mike Hearn

Contents

Note to
the Reader

MY SON ANTON AND I collaborated in the writing of this book. Although
the text was written together, we have chosen to use the first person
singular throughout the book.

The word 'rhinoceros' is derived from the Greek words ῥῖνο (rhin),
referring to nose, and κέρας (keras), meaning horn, hence 'nose horn'.
The plural can be rhinoceri, rhinoceroses, rhinoceroi or, in our case,
rhinoceros. Rhinoceros, with due respect, becomes a bit of a mouthful
after continual use, however, and as they are generally known as rhinos,
this is the term we will use henceforth.

Prologue

My rhino journey began in 1956 in the library of my mentor, Hans Bufe, while looking at black-and-white photographs of hunting expeditions in what was then part of Northern Rhodesia and is now Zambia's Luangwa Valley. A section of the reserve was set aside as a controlled hunting area in 1951 at the instigation of the late Norman Carr, who was the warden at the time, with ensuing benefits going to the relevant local tribal authorities. Carr's proposal was unique at the time and in addition to game species such as lion, elephant and buffalo, one could take a trophy black rhino on licence, at a price. One of the photographs depicted a dead black rhino with a game scout standing smartly to attention behind the fallen animal. Hans, an accomplished big-game hunter, was of German descent and had accompanied an Austrian count on safari as companion and interpreter. The black rhino was common in the valley at the time and no one considered the possibility that the species could become extinct throughout Zambia in the not too distant future.

My second encounter was in Kenya's Tsavo National Park in 1960, which was home to no fewer than 9,000 black rhino. From Poacher's Lookout I counted ten black rhinos in the shade of the thorn trees below with Mount Kilimanjaro rising in the distance. The irony of the name was to prove prophetic as poachers eventually succeeded in killing every rhino in the park.

At an International Union for Conservation of Nature (IUCN) rhino and elephant conference in Tsavo 20 years later, it was revealed that the population of black rhino throughout Africa had plunged from 100,000 to less than 15,000. Suddenly everyone was very concerned.

I had, by this stage, already come face to face with both black and white rhinos in Zululand while on a wilderness trail, and in 1973 I founded the Endangered Wildlife Trust (EWT). I had more than a passing interest in the plight of black rhinos after meeting members of the Natal Parks Board field staff, led by Ian Player and the likes of Peter Hitchins, who were to awaken a deep sense of awe in an animal that had a very bad, and misunderstood, reputation.

From 1973 to the present my family has been swept up in the world of both black and white rhinos in Africa. The work of the EWT, and that of the Rhino & Elephant Foundation (REF), which was founded by Dr Anthony Hall-Martin, Peter Hitchins and myself in1987, has played a significant role in protecting both rhino species. The establishment of Lapalala Wilderness in the Waterberg in the Limpopo province, by Dale Parker and myself in 1981, was especially significant as it was the first-ever private black rhino sanctuary in South Africa. My son Anton grew up at Lapalala, which became his second home from the age of 12, and today manages the 36,000-hectare rhino sanctuary. The reserve is a testament to the passion and commitment of the late owner, Dale 'Rapula' Parker, who often remarked that 'rhino conservation was not for the faint-hearted'.

The founding of the Lapalala Wilderness School allowed thousands of children to come face to face with a black rhino whose nursery was in our backyard. Karen Trendler hand-raised the calf, named Bwana, until he was six months of age. His care was then taken over by my wife, Conita Walker, who succeeded in raising him to adulthood when he became South Africa's first 'rhino ambassador'. Bwana was followed by a white rhino calf, a hippo and a female black rhino calf, named Moeng. Sadly, Moeng was brutally slain by poachers at the age of four at the commencement of the current rhino crisis. Metsi, a black rhino male who was also under Conita's care at the time, survived the attack.

There is a great deal of scientific and technical literature devoted to the rhino, far more than you may imagine, and this book is not intended to add to this already well-researched body of academic work. Rhinos have not enjoyed the popularity of lions or elephants, however, and this is reflected in the unfortunate shortage of rhino books that are accessible to the general reader. This book, therefore, is an account of my own personal exploration and experiences of rhinos and will explore its journey since before the first Europeans arrived at the foot of Africa. While it is not a scientific work, I have made every effort to ensure that the biological and other information is accurate. I have tried to be as objective as possible and in no way intend to offend, anger or disturb anyone. I hope, at least, that the book will help to clear up some misunderstandings, raise pertinent questions, look at both sides of the story and stimulate thought and debate about how best to ensure the long-term survival of the rhino.

My journey has not been undertaken alone, and I have been privileged to travel with some amazing people, all of whom I consider to be 'rhino keepers'. These are the scientists, game rangers, wildlife managers, guides, field rangers, journalists, artists, conservationists (a conservationist, in this context, is anyone who is passionate about nature, and can be a school teacher, plumber, school kid or even, on rare occasions, politicians), wilderness walkers and hunters (although not all hunters, mind you) whose contributions, whether large or small, have helped to protect the rhino.

Several very well-known personalities, not to mention the countless unknown, all share the same interest in saving the rhino. The exception to this rule is the poacher and the faceless millions of consumers of rhino horn who know little about this extraordinary animal and probably have no idea what it even looks like. This book offers no silver-bullet solution to the rhino problem, but seeks rather to convey the reasons why I believe these amazing creatures are worthy of our highest respect and protection.

It is once again five minutes to midnight for the world's surviving rhino, and we all know that the clock is ticking. Once they are gone, they will be gone forever. The choice is ours. Should you read this book, keep an open mind and heed the words of the great American poet Walt Whitman who said, 'You must not know too much, or be too precise or scientific about birds and trees and flowers. A certain free margin . . . helps your enjoyment of these things'.

Clive and Anton Walker
Islands, October 2011

List of Acronyms

AfRSG – African Rhino Specialist Group
AROA – African Rhino Owners Association
AsRSG – Asian Rhino Specialist Group
CITES – Convention on International Trade in Endangered Species
   of Wild Fauna and Flora
CoP – Conference of the Parties
DEA – Department of Water and Environmental Affairs
DSWF – David Shepherd Wildlife Foundation
ESPU – Endangered Species Protection Unit
EWE – Educational Wildlife Expeditions
EWT – Endangered Wildlife Trust
GRAA – Game Rangers Association of Africa
IRF – International Rhino Foundation
IUCN – International Union for Conservation of Nature
NPA – National Prosecuting Authority
NPB – Natal Parks Board
NWCRU – National Wildlife Crime Reaction Unit
NWT – Namibian Wildlife Trust
PROA – Private Rhino Owners Association
REF – Rhino & Elephant Foundation
RMG – Rhino Management Group (of the SADC)
SADC – Southern African Development Community
SAHGCA – South African Hunters and Game Conservation
   Association

SANF – South African Nature Foundation
SANParks – South African National Parks
SAVE – Save Africa's Endangered Wildlife
SRI – Save the Rhino International
SRT – Save the Rhino Trust
SSC – Species Survival Commission (of the IUCN)
TRAFFIC – Trade Records Analysis of Flora and Fauna in Commerce
WESSA – Wildlife and Environment Society of South Africa
WRSA – Wildlife Ranching South Africa
WWF – World Wide Fund for Nature

CHAPTER 1

The Flight of the Unicorn

THE UNICORN WAS FIRST mentioned by the ancient Greeks in what was to become Europe, not in their mythology but in their accounts of natural history. The earliest description of a unicorn is perhaps from the Greek physician Ctesias in 416 BC. Both Aristotle (384–322 BC) and Pliny (AD 23–79) were convinced of its existence and believed that 'like the rhino, the unicorn was endowed with enormous strength, but this was concentrated in its single horn'. Some 500 years after Aristotle, the Roman scholar and teacher of rhetoric, Aelian, mentions the unicorn on several occasions in his 17-volume *On the Nature of Animals*. This mystical creature later became an important symbol in both the Middle Ages and the Renaissance period and was described as an extremely wild creature, possessed of purity and grace. Even the genius of Leonardo da Vinci (1452–1519), writing in one of his notebooks, was taken in by the belief: 'The unicorn, through its temperance and not knowing how to control itself, for the love it bears to fair maidens forgets its ferocity and wildness, and laying aside all fear it will go up to a seated damsel and go to sleep on its lap, and thus the hunters take it'. The one thing that Da Vinci got right was the unicorn's wildness, and it can certainly be ferocious.

We know that medieval knowledge and belief often stemmed from ancient Biblical sources that reference the unicorn on a number of occasions. Kelly Enright, in her excellent work entitled *Rhinoceros*, places it perfectly into context: 'The Greek translation of the Hebrew Bible (second century) translates re'em as "monoceros" or single-horned. In the Latin Vulgate Bible, the main version used from 400 through to 1400 CE, re'em, or monoceros was translated to "unicornis", the Latin word for single horn'.

As Latin was the official language of the church, *unicornis* became the accepted word and took on the meaning as evidenced in Numbers 24:8, 'He hath as it were the strength of a unicorn' and again in Isaiah 34:7, 'And the unicorns shall come down with them, and the bullocks with their bulls: and their land shall be soaked with blood'. In Job 39:9–11 we perceive another element, 'Will the unicorn be willing to serve thee, or abide by thy crib? Canst thou bind the unicorn with his band in the furrow? Or will he harrow the valleys after thee? Wilt thou trust him, because his strength is great?'

These Bible passages leave one with an impression of the unicorn as an animal possessed of immense strength and violence. Consider how far back these writings go. Numbers recounts the 40 years that the Israelites wandered in the desert after they left Mount Sinai. They had rebelled against God and his appointed man, Moses. Both Numbers and Isaiah conjure up a sense of great power and retribution for those who disobeyed. But perhaps the unicorn was also imbued with another property, as in Psalm 92:10, 'But my horn shalt thou exalt like the horn of a unicorn: I shall be anointed with fresh oil'. Perhaps we should leave the interpretation to more learned scholars.

There are so many legends attached to the origin of the unicorn that I would argue that the rhino should be considered a candidate for the honour. The popular portrayal, of course, is that of a beautiful white horse with a goat's beard and a large spiralling horn protruding from its forehead which could, apparently, only be captured by a virgin. Does it surprise anyone, therefore, that it is generally portrayed as such and certainly not in the likeness of a rhino?

Da Vinci had clearly never seen a unicorn, and neither had anyone else of his time until the return of the celebrated Venetian traveller Marco Polo. While travelling in Indonesia, in the 13th century, he described a unicorn as:

scarcely smaller than elephants. They have the hair of a buffalo and feet like an elephant's. They have a single black horn in the middle of the forehead . . . They have the head of a wild boar's. They spend their time by preference wallowing in mud and slime. They are ugly brutes to look at. They are not at all such as we describe them when we relate that they let themselves be captured by virgins, but clean to the contrary to our notions.

What Marco Polo had seen turned out to be a Javan rhino, which evidently did not fit his perception of a unicorn.

As so often with myths and legends, ideas are developed and passed down from one generation to another, one storyteller to another, one writer to another until they eventually take on a reality of their own. What starts off as a *myth* becomes in the end a *fact*. We know today that no such animal as a unicorn exists, and if by any chance the rhino can lay any claim to the origin of the legend, no virgin in her right frame of mind would go anywhere near one, especially not a black rhino. As a child, it was a great story, but as you grow older you realise that your local zoo, or for that matter any zoo, doesn't have one.

Right up to the beginning of the 19th century, a strong belief in the existence of the unicorn was widespread among writers, poets, historians, alchemists, physicians, theologians and no doubt a fair number of travellers.

In books on traditional Chinese medicine, beginning with the oldest, the *Shennong Ben Cao Jing* (attributed to the Chinese emperor Shennong, who lived around 2800 BC, it was only compiled into three written volumes in the late Warring States and Western Han periods from 475 BC to AD 9), rhino horn is classified as a cold drug, indicated for hot diseases and thus suitable for cooling the blood and counteracting toxins. In the poem 'Juan Er' from the *Shi Jing* (Book of Songs) it says 'Just for a moment, I pour from that rhino-horn cup, so as not to hurt forever'. This may be the first written evidence confirming the fact that by the Eastern Zhou Dynasty (770–221 BC) at the latest, the Chinese were using cups made out of rhino horn. That is more than 2,200 years ago. Another written reference to rhino horn is found in the *Hou Han Shu* (official dynastic history records) dating to the Xin Dynasty of Wang Mang (AD 9–23) where it is mentioned as an ingredient in a recipe for longevity.

So, because of the dramatic decline of the Chinese rhino population during the Eastern Zhou Dynasty, the Han were importing rhino horns by sea from Sumatra. By the Western Han period, rhino-horn cups were being buried with their owners, as they were deemed more valuable than jade. The rhino became mythical, and its horns came to be considered magical. Based on the power of their respective horns, images of Zhi, the mythical Chinese goat-unicorn, were transformed into mythical rhino-unicorns.

While the Western Han were conquering and colonising the south, the tide of human influence turned and began to flow mainly from the East to the West via the land routes of Central Asia and the developing maritime silk route, as traders of Mediterranean origin began to use the south-west monsoon winds to sail right through to southern India. Due to the nature of these trade winds, the merchants and traders had to remain ashore in southern India for several months before the turn of the winds. This had an enormous impact on later unicorn myths.

This southern India trade route was not only a conduit for spices, silks and other valuable goods such as rhino horn and elephant ivory, but also for stories and information. As stories of the mythical Chinese unicorn moved westward, they filtered through Indian culture and acquired new erotic and aesthetic aspects from the old Indian story of the gentle one-horned hermit Rishyasringa from the third volume of the *Mahabharata* written in about 400 BC. As such, certain aspects of the European unicorn myths, especially its gentleness and its supposedly easy capture by a maiden, were probably of Indian inspiration. So profoundly was the myth of the Chinese unicorn transformed by its passage through southern Indian culture that knowledge of its origin in China was gradually superseded.

The belief in the power of rhino horn as an aphrodisiac must have originated within the greater Indian sphere of influence. From ancient times in China, rhino horn was believed to serve the practical medical functions of lowering fevers and counteracting toxins, but people in the West somehow came to believe that rhino horn was used in China as an aphrodisiac. This idea is completely unfounded, as there is no mention of using rhino horn as an aphrodisiac in any texts on traditional Chinese medicine.

Rhino / unicorn horn acquired additional magical powers when Ge Hong (AD 283–343), best known for his interest in alchemy and techniques of longevity, wrote his *Baopuzi* (Book of the Master Who Embraces Simplicity). Rumours of these magical powers began to spread westward.

The horn of the narwhal (*Monodon monoceros*), which is actually a tooth and not a horn, came into China from the north-east Arctic seas as early as the Tang Dynasty (AD 618–907), and was used, like rhino horn, for medicine and for carving. Soon rhino horn and narwhal horn became linked due to their use as medicine and, as a result, narwhal horn acquired the magical aspects of rhino / unicorn horn. Knowledge of these magical qualities reached the Muslim world via the Turkic tribes of Central Asia, and by the early 11th century the Arabs had come to consider rhino horn and narwhal horn (which they called *khutu* and was carved to make their knife handles) as one and the same. During the 12th century, rumours about the magic of rhino / unicorn / narwhal horn spread to Europe from the Arab world, and images of unicorns with spiral horns began to appear in medieval European art.

While unicorns only exist in our imagination thanks to myth, legend, fairy tales, art and literature, rhinos still exist today. All rhinos belong to the mammalian order *Perissodactyla*, which comes from the Greek περισσός (perissós), meaning uneven or odd number, and δάκτυλος (dáktylos), meaning finger or toe. In other words they are odd-toed ungulates. Other extant *Perissodactyla* are tapirs and equids (horses, zebra, etc.). We know from the fossil record that the world's five

remaining rhino species were once widespread and numerous. Rhinos have been around for at least 50 million years. They appeared during a long series of geological time frames comprising three Periods and seven Epochs known as the Cenozoic Era. This Era, which we know as the Age of Mammals, began 65 million years ago.

Rhinos were once a diverse group of mammals ranging over a wide variety of ecosystems in North America, Europe, Asia and Africa, although they were never found in South America or Australia. The earliest rhinos had no horns and some were only the size of a dog. The largest and most spectacular, the *Paraceratherium*, also commonly known as the *Indricotherium*, stood 5.5 metres at the shoulder, was over 8 metres long with a 1.8-metre-long skull and weighed in at about 20 tons. To put it into perspective, that's more than the weight of three African bull elephants.

The woolly rhino (*Coelodonta antiquitatis*), a two-horned animal with the anterior horn measuring up to a metre long, was larger than today's white rhino (*Ceratotherium simum*), and was on average some 3.7 metres in length, around 2 metres tall and weighed 2–3 tons. The woolly rhino was well adapted to the steppe tundra, with short stocky limbs and a thick woolly coat, and first appeared in China about a million years ago, later spreading to Europe where it became common along with the woolly mammoth. With powerful neck muscles, it used its large horn to sweep aside the snow in order to eat the underlying vegetation. The long horn was comprised of keratin, as are the horns of rhinos today, and was likewise used as a defensive weapon. They were supremely well adapted to the cold climate of northern Eurasia and the arid desert regions of southern England and western Siberia. We know that the woolly rhino was observed by humans, as they are depicted in the cave art of Europe dating back, in one case, some 30,000 years.

In the valley of Ardeche in France, set in a limestone cliff above the former bed of the river of the same name, is the Chauvet Cave. The cave was only explored in December of 1994 and it revealed the most stunning examples of early cave art, depicting cave lions, mammoths, bison, cave bears, horses and the most superbly executed woolly rhinos. While it has never been my good fortune to see these depictions, they have been described as exceptional both in quality, condition and quantity – 53 of the images are of woolly rhinos. Chauvet and the other caves of Europe surely rank as the world's first known art galleries, dating back to the Upper Paleolithic (Late-Stone Age). Although artistic creation may not have been the original inhabitants' intention, who is to say the creators were not a little satisfied with their handiwork. In my opinion, as an artist rather than a scientist, they are breathtaking in both their line and form.

In 1940, a cave was discovered near the village of Montignac in France by four teenage boys, Marcel Ravidat, Jacques Marsal, Georges Agnel and Simon Coencas, as well as Robot, Marcel's dog. What they had stumbled upon was beyond their wildest imagination, for within its vast, pitch-black interior the caves were to reveal some of the best known Upper Paleolithic art ever found in Europe. Some of the artworks had been incised into the stone, but most had been painted using mineral pigments. The paintings of the Lascaux Caves, which are estimated at being over 17,000 years old, comprise some 2,000 images of which 605 have been precisely identified. Of the images, 364 are equines and among a collection of other images are seven felines, a bird, a bear, one human being and one rhino. The most stunning images are of four huge black bulls – one is 5.2 metres long, making it the largest animal cave art known. The black bulls, or more correctly aurochs (*Bos primigenius*), now a long-extinct giant ox, are known from the fossil record to have lived in the region and are the dominant feature among the 36 other animal species to be found in 'The Great Hall of the Bulls'. It is believed that the aurochs were driven to extinction by man.

Another Asian species, the giant unicorn rhino, (*Elasmotherium*) or thin-plate beast, stood over 2 metres high at the shoulder, up to 6 metres long, weighed 5 tons and had an enormous single horn, up to 2 metres long. They first appear in the fossil record some 2.6 million years ago. This long-legged rhino displayed horse-like behaviour and occupied the steppes of Siberia. So, *Elasmotherium* may be the only species of (now extinct) rhino known to early humans that can lay claim to the title of unicorn as it resembled a horse and had a single large horn on its forehead. Apart from one image in the Rouffignac Cave in France, no extensive cave art exists to reveal what it may have looked like. We have to rely on the reconstructed form based on the fossil remains and the written record of one medieval traveller by the name of Ahmad ibn Fadlan. He set out from Baghdad in June AD 921, as the secretary of an ambassador, destined for the towns of the Bulghars at the three lakes of the Volga. His journey was both illuminating and hazardous and upon eventually reaching the Volga River in May AD 922, he wrote:

> Near the river [the Volga] is a vast wilderness wherein they say is an animal that is less than a camel and more like a bull in size. Its head is like a camel, and its tail is like the tail of a bull. In the centre of its head it has a thick horn, which as it rises from the head of the animal gets to be thinner until it becomes like the point of a lance . . . I saw in the king's house three large bowls which looked like [they were made of] the onyx of Yemen. The king informed me that it was made from the base of the horn of the animal. Some of the people of the country told me that it was a rhinoceros.

Elasmotherium and the woolly rhino both died out about 10,000 years ago. Apart from possible climatic change, although their extinction does not coincide with the end of the last ice age, the woolly rhino, the *Elasmotherium* and the woolly mammoth were, in all probability, bundled into extinction by humans.

The *Liber de Spectaculis* (On the Spectacles) is dated to AD 80 and was written to celebrate the 100 days of games held by the Roman emperor Titus to inaugurate the Flavian Amphitheatre, or the Colosseum as we know it. Written by the poet Martial, it gives a complete account of what was intended as an illustration of Titus's power and benevolence:

> Now while the rhinoceros is entertaining to observe, when undisturbed it is naturally diffident [shy] and seems to be a disappointing animal for the games. A strict vegetarian, in nature it attacks no other animal for food but is content to munch the placid shrub. This is not very promising for the arena. But the unexpected aspect of this preposterous

quadruped is its explosive anger and incredible power when annoyed. Its temper is uncertain: you might have to work at disturbing it, but when sufficiently provoked it attacks ferociously, propelling its tonnage at 30 miles per hour, an attack which hardly anything in nature can withstand, while bellowing a variety of frightening noises.

The expectant Roman audience could rely on the usual lion or bull or bear to maul, dismember and (save for the bull) devour its helpless victim, man or beast, with gratifying savagery. But the lion fled in terror from the rhino and the bear was tossed in the air like a bundle of straw. Martial notes that 'he lifted two steers with his mobile neck, to him yielded the fierce buffalo and the bison'. It is clear from Martial's vocabulary that the triumph of the rhino is emphatic: 'The rhinoceros has to be provoked, but once that is achieved nothing can withstand it and it puts on a wonderful show'.

Titus's games were not the first time the rhino had been included in the assortment of animals exhibited at inauguration games. A rhino was at the games of the Theatre of Pompey and Caesar Augustus exhibited one in the Saepta. But the rhino was always unfamiliar. Interestingly, back then, when Roman audiences were so jaded that they expected animals in any set of games to be slaughtered in their thousands, the rhino had an 'advantage over the other beasts' because it was 'so difficult to acquire, was expensive and put on such a good show'. It was therefore 'preserved to be produced publicly on more than one occasion'.

In Africa today, the black rhino has a reputation of being a particularly nasty customer and should be avoided at all costs if you are on foot and not intent on killing it. Some 19th-century hunters considered hunting it a 'tame affair' and placed little stock in it as a worthy trophy. Take the gun away from the same hunter and let him blunder about in the bush where black rhinos occur and it's very likely he will never want to set foot there ever again.

When it comes to the question of good looks, most people would agree that only a rhino could love another rhino. Considering that the unicorn is universally portrayed as a beautiful white horse, it's not surprising that the poor old rhino has had a bad PR rap and lost out to his equine opposition. Is it deserved? After all they are related. As to being good looking, well, rhinos have their moments. Nothing will arrest one's senses and focus one's attention more acutely than coming upon a black rhino in its own space when it is on its feet and facing you directly with head held up high, beady eye straining forward and ears twitching. While this is the perfect opportunity to decide for yourself on the rhino's aesthetics, you won't have much time to make up your mind. In this moment, two possibilities exist: the rhino will either give a sharp snort, about-turn and vanish, or it will give the same snort and you will discover very, very quickly what is meant by a bullet train. The options thereafter will be few. To me, that is true beauty and it has nothing to do with good looks.

While the first European-recorded rhino sighting in southern Africa dates back to 1647, the San left us an amazing record in rock-art depictions of primarily the black rhino, which they regarded as a 'heavy rain' animal, as well as the white rhino, which was regarded as a 'soft rain' animal. The largest concentrations of these painted forms are to be found within the Limpopo basin, south-western Zimbabwe, south-eastern Botswana and the Makabeng and Waterberg escarpments where I live. Traversing this beautiful region of mountains, sandstone and granite outcrops, deep incised krantzes, arid sandy plains supporting a diverse range of habitats from dry mopane woodland to dense riverine and mountain forests, one finds many seasonal streams and rivers of which the Limpopo is by far the most prominent. Here the hunter-gatherer San reigned supreme for over 5,000 years before the arrival of the hunter-herder Khoe with their livestock about 2,000 years ago and the arrival of the first Bantu-speaking peoples who crossed the Limpopo in about AD 300. Changes in occupation of the land began when the colonisers, more skilled in iron-making and agriculture, set about altering the landscape of the original inhabitants forever.

Commencing with the San, each group imprinted on the region their own unique rock-art style. Both the Khoe and the iron-mining agro-pastoralists sought to leave their mark by way of painting in various forms and rock engravings. They left us hundreds of superb art galleries with some of the most beautiful rock art to be found anywhere within southern Africa. Sadly the San were not able to adjust to this invasion of their wilderness and in time were either exterminated or absorbed into the more dominant and powerful occupiers. Today the San no longer exist here as an ethnic group and all we have of their former existence is their rock art.

The study of rock art is well understood in South Africa and, as the images occur in important places associated with shamanistic rituals, mythology, rainmaking, medicine-making and experiences such as trance dances, most researchers agree that the depictions are not simply art for art's sake. Dr Sven Ouzman put it most succinctly to me in an email: 'We know much of the rock-art works on symbolic and religious levels. Just like the "lamb" in Christian iconography. The engravings plus the place it was engraved combined to help people think about their world'.

I find his view most profound, particularly his opinion that not all species were necessarily 'menu' animals, which suggests that other forces were at work in the lives of the painters. One only has to look at the symbols representing a belief system such as idols, tomb paintings, cave art, tapestries, scrolls, small stone seals inscribed with elegant depictions of animals, including a unicorn-like figure dating back to a 2500 BC Indus Valley civilisation, to see how closely associated art and religion were in their development. Human beings throughout history have always sought out something, be it water, food, shelter, land, possessions or wealth. Is it possible that art as self-expression started out as a means of reaching out to a higher being in order to acquire these needs?

The rhino, it is suggested by archaeologists, was considered by the San to be an animal of great potency, possibly because of its size and, in the case of the black rhino, its aggressive nature. They had great empathy with the animals that occupied the same landscape as they did. Their very survival depended on their ability to accurately determine their habits and the space they needed to be given in order to avoid any confrontational situation. The art of the San left us evidence, in the absence at times of the written word from travellers and hunters, of the existence of rhinos. At least four depictions of the black rhino have been found on the north side of the Waterberg plateau of the Limpopo, which played a minor role in the decision to reintroduce the species back into these densely wooded hills and valleys.

To the east of the Waterberg massif lies a mountain range known as Strydpoort. This island mountain range is approximately 19 kilometres long and 10 kilometres wide. Within this range of rugged folded hills and deep bush-clad ravines, known as the Makapan Valley, lies the farm Makapansgat. The farm is important due to the tragic interracial conflicts in the middle of the 19th century and the discovery of a palaeontological and archaeological site of mind-blowing proportions. Secluded among the hills are numerous ancient caves formed by the dissolution of the surrounding dolomite rock by percolating water. Preserved within the sediments filling these caves is an astonishing fossil record spanning more than 3 million years including extinct species such as elephants, sabre-toothed cats, giant porcupines and dassies, as well as proto-humans and humans from *australopithecine* to the present. No extinct rhino fossils are evident in the record, but the caves have revealed fossilised teeth of both species of today's white and black rhino.

About 200 kilometres north of Makapan, and more than 1,000 years ago, Mapungubwe was the centre of a thriving, powerful kingdom with wealth created by trade with the Arabs on the Indian Ocean coastline. The remains of high-quality trade goods have been found at Mapungubwe including items from China, India and the Middle East. Glass beads, Chinese ceramics and cotton cloth would have been traded for ivory, copper, hides and in all probability rhino horn, for we know from the written record that rhino horn was sought after by Arab traders for centuries. Gold was similarly coveted by the Arab traders from their base on the coast of Sofala in present-day Mozambique. This was the fabled land of Monomotapa of the legendary *King Solomon's Mines*. Slaves were also very much in demand for later trading and one must remember that someone had to carry the goods to the coast, which was a very long way away.

From AD 1300, with a population of some 9,000 inhabitants, a new type of social hierarchy emerged. Coupled with the onset of climate change, which resulted in drought and crop failure, Mapungubwe began to wane and a shift of regional power to Great Zimbabwe resulted in the ultimate collapse of the kingdom. Today Mapungubwe is a World Heritage Site and a national park under the control of the South African National Parks. The site is on the south bank of the Limpopo River bordering Zimbabwe in the north and Botswana in the west. The meaning of the name Mapungubwe is a mystery. It has been referred to as the 'Place of Jackal', although the origin of the word is neither Venda, Shona nor Karanga, and most likely comes from a dialect not as yet recorded by linguists. A place of haunting beauty, which locals believed was sacred to ancestral spirits, Mapungubwe was shrouded in the past with mystery and a degree of fear, not to mention the hidden treasure that ultimately led discoverers to it.

In 1932 local farmer Jerry van Graan discovered the site. Being from an educated family, he informed the Transvaal University College (now the University of Pretoria), who have been the custodians of the unbelievable relics and treasure trove of golden objects recovered from a hidden grave for more than 70 years. Among the enormous number of golden objects found was a beautiful gold-plated rhino. According to Sian Tiley-Nel, curator of the Mapungubwe Museum at the University of Pretoria, this golden rhino was:

> once a symbol of royalty [and] lay buried for seven centuries in a sacred grave on Mapungubwe Hill until it was unearthed in 1933. This fat-bellied rhinoceros is about 15.2 centimetres in length and shaped out of two finely beaten sheets of gold foil only 0.5 millimetres thick and was fashioned around a soft core, probably sculpted wood, and held in place with minute gold nails.

This is the only complete and restored animal found at Mapungubwe, although two other torsos of rhinos were recovered. The animal has a single gold-foil horn and a solid gold tail. The shape of the rhino, with characteristically lowered head, powerful shoulders and fat belly, depicts a white rhino in my opinion. The white rhino most certainly occurred in the region, as evidenced by the rock-art sites and the records of 19th-century hunters. The one confusing aspect, however, is the single horn, which is only found on the Javan and greater one-horned rhino today. Both of these single-horned Asian rhinos were, at one time, widespread across Asia. Given the discovery of a vast number of glass trade beads originating from India, Persia, Egypt and Arabia via the east coast trade merchants, is it possible that there was some influence from this quarter? The single horn is indeed fascinating. The golden rhino of Mapungubwe was to become not only the symbol of a once-flourishing empire but a symbol of the once-numerous rhinos alongside the painted images of a now extinct species emblazoned on the sandstone cliffs and overhangs by the artists who followed the same fate.

At the confluence of the Limpopo and the Shashe rivers, there is an island whose ownership was disputed by Botswana, Zimbabwe and South Africa at one stage, and largely disowned by all three. Willem Coetzer, the private owner on the Botswana side, who was a great friend to Educational Wildlife Expeditions (EWE), and allowed us to run trails on his property, proposed setting up an independent state with its own flag and stamps. His suggestion was more tongue in cheek than serious. This beautiful island covered in magnificent trees was directly opposite what was to become the Mapungubwe National Park and the haunt of elephant, impala, baboons and bushbuck. Amid the vegetation and outcrops of sandstone, a San painting of a rhino and a single human figure was found – further evidence of the importance of the rhino in San belief and of the ultimate disappearance of both. The dispute was eventually settled with ownership residing with Botswana.

After an absence of more than 100 years, the black rhino was successfully reintroduced to Venetia, the De Beers reserve to the south of Mapungubwe National Park, in 2003. Venetia remains a separate, closed system. I was a member of the South African National Parks Board, which was on a conservation committee visit to the park, and we all witnessed the release of the rhinos into the holding pens. For most of our committee this was their first-ever opportunity to see a living black rhino. As part of the planned international transfrontier park embracing Zimbabwe, Botswana and Mapungubwe, the black rhino should hopefully one day be seen again within the rugged, beautiful sandstone landscape, roaming free as it did more than 1,000 years ago. We will have to be patient as this has yet to become a reality.

To the west near the Motloutse River, a tributary of the Limpopo, the artist and explorer Thomas Baines recorded the following in his diary of 1871, 'We breakfasted under a leafless baobab, about 40 feet in circumference, and passed others beginning to show young foliage, some of them 50 feet in girth; we saw a rhinoceros, two giraffe, and some antelope.' He subsequently produced an excellent oil painting of a black rhino in 1874, which is now in the Sanlam Art Collection and forms part of a series he produced from the region. The hunting of rhino for meat (the best part being the tongue, well salted and boiled), the hide for sjamboks (whips for horse riding and punishing wrongdoers, no doubt) and the horn for trade, is well illustrated in an earlier painting he produced in 1850 of the market square in Grahamstown.

The story of the rhino in southern Africa has been a bloody one since the arrival of the first European settlers in 1652. The rhino has survived largely due to the far-sighted and timeous interventions of individuals who recognised that the species would not survive the hand of man if action was not taken. The tsetse fly and malaria played an important part in the survival of the last pocket of white rhino and perhaps less than 100 black rhino in the wilderness of Zululand in 1895. One black rhino female survived in the Kruger National Park as late as 1936. With the exception of the remote desert regions of the Kaokoveld, the rhino of Namibia was extinct by the turn of the 19th century. Botswana did not do much better with occasional sightings in Ngamiland up to 1994, when it finally became extinct there. Zimbabwe and Zambia fared far better, thanks to dedicated field men and the old ally, the tsetse fly.

All that changed very dramatically when Zambia lost all their rhino in the 1980s, and very nearly the same thing happened in Zimbabwe. Mozambique has always been a bit of a mystery, a protracted bush war did not help and most certainly the species did not survive very long into the 20th century in the southern part of the country. When I hunted in the area in the 1950s, the animal was unheard of, although they did occur in low numbers in the north. In Malawi, the species was regarded as extinct.

Where are we today? And what has been achieved since the beginning of the 20th century? There are never any easy answers in a continent bedevilled by poverty, corruption and greed. In the case of the rhino, the problem is not entirely of our own making in Africa, in spite of all our faults. As long as the belief exists, far away in another place, that rhino horn is essential to good health, someone is going to seek it. The stakes are very high and all options, even those that are anathema to many, need to be put on the table and debated for the sake of the rhino's future. There is perhaps no other living creature with as high a price tag on its head as the rhino and, no matter how beautiful, no amount of rock art or golden objects will ever replace the living animal.

CHAPTER 2

The Last
Living Rhino

OF THE FIVE LIVING SPECIES of rhino, the Sumatran rhino (*Dicerorhinus sumatrensis*) is considered to be from the oldest and most archaic form and first appeared in the fossil record in the lower Miocene Epoch 20–16 million years ago. The Sumatran rhino as we know it appeared about 2.5 million years ago. The single-horned rhino (*Rhinoceros*) first appeared in the middle Miocene about 14 million years ago with the greater one-horned rhino (*Rhinoceros unicornis*) and the Javan rhino (*Rhinoceros sondaicus*) appearing around 2 million years ago. The two African species belong to the *Dicerotini* group and also first appeared in the middle Miocene. The white rhino (*Ceratotherium simum*) first appeared 3 million years ago and the black rhino (*Diceros bicornis*) about 4 million years ago, making it among the most stable and long-lived species on the African savannah.

Black/White grey

I would like to clear up one aspect of the African rhino that has been the topic of much discussion since before the turn of the 19th century: the terms 'white' and 'black' used to describe the two species. In truth, they are both more shades of grey than black or white, and there is not much to distinguish them by colour. The apparent colour of both species is most often due to their frequent mud wallowing, which

17

wide Rhino

colours their hides in the hues of the local soil and further confuses the issue.

Some, if not most, of the confusion seems to arise from the incorrect belief that the Dutch word for wide, *wijd* (also *weid, weit, wyd*), became corrupted to *wit* and was then translated into English as white. 'White rhino' was first written in English by John Barrow in 1801, when describing his travels in the Calvinia area of the northern Cape during 1798, where he met a Griqua Afrikaner who told him that in his youth he had killed 'seven camelopards [giraffes] and three white rhinoceroses in one day'. Petrus Borcherds, assistant secretary and scribe to the commissioners of the Truter-Somerville expedition of 1802, describes the killing of a 'white rhino', but also makes reference to the 'black variety' of rhino. The report was submitted in English, but was no doubt drafted in Dutch – *wit* to white and *swart* to black. Frederick Courteney Selous, the 19th-century hunter and naturalist, made the following observation in Rowland Ward's *Great and Small Game of Africa* in 1899:

> It is true that when standing in the open ground on a winter morning, with the sun shining full upon them, they look very white, and as the Boers must first have encountered these animals on the open plains in the neighbourhood of the Vaal River, this fact may have appealed to them, and caused them to bestow upon the square-mouthed rhinoceros a name which has always appeared to me singularly inappropriate.

He goes on to state:

> I have often seen large sheets of hide from freshly-killed specimens of both species of African rhinoceros lying in camp side by side, waiting to be cut into sjamboks, and certainly never noticed much difference between the two in colour of the epidermis, though the hide of the square-mouthed rhinoceros was a good deal thicker than that of the prehensile-lipped species.

Perhaps the issue may best be summed up in part by Jim Feely who wrote, in his paper, 'Black rhino, white rhino: what's in a name?':

> Short and pithy, *swart*/black with their opposites *wit*/white have remained firmly in everyday use to distinguish the African rhinos for more than two centuries. Thus the name will no doubt continue in common usage, whatever their etymology or alternatives preferred by zoologists. One thing is certain, no African animal has attracted so much attention to its name as has the white rhino.

❀

3 tonnes .

The white rhino (*Ceratotherium simum*), second only in size to the African elephant, can attain a shoulder height of up to 1.8 metres, weigh up to 3,000 kilograms and have a large head with a broad chest and short neck. They have a massive nuchal hump on their shoulders with stocky, powerful legs. In spite of their size they are swift-running animals, reaching speeds of up to 40 kilometres per hour. Never underestimate their supposedly docile nature. They do not take kindly to being held in enclosures when first captured and are potentially extremely dangerous. Their eyesight is poor, and they rely on their excellent hearing and sense of smell, which is highly developed. Birds are an early warning system for them, especially the red- and yellow-billed oxpecker.

They carry two horns on their snout, which are not attached directly to the skull. The horns, as in the case of the extinct woolly rhino, the black rhino and the three Asian rhinos, are comprised of keratin – the same type of protein that makes up human hair or fingernails. Should a rhino break off its horn, or is dehorned for whatever reason, it will regrow at the rate of 6–10 centimetres, or 750 grams, per annum. This is subject, of course, to normal wear through rubbing, and varies according to the individual animal's behaviour and environment. One of the first white rhinos introduced to Lapalala Wilderness in 1982 broke off its beautiful anterior (front) horn at the base while in transit from Zululand. Over the ensuing years, the horn steadily grew back but was never the same graceful shape. At the time of her death many years later, when she and her calf were killed outright by a lightning bolt, the horn was massive and bulky.

A single calf is born after a gestation of about 18 months, and the calf remains with the mother for up to three years. One will notice that the calf runs in front of the mother when moving. While oxpeckers rid them of ticks on the land, the role is taken over by terrapins when they are in mud wallows. Broken tree stumps make excellent rubbing posts and help to further remove parasites and keep their skin healthy. As with all rhinos, their skins are thick and tough, which is one of the reasons why they were hunted. If not fatally wounded, the skin closes over the entry wound and later causes serious infection, invariably leading to the death of the animal. Poachers today use modern rifles that fire light-calibre bullets, which leave even smaller openings.

They are grass-eaters, preferring open areas, and they deposit their dung in large communal middens with the dung turning quite dark in colour with age.

Their former range extended over much of southern Africa with the exception of the southern and Eastern Cape, parts of Namibia, Botswana and Angola. Both Zimbabwe and Mozambique provided good habitats for the white rhino. Aside from the last surviving population in the bushveld of Zululand, they were totally exterminated by the turn of the 19th century. Mozambique had the dubious distinction of having the species go extinct twice. In 1903, it was estimated that there were less than 50 white rhino left in southern Africa. Today there are over 20,000, but more on this success story later.

The northern white rhino (*Ceratotherium simum cottoni*) was formerly found in north-western Uganda, southern Chad, south-western Sudan, the eastern parts of the Central African Republic and north-eastern Democratic Republic of Congo. In 1960 there were over 2,000 northern white rhinos in the wild. By 2005 there were four. There has been no sign of the four since 2007. In 2009 four of the six rhino from Dvůr Králové Zoo in the Czech Republic were relocated to a highly

20 ⌐ what aend survey told us this?

protected sanctuary in Kenya, in the hope that the return to a natural environment would stimulate reproduction. With the three captive animals left in two zoos, the world total is seven. *NOW 3.*

In his 1910 book, *African Game Trails*, former US president Theodore Roosevelt wrote, 'I do not see how the rhinoceros can be permanently preserved, save in very out-of-the-way places or in regular reserves'. His words proved disastrously prophetic when the species in the wild was declared biologically extinct in 2010. What he omitted to add was the number of northern white rhinos that he and his son Kermit killed on his long-planned and prolonged safari, with his big-game hunting friend Frederick Courteney Selous. They shot and killed a total of nine of the very species that is now extinct, which is well over the permitted limit. This slaughter was excessive by any standards, and more so given their scarce standing, even at that time. It is noteworthy, however, that as a politician he stands head and shoulders above most, for his far-sighted vision and action in declaring reserves and national parks in the USA.

BLACK RHINO.

There are only three sub-species of black rhino surviving in Africa today. Over 95 per cent of all Africa's black rhino are conserved in only four countries: South Africa, Namibia, Zimbabwe and Kenya. The south-central subspecies (*Diceros bicornis minor*) is the most numerous, and once ranged south from central Tanzania through Zambia, Zimbabwe, Mozambique, Malawi and Botswana to north and south-eastern South Africa. The south-western subspecies (*Diceros bicornis bicornis*) ranged through Namibia, southern Angola, western Botswana and the north-western Cape. Historically the range extended as far south as the Cape peninsula, and would have included Addo Elephant National Park and the Karoo. The East African subspecies (*Diceros bicornis michaeli*) ranged from southern Sudan to central Tanzania, but today Kenya is the current stronghold with an estimated 600 rhino. The West African subspecies (*Diceros bicornis longipes*) was formally declared extinct by the International Union for Conservation of Nature (IUCN) in November 2011.

During the 20th century, the black rhino was considered the most numerous of all the five extant species of rhino. At the turn of the 19th century there were conceivably several hundred thousand living throughout their range. During the mid-20th century their numbers were about 100,000. By 1970 they were down to 65,000. Ten years later, in 1980, their numbers had plummeted to around 15,000. Between 1970 and 1980, black rhino were being poached at over 5,000 per year.

The black rhino is smaller than the white rhino, standing between 1.4 and 1.7 metres high at the shoulder, measuring between 3.3 and 3.6 metres in length and weighing between 800 and 1,400 kilograms. The head, which is much smaller than the white rhino's, is held high. The females are smaller than the males, but both are extremely swift, reaching speeds of up to 56 kilometres per hour. They are highly agile and are capable of turning on a dime, so to speak. Unlike the elephant, they are quite capable of leaping. If you are on foot and charged by one, you may with some considerable effort dodge a black rhino at the last moment, but that is certainly not your best option. Flying away would be ideal, but we know that's not possible. The only option is to get up a stout tree immediately, regardless of any possible thorns. When walking, make a mental note to observe climbable trees nearby and avoid turning around while running in the event of a charge. You should never go walking in any area where black rhinos occur unless you are with an experienced wilderness guide.

Both males and females have a reputation for being extremely aggressive. They will charge if they feel threatened, but their habit of attacking is simply their defensive mode; they do not possess good eyesight, which causes them to be wary of strange sounds if they are not able to detect the disturbance by scent. Black rhinos have a wide range of vocal sounds, which they use to communicate to one another and a few to express their displeasure. Long snorts with the attendant swift expelling of air may indicate anger or awareness of an approaching threat. Erect ears will indicate that the animal is trying to locate the source of the intruder, followed by ears pressed flat back if it is responding aggressively. In the event of a charge, they are capable of attaining a top speed in a very short distance and on the point of contact propel their head up with incredible force by means of very powerful neck and shoulder muscles.

Black rhinos unfortunately carry a great deal of baggage, largely from ill-informed travellers and hunters who became writers during the 19th century and the early part of the 20th century. They have, as a result, become extremely misunderstood and few zoology students choose to study them. I believe that this is due to a fear of the animal's reputation and its preferred habitat of dense bush. I am convinced that their reputation is undeserved, and the people who have had the privilege of working with wild and captive black rhinos will testify to this. Contrary to popular belief, black rhinos are intelligent creatures. They are able to communicate with one another at a level inaudible to humans, and although they are generally solitary they will interact with one another on occasion. Large African animals should always be looked upon as potentially dangerous, but this does not necessarily mean that they are bad tempered, stupid, dumb or brutish.

Although their eyesight is poor, their senses of hearing and smell are excellent. Their ears have a wide rotational range, enabling them to detect sound from all around. If observed while lying down and seemingly asleep, one will notice the rhino's ears constantly rotating. As with the white rhino, birds are their best warning of danger, especially the red- (*Buphagus erythrorhynchus*) and yellow-billed (*Buphagus africanus*) oxpeckers. These birds will instantly raise the alarm at the approach of any danger by flying off and emitting a loud hissing call, which will immediately alert the rhino. Another ally is the fork-tailed drongo (*Dicrurus adsimilis*), a noisy and aggressive bird.

Black rhinos are browsers, which accounts for their habitat preference where they are able to use their prehensile lip, and horn, to good effect. Otto Friedrich Mentzel, a government official in the Cape from 1733 to 1741, wrote that 'the upper lip can be stretched half a foot, and ends in a pointed fleshy protuberance, which it uses as a kind of hand and imperfect trunk for taking up its food and putting it into its mouth'. They will use their horn to pull down branches and will use their chest to push over small trees to reach twigs and foliage. They eat a wide range of plants – up to 220 have been recorded – including certain poisonous varieties, twigs, branches, leafy plants, forbs and shoots. Peter Kolben, appointed the first official astronomer in South Africa in 1705, noted that 'his mouth is like that of a Hog, but somewhat more pointed . . . He is not fond of Feeding on Grass, chusing rather Shrubs, Broom and Thistles. But the Delight of his Tooth is a Shrub . . . the Rhinoceros-Bush'.

They will drink daily, consuming as much as 30 litres, but are capable of going for many days without water, as with the rhinos in the arid zones of Namibia. They are particularly fond of mud wallows and will spend lengthy periods lying up, thus keeping their body temperature down. The mud is of importance to the health of the animal's skin and warding off biting flies. In the absence of mud they will happily wallow in dust bowls.

A single calf weighing 35–50 kilograms is born to the female after a gestation period of 15–16 months. The calf is weaned at around two years, but will remain with the mother for up to three years. This can be a very vulnerable period for calves, who are particularly at risk from males wishing to mate with the mother. Black rhinos have the highest rate of combat-related encounters of any mammal, and deaths have been recorded in both sexes. Calves may be killed or seriously injured during these contacts. Calves may also be vulnerable to lions or hyenas due to their nature of following behind the mother. Adult black rhinos have no natural enemies other than humans intent on killing them for their horns.

The greater one-horned, or Indian, rhino (*Rhinoceros unicornis*) once ranged over a vast area of the northern part of the Indian subcontinent, from Pakistan in the west to the Indian-Burmese border in the east, including parts of Nepal, Bangladesh and Bhutan. Their presence was possible in southern China, Indo-China and Burma (now Myanmar) according to the literature. Today they are extinct in most parts of their former range and are confined largely to unfenced parks that are, in effect, islands in a sea of humanity. Being surrounded by human-dominated land renders them vulnerable to poaching, but also exposes them to the greater danger of wandering into adjacent farmland where they are a potential threat to humans. They have been known to kill people, although the one-horned rhino is a reasonably placid creature, especially when compared with the black rhino.

The horn of the Indian rhino is considered by the Chinese to be far more valuable than that of its African counterparts and a great deal of the credit for its survival is due to the international NGOs who have assisted the authorities and the dedication of the staff of the various parks. Rhino numbers in South Africa's national parks are not made public due to the high demand for rhino horn. In a country where people have been killed for their cellphones, the less public rhino numbers are the better, especially when considering that rhino horn sells for up to US$60,000 per kilogram. In the case of the Asian species, this is difficult due to the very low surviving numbers; there are only two really viable populations of the one-horned rhino. Of the current world population of just over 3,000, the bulk are to be found in Assam's Kaziranga National Park, in India, with smaller populations in Orang National Park and Pabitora Wildlife Sanctuary. The Chitwan National Park, in Nepal, has over 500 animals, while the Bardia National Park only has 24.The Indian populations have benefitted greatly from support from the US- and UK-based Save the Rhino International (SRI).

The one-horned rhino is similar in size to the African white rhino and weighs in at between 2,200 and 3,000 kilograms and attains a height of 1.7 to 2 metres. They are taller than the white rhino, but weigh slightly less on average. A single horn is present in both sexes, hence the name. No other member of the rhino family comes remotely near this species' prehistoric appearance. The skin is a silver-brown colour, becoming pinkish near the large skin folds that cover the body. These folds are especially well developed in the males, giving them the appearance of being armour-plated. The German name for the one-horned rhino, fittingly, is *panzernashorn*, or 'armoured nose-horn'.

They have attributes of both the black and the white rhino, in addition to several unique characteristics. They are excellent swimmers, and are happy to wallow and feed in lakes, streams, rivers and mud pools, where they plunge their heads under water for up to 45 seconds. They are primarily grazers, but are known to eat leaves, branches of shrubs and trees, agricultural crops, fruit and submerged and floating vegetation.

It would indeed be pleasant to record that the species represents a success story, for that was the case in the 1980s, certainly in the Chitwan National Park where they became so plentiful that they became a positive menace to farmers surrounding the reserve. The species enjoyed special protection, which included the added benefit of the presence of the Nepalese army, and numbers increased from approximately 95 in the 1960s to 612 in 2000. The Maoist uprising, from 1996 to 2005, resulted in the decline of the military presence in the park and led to the slaughter of many of the rhino. Poachers claimed 108 rhino from 2001 to 2005.

In 1984, my son Anton and I went on an EWT explorer trip to India and Nepal. The assassination of the Prime Minister of India, Indira Ghandi, the week of our departure put the country into a state of turmoil. Our group of 17 South Africans were understandably more than a little apprehensive. The Indian ambassador in Mauritius gave us the green light, although our itinerary was altered, which meant that we were unable to visit Kaziranga or the Corbett Tiger Reserve. The trip centred around endangered wildlife, starting in Mauritius with the Mauritius kestrel and the pink pigeon, both highly threatened, and the opportunity to view a skeleton of the extinct dodo, lest we forget its demise.

Our flight was cleared to Bombay (Mumbai) at midnight, which meant that we would arrive in a city of 9 million inhabitants at 4 a.m. If anyone is in doubt about the world's population crisis, a trip to India will clarify the issue very quickly, especially if you land at the Mumbai airport in the early hours of the morning. The population of India in 1984 was around 800 million.

We suffered more apprehension after we landed at the Bombay airport. We were told never to let our luggage out of our sight; everyone wanted to help us carry our luggage and was apparently equally happy to relieve us of it permanently. To add to the confusion everyone seemed to be yelling instructions. It was bad enough worrying about the murder of the prime minister without the din. 'Welcome to India' the sign said as we bundled into our waiting bus.

As we proceeded into Bombay we saw hundreds of white-linen-clad forms lying in doorways, on pavements, on benches and on the beaches. Those who were awake were playing cricket before going to work or school. Children relieved themselves on pavements as their mothers drew up water from nearby wells. The press of humanity was overwhelming. How, we thought, could this country, with its poverty and malnutrition hope to save the tiger, let alone the rhino? India's human population, 27 years after our visit, is over 1.2 billion and the tiger and rhino are still with us.

With population levels of those proportions, where today half of its children are undernourished and half the population live below the international poverty line of less than US$1.25 a day, how does one hope to ensure the survival of the tiger or the greater one-horned rhino? As economies accelerate and population growth remains high, the demand for rhino horn increases, which ensures that the one-horned rhino remains highly endangered. Sport hunting back in the 1800s most certainly played a role in the decline of the species. One English sportsman, Colonel Fitzwilliam Thomas Pollok, slaughtered no less than 47 rhino in Assam, and in Bengal the Maharajah of Cooch Behar outdid himself by shooting no less than 207 over a period 26 years. In 1896 the Bengal government was paying bounty hunters 20 rupees for every rhino shot. Worse still was the clearing of prime rhino habitat to establish tea plantations. In 1910 the British colonial government outlawed rhino hunting. India has some 500 sanctuaries and 13 biospheres today and international funding comes from various quarters, with a high awareness of the rhino's plight at various levels. The diversity of wildlife on the Indian subcontinent is astonishing and is deserving of every bit of support and encouragement it receives. Of course one has to ask how well they are run in terms of staff, and whether there is sufficient concomitant funding to adequately conserve these areas and species in the face of pervasive and ecologically devastating human encroachment. One of the tiger sanctuaries we visited had a population of 30 tigers, but today they are extinct in that park.

From Bombay we travelled by coach to Delhi and then north to Kathmandu, gateway to the Himalayas and the jungles of Chitwan, which means 'heart of the jungle'. The Chitwan National Park is Nepal's most famous reserve and is home to over 500 one-horned rhino and some 40 tigers. There are three ways of getting around Chitwan: from the back of an elephant, trekking through the jungle on foot and going on a traditional game drive. Our group chose the back of an elephant without hesitation. Anton and I later spent three days on foot, jungle trekking with a guide and four porters. We skipped the game drives as we could do that back in Africa. The last time I rode on the back of an elephant was in the Johannesburg zoo at the age of six, but this was a different proposition altogether and I couldn't wait to try the real thing. The size of the elephant determines the number of people he or she will carry, and for the next two days we split the group over five elephants. My favourite elephant for rhino spotting was a regal specimen called Shamshahar. We would set out each morning, and again each afternoon, from the front lawn of our game lodge, Tiger Tops, with the attendant mahouts in search of rhino. The grass through which the elephants find their way is incredibly tall and they show no fear of the rhino, which don't appear all that big when you see them. One forgets that you are more than two metres above the jungle floor, swaying as you do in tune with your elephant's gait.

Two days later, after most of the group had gone mountain trekking, Anton and I set off on foot with Dan Bahadur, our expert jungle guide. We were accompanied by three porters carrying tiny one-man tents and our supply of food, which was mainly rice and four live chickens in a bamboo cage. We were in this jungle wilderness for three days. The porters took a different route and left us with Dan, who spoke good English. This part of Chitwan comprised tall sal forest, which was dominated by one species, *Shorea robusta*, rising up more than 40 metres, often closing at the top and shutting out the sunlight as brilliantly coloured scarlet minivets flitted in and out of the forest canopy. The birdlife of the Indian subcontinent is astonishing. Down below we followed jungle trails in and out of dense vegetation. Apart from tigers, a host of species live here. One tiger passed by our camp on the first night and we came across a sloth bear (*Melursus ursinus*), which in Nepali is called a *bhalu*. Dan whispered that they can be unpredictable and nasty if they so choose. They weigh about 135 kilograms and have a distinctive 'V' or crescent on the chest, set off by a shaggy black coat. This one had his rear end up in the air, furiously digging into a termite mound. We quietly left him to his task.

Each evening we would arrive at our camp, which was duly set up minus two chickens who had been taken care of with a very wicked-looking knife the guides called a kukri. Chicken Nepalese-style with wonderful spices was served in due course with mounds of steaming rice. To keep weight down I carried miniature bottles of Johnny Walker whisky, courtesy of Air India, to which I added pure jungle water from a nearby stream. Anton, being a schoolboy at the time, had to contend with tea.

On our last day as we headed back to Tiger Tops we encountered a large male one-horned rhino at close range. On foot, one is suddenly very conscious of their size, which is even more impressive given the body folds. There was not an awful lot of space between us but Dan was unperturbed. The rhino was below us and feeding on bamboo in a densely wooded stream with more than half his body in water. We watched him for more than half an hour. Dan had managed to get us so close to the animal and it had no idea of our presence. I was reminded of how easily they can be killed by hunters.

According to my long-time friend K. K. Gurung, who at the time of our visit was manager of Tiger Tops, the rhino is a sacred animal in Nepal. We had dinner with K. K. on our last night and he gave us each a copy of his excellent guide to the park. In the chapter on the one-horned rhino he says that it's an 'object of great veneration, and the possessor of magical powers'. Its unique reputation derives from the belief that it got its horn from Parvati, the consort of the god Shiva. There is much we don't realise about the customs of other countries, and go about imposing our beliefs on long-held traditions, which is most often the cause of confusion and misunderstanding. One needs to pause here and think carefully when we pronounce our views on traditions that go back a very long way.

What many people don't realise is that the horn is not the only body part of a rhino that is prized in Southeast Asia. Poachers waste little time, other than to remove the horn as quickly as possible and to vanish. According to K. K., though, when a rhino died from natural causes and the powers that be authorised the villagers to remove the body, the rush to get at the carcass often resulted in knife wounds. The usages are varied and make for compelling reading. The blood is used to treat menstrual and excessive bleeding after childbirth; urine is used as a remedy for asthma, stomach pains and tuberculosis; and the dung is used as a laxative or to cure coughs when mixed with tobacco and smoked. The skin is highly sought after and the meat, even if stinking and covered in maggots, is consumed with relish.

Esmond Bradley Martin, a recognised trade specialist, noted in a report first published in 1981 that 'the Chinese regarded the horn of *R. unicornis* as the best of all the rhino species'. In spite of the continued media belief in the West, it is amazing how the myth of the horn being sought by the Chinese as an aphrodisiac persists. The principal use of rhino horn is traditional Chinese medicine. If it was used as a sexual stimulant the rhino would, in all probability, have disappeared a very long time ago.

The systematic elimination of malaria from Chitwan in 1954 was so successful that by 1960 the area was declared malaria free. As a result, thousands of hill people poured into the region and set about the inevitable destruction of the habitat. Approval to establish a national park to protect both flora and fauna was given by the late King Mahendra in 1970 – it is a real plus when the head of state is on your side. The Royal Chitwan National Park was officially gazetted in 1973, becoming the first national park in Nepal. It came just in time to save the one-horned rhino and the third that was left of the Chitwan forest. A great deal of the credit for the establishment of the park must go to the Fauna Preservation Society and the IUCN. Establishing the park was no easy matter and required the removal of over 22,000 locals in 1964, which was met with a great deal of resentment and would have been extremely difficult to achieve today.

Moves to establish the park were largely due to the serious decline of the rhino and other species of wildlife, as evidenced by a survey produced in 1969 by G. H. Caughley and H. R. Mishra, who estimated that there were only between 81 and 108 animals. They believed that the one-horned rhino would be extinct by 1980. At the time of our visit in 1984 some 350 rhino occurred within the park. Tough choices had to be made. Are rhinos more important than people? In this case the answer was yes, given the past history of slaughter. The 'bag' at the time of King George V of England's visit in 1911 at the invitation of the Ranas, who were the de facto rulers between 1846 and 1950, was considerable. The party killed 39 tigers, 18 rhinos, 4 bears and several leopards. An all-time record was achieved on the occasion of Lord Linlithgow and party's visit in 1938–39 with a bag of 120 tigers, 38 rhinos, 27 leopards and 15 bears. Fortunately the hunts were not all that frequent. The Ranashad accorded the Chitwan valley the status of 'private hunting preserve' and maintained it for the privileged class. Anyone caught hunting a rhino received capital punishment, which I presume was fatal. What they did achieve, however, was a measure of protection for the wildlife, not unlike the Zulu kings of old who set aside the areas we know today as the Hluhluwe-Umfolozi Game Reserve. The important aspect was that the habitat remained unchanged until the eventual elimination of malaria in Chitwan. Today, Chitwan is the second-most important sanctuary conserving the Indian rhino.

Petrus Camper first suggested that there were two species of Asian rhino in 1771, but the first scientific description of the Javan rhinoceros, by Anselme Desmarcst, would only appear in 1882. The Javan rhino (*Rhinoceros sondaicus*) is the most critically endangered of the five extant species of rhino and probably the rarest large mammal on earth. It is likely that there are only about 40 surviving in Ujung Kulon National Park on the island of Java in Indonesia, their only remaining range. The species belongs to the same genus as the one-horned rhino and has a similar likeness in terms of its armour-plated appearance. It is hairless with grey-brown skin that falls in folds to the shoulder, back and rump. The neck folds are less conspicuous than those of the one-horned rhino.

Few measurements of weight are available, but a range of 900–2,300 kilograms is generally accepted. They measure up to 3.2 metres in length and have a shoulder height of 1.2–1.7 metres. The females have a birth interval of four to five years, and weaning occurs at 12–24 months. The Javan rhino is a generalist browser and consumes little to no grass and few herbaceous species, preferring leaves, shoots and twigs of woody species. In 1985 Hartmann Ammann listed 190 species in their diet, of which just four made up 44 per cent of the food consumed. Salt is an important aspect of its diet. As with all rhino, they are very fond of wallowing. This enables them to control body temperature and keeps their skin free of disease and parasites. They are a solitary and shy animal, although they have been known to demonstrate aggression when approached. They carry a single horn, which may grow to about 25 centimetres over their life span of 30–45 years.

The Javan rhino was once the most widespread of all the Asian species, and was found in India, throughout Southeast Asia, the islands of Indonesia, China and even the Indian Sundarbans. Thomas Horsfield, in 1824, noted that the Javan rhino was not limited by region or climate with 'its range extending from . . . ocean to the summit of mountains of considerable elevation' and typically with 'a profuse vegetation'. Arthur Adams, naval surgeon and conchologist, gave an account of his visit to Mew Bay (Meeuwenbaai) in western Java during his voyage on board the *Actaeon* in 1857 stating, 'There is a legend among the sailors of a rhinoceros having charged a party watering here some time previously'. Although this could have been an unfounded rumour, he also found the ground 'literally ploughed up by the tracks of these unwieldy pachyderms'. Richard Lydekker chronicled in 1907, 'the

Javan rhinoceros prefers forest tracts to grass-jungles, and is generally met with in hilly districts, where it apparently ascends in some parts of its habitat several thousand feet above sea-level'.

Rhinos were often shot in the southern part of Bantam, western Java, in the early part of the century. H. M. Van Weede hunted rhinos in 1908 on the south coast, stating his regret that the numbers were diminishing. It is widely accepted that the last rhino in southern Java was shot in January 1934. In Sumatra, the last known individuals were killed between 1927 and 1933. It was uncommon or extinct in Malaysia by the 1930s. In the 1970s, it was still reported by local villagers of south-western Thailand and in Burma it was common in the mid-1800s, but very uncommon by the 1920s. The Javan rhino was well known in Laos and Cambodia with the last known individual being shot in 1930. In Vietnam, where historically it may have occurred up to the Chinese border, it was declared extinct in October 2011.

The zoological gardens of the Royal Zoological Society of London, established in 1828, paid £800 for a Javan rhino in 1874. The last known captive Javan rhino lived at the zoological gardens in Adelaide, Australia, and died in 1907. It was exhibited as an Indian rhino for most of its 21 years in captivity.

The Sumatran rhino (*Dicerorhinus sumatrensis*) is the smallest of all the rhino, standing about 1.2–1.45 metres at the shoulder and weighing only 500–800 kilograms. The animal carries two horns that are 15–25 centimetres in length. They have very low reproduction rates with a single offspring produced every four to five years and a gestation of 15–16 months. The rhino's skin is relatively thin and largely covered in reddish-brown hair. Solitary by nature, they once inhabited rain and cloud forests and swamps in India, Bhutan, Laos, Bangladesh, Burma, Thailand, Malaysia, Indonesia and China. In the early 1980s it was estimated that there were between 800 and 1,000 Sumatran rhinos across their range. By 1993 this was down to less than 500. Their solitary nature makes them difficult to count, but the total population today is estimated at between 150 and 200.

The first English explorer to write of the Sumatran rhino (albeit a dead one) was Daniel Beeckman in 1718. In describing Borneo he wrote:

> In this Garden is likewise a House, build for that purpose, wherein are kept a Collection of the Skins of a multitude of strange Beasts which Africa is famous for, so artificially and nicely stuff'd, that at first you would be surpriz'd at them, and would believe them to be really live Creatures, viz. Lions, Tygers, Leopards, Elephants, Rhinoceros's, wild Cats.

Then in 1793, William Bell, the surgeon in the service of the Dutch East India Company, gave a 'Description of the double horned Rhinoceros of Sumatra':

> The head much resembled that of the single horned rhinoceros . . . The horns were black, the larger was placed immediately above the nose, pointing upwards, and was bent a little back; it was about nine inches long . . . The whole skin of the animal is rough, and covered very thinly with short black hair.

The description was accompanied by very good drawings of the animal. It was, however, only 21 years later, in 1814, that the Sumatran rhino was given its official scientific name, by Johann Fischer von Waldheim.

Only six substantial populations exist, four on Sumatra, one in Borneo and one in the Malay Peninsula. It is the most vocal of all the rhino. It is agile and quick, easily climbing mountains, steep slopes, ravines and river banks. In 1823, Caspar Reinwardt wrote of the Sumatran rhino:

> The rhinoceros has a habit to push on to the end of the highest mountain, and its paths have often been useful to us in the dense forest. These paths even extended to the top of the Patoeha and across the difficult Goenoeng Goentoer, over the sharp lava along the crater.

Given the nature of their terrain, they have not been easy to study. Through the fantastic study by Nicolaas van Strien in 1986, and that of several other field researchers, there is now a better understanding of the species. They are very good swimmers, taking full advantage of riverine and aquatic vegetation. They spend much of the day wallowing in mud and feed mainly at night browsing on more than 150 species of trees and shrubs. Being shy and solitary, they do not appear to defend territories through fighting and appear somewhat docile. Males are more nomadic, and visit the females' territory to mate.

The question of habitat loss and disturbance is often overlooked when considering the long-term survival of the five remaining rhino species. It is obvious that all five species were once numerous and enjoyed a vast range. Hunting for the horn has been the major cause of their decline, but by the same token human expansion has had a disastrous effect. It is highly unlikely that they could ever have hoped to retain their geographical range in the environment we face today – even if the horn was worthless. If you add to this the Asian belief in traditional medicine, is it any wonder that rhino populations are now at such alarmingly low levels?

The rhino is a flagship species and if we cannot ensure its survival, then in the end it may well be a barometer of our own. Fortunately for the rhino it is easier to raise funds for their conservation as they are mega fauna 'superstars'. The real problem is that there are very few rhinos left. Will the world carry on if the rhino goes? Of course it will. Most of the people in the world are too busy trying to get by to spare a thought for the extinction of the rhino, save perhaps for those who believe in the efficacy of rhino horn and will only miss it when it is no longer available.

CHAPTER 3

Extinction at the
Hand of Man

THERE HAVE BEEN AT least five major mass extinctions over the past 540
million years of life on earth. The first mass extinction was the End
Ordovician event that occurred between 450 and 440 million years ago,
and is believed to have exterminated nearly 60 per cent of all genera.
The second, which lasted 20 million years, was the Late Devonian
event around 360 million years ago. The third was the Permian-Triassic
event 250 million years ago, known as the Great Dying, during which
90 per cent of all known species became extinct. The fourth was the
End Triassic event about 205 million years ago, which saw the end of
most non-dinosaurian land quadrupeds. The fifth, the K-T extinction
event at the end of the Cretaceous-Tertiary period 65 million years
ago, is probably the most famous and saw the demise of all non-
avian dinosaurs. The dinosaurs are extinct, although no man-made
catastrophe was responsible for their demise. The Neanderthals are no
longer with us, neither are the proto-humans who are reflected in the
fossil records for more than 3 million years. The fossil record reveals,
beyond our wildest imagination, just how astonishing life here on earth
has really been.

Recent studies conclude that apart from complete destruction of
the globe, no single event is likely to cause human extinction. Unless
there is a succession of global catastrophes – pandemics, runaway
global warming, nuclear wars, collapse of resources, an asteroid

impact – *Homo sapiens* is currently in no danger of extinction. Humankind has colonised virtually every corner of the globe, except the deep oceans. Regardless of conditions, we have become more successful than parasites, cockroaches, bugs, rats, mice and a host of other undesirables. We are able to overcome most catastrophes, suffer unbelievable hardships and are extremely good at giving it back to one other and, in particular, to the fragile environment that supports us like a long-suffering, patient aunt.

According to the IUCN, at least 784 documented extinctions have occurred since AD 1500, most through habitat loss and over exploitation. The last 100 years or so have seen an unprecedented level of species disappearances across the globe, including nearly 90 mammals and 17 birds – not due to climate change, earthquakes, tsunamis or meteorites, but by the hand of man. There are numerous factors behind the enormous loss of life on earth. The view is widely held that the uncontrolled human population expansion, and the subsequent loss of habitat, is a leading factor in biodiversity collapse. Africa, for example, has the distinction of being the continent with the fastest human population growth in the world. Most African governments have done very little about this problem or have simply ignored the fact. How do you begin to tell someone that having numerous children is not in the family's best interest and certainly not in the best interest of the child?

Sensible people and sensible governments know that we have an enormous problem. In Africa, the issue is too thorny, and few, if any, politicians are prepared to stick their necks out to confront it. Can we not, as individuals, do something about it? Or do we believe it is the responsibility of the government to lift people out of poverty and degradation? Do we leave it to them to ensure that everything will turn out right?

Four days ago as I penned this, persons as yet unknown shot a white rhino in a holding pen, 7 kilometres away from our home with a crossbow; they did not want to be detected and crossbows are silent. White rhino are fairly tough animals though, and in spite of being shot with four bolts he survived. Who on earth would do this, and with such a weapon? It's unfortunately quite simple: it's all about money, and lots of it. If they had been successful, they would have cut the horns off, scrambled over the wall and vanished. The horn of this seven-year-old male probably weighs about 2 kilograms and has a value of around US$10,000 to the poacher. Anything that is in demand has value, and in this case the rhino's horn put the animal in jeopardy. It is a very difficult issue. Can you be poor and remain honest? Likewise if you are rich? If it's there for the taking, even if it is a protected species, why not help yourself? Of what consequence is the slaughter of an animal when its death will relieve the poverty of your family? These products all have a street value and as long as there are hungry men in the front lines, there will always be greedy men in the backrooms.

I recently travelled to a once-remote area in northern KwaZulu-Natal to view a sanctuary that houses both species of African rhino and is home to 250 elephants, the last remnant of the great herds that inhabited that part of the province in the 19th century. When I travelled to the area 30 years ago, it was very sparsely populated. I set off from the small village of Jozini, high up in the Lebombo Mountains of Maputaland, and took the sand road for 60 kilometres to a T-junction where there was a single trading store and nothing much else. I carried on to Ndumo Game Reserve on an even sandier road. I turned off at Makanes Drift and drove over the Pongola River, passed a few more dwellings and proceeded to Sihangwane, which was situated at what was eventually to become the entrance of the Tembe Elephant Park. There were wandering cattle and goats and the ubiquitous chickens, but very few people, and even fewer dwellings, and most of these were hidden in the bush. Kilometre after kilometre with not a soul in sight, and the bush on either side of the road was pristine. You could be forgiven for thinking you were in the middle of nowhere.

The locals utilised the natural resources of reeds and thatching grass to build their beautiful beehive-shaped huts, and each family occupied their own private forest clearing. Most of the young men were either unemployed or worked further south on farms or had moved to the cities, leaving the women and children and old men to carry on with the age-old customs of family life. There were some 51 kraal sites and I set about documenting their traditional dwellings and many of the inhabitants themselves. There existed here a tremendous wealth of indigenous knowledge, which was beyond my scope to capture. What I did capture, however, was a microcosm of a way of life that I did not realise was to slowly vanish. Even though I knew these people would one day have to give way to the elephants and move away, I certainly did not imagine their way of life could ever become extinct.

Moving people to make way for animals is always going to be an issue in Africa. But make way they did and today, thanks to the far-sighted vision of various individuals who pressed their governments (in this case the KwaZulu Bureau on Natural Resources supported by the Minister of Economic Affairs and Chief Minister, Mangosuthu Buthelezi), the Tembe Elephant Park was proclaimed in October of 1983. If action had not been taken, no matter how controversial at the time, I am certain a unique area would have been lost forever and along with it a large slice of its biodiversity.

When I returned in October of 2011, the elephant sanctuary was a reality and the local people had been relocated. A valuable asset has been preserved in the establishment of this 30,000-hectare reserve, which represents one of the finest examples of tropical dry forest in southern Africa. Important plants, rare species of birds and a wide variety of introduced animal species, formerly absent, have found a safe haven here. The black and white rhino once occurred here, but were long ago shot out. The only large mammal to survive were the elusive elephants, which are now flourishing within the electrified perimeter fence. In establishing the park for elephants, the authorities also provided a sanctuary for rhinos.

Today the picture is very different. From Jozini, after crossing the dam wall, right through to Makanes Drift, one can hardly get away from the rows and rows of houses (breeze blocks and iron roofs, many pretty smart), the vehicles and the people. This area is described as the Pongola Zone after the river of the same name, which is the most important feature of this extremely rich floristic region. In 1990 Alan

Mountain, in his important book *Paradise under Pressure*, wrote the following: 'The ecology of the Pongola floodplain is finely tuned and, sadly, the careful balance struck by nature is being increasingly disturbed, not only by the damming of the Pongola River at Jozini, but also by the increasing population pressure on the floodplain'. Those words were penned 21 years ago and what we saw then was more than a little disturbing.

One does not have to be a trained ecologist to recognise the changes that have taken place in the last 30 years. If one has to justify the protection of an area solely on the grounds of so-called sustainable utilisation and use that as an example for an area's right to exist, then extinction is a real possibility. Why does one so often hear that if it pays, it stays? That mindset is often driven by political considerations, and stems from the poverty that arises from population growth and high unemployment.

Most of the KwaZulu-Natal reserves are living repositories of biodiversity surrounded by the encroaching human population – all the more reason to hold onto and conserve what remains. But how do you tell a woman who is the head of her household, on the last leg of her journey to Tembe Elephant Park, who earns less than R170 a month, that cutting down the Lebombo wattle (*Newtonia hildebrandtii*), a protected tree mind you, is not a very sensible thing to do? If she has a family to look after, and there is no possibility of gaining meaningful work, and the trees are occupying her space, then who is to tell her not to support her family? The wood is not sold to the reserve's lodge guests, they have no need of it. It is for sale to campers and sport fisherman heading to the coast.

To this end one is reminded of the words of Ann Crittendon:

Like a modern Midas, it [tourism] has transformed much of the world's natural beauty into pure gold. In the process, the industry may have planted the seeds of its own destruction. For the suspicion is growing, ever so slowly, that the more tourism succeeds, the more it cannibalises the very basis of its own existence.

The point is that there are many issues that may lead to extinction and there are equally increasing threats as our world gets more crowded. On the 31st of October 2011 the world population passed the 7 billion mark. We are going to eventually jostle ourselves to death in search of food and accommodation. Earth can't sustain the trend in human population growth. The planet is reaching its human carrying capacity. Unless governments place the topic of population pressure at the top of the agenda, the world is in for a bumpy ride.

Before the turn of the 19th century, South Africa witnessed the extinction of several species of mammal. The most famous was the quagga (*Equus quagga quagga*).The word quagga is derived from the Khoe *khoua khoua*, an imitation of the species' bark-like cry. The quagga differed in colour from the Cape mountain, Hartmann's and Burchell's zebras, and had no markings or stripes on its legs or hindquarters. It once abounded all over the Karoo of the Cape and the plains of the Free State, where it may have survived as late as 1878. It was shot to extinction and the tragedy is that the only specimen in South Africa is the skin of a foal in the Iziko South African Museum in Cape Town.

The so-called Cape lion (*Panthera leo melanochaitus*), a subspecies, was notable for its huge black mane that covered the shoulders entirely and traversed the abdomen to the hind legs. What distinguished the animal was the short, broad head. Lions and cattle don't mix well and the expanding settlement in the Cape meant that the lion became a prime target for irate stock farmers. Its demise probably had little to do with collecting or sport hunting – it was simply a nuisance. It became extinct in the Cape by around 1858 and in Zululand in 1865. No specimen exists in any South African museum.

In many respects the most dramatic extinction was the blue buck or *blauwbok* in Afrikaans (*Hippotragus leucophaeus*). The animal stood about 1.27 metres tall and was bluish-grey in colour with no face markings and slender curved horns. It was largely confined to the south-western Cape and disappeared before science had any, or very little, opportunity to study it. It is believed not to have survived beyond 1800, and was thus the first of the African mammals to become extinct. Sadly, no mounted specimen is to be found in South Africa.

Since then we have nearly added both species of rhino, the bontebok (*Damaliscus dorcas*) and the Cape mountain zebra (*Equus zebra zebra*). Conservation of southern Africa's wildlife during the 20th century has certainly had its up and downs. The rhino, we are told, is already in an evolutionary cul-de-sac in terms of the 10 million years generally allotted to individual species. There is not a great deal we can do about that at present, but hopefully we can accommodate them for the foreseeable future.

There have been many hard-fought battles, especially for the rhino, and not forgetting the elephant. Unfortunately for both, mankind has had a love affair for a very long time with both species because he covets the horn and the tusk. Extinction at the hand of man is not a late phenomenon. Today we are witnessing the extinction of thousands of species as humanity slowly but surely grinds the world's species to dust. Unlike the Neanderthals who drove the woolly rhinos to extinction trying to survive, modern-day extinctions occur for a number of reasons: over exploitation, degradation, survival and the most insidious – greed.

CHAPTER 4

Path of Blood

In March 1647 the Dutch ship *Nuwe Haerlem*, en route from Batavia to the Netherlands Republic, was wrecked in Table Bay. Although the ship could not be salvaged, the captain and crew managed to reach land safely. The captain left for the Netherlands on a ship that was on its return journey, but junior merchant Leendert Janssen and 60 sailors had to stay behind for over a year. Janssen wrote that a rhino was shot 'near the fort' and that 'the flesh was firm and tasty'. 'Near the fort' must indicate that the rhino was seen on or very near the peninsula itself – this was the first written record of the rhino at the Cape.

Jan van Riebeeck arrived at the Cape of Good Hope on the 6th of April 1652 as a result of the Janssen report, which stirred up the Dutch East India Company. The company had sent him and his crew out to set up a trading station, a fort and a garden; zoology was not part of his brief. Van Riebeeck's first record of the rhino in the Cape came in September of 1652 from one of the men tracking down three deserters of the settlement, near what is today Somerset West, 'In the evening marched 7 miles. Saw two rhinoceroses which charged us and threatened to destroy us, but God protected us. Jan Verdonck had to abandon his hat and sword'. They were all condemned to work as slaves in irons for two years and Jan Blanx, the architect of the desertion, was keel-hauled and got 150 lashes. Thus ended the first expedition away from the fort. It was two years later, in March 1654,

43

that the second record of rhino appears in Van Riebeeck's diary. As Johan Nieuhof reported, 'We heard that a rhinoceros, or nose-horner, was fallen in a marsh and, because of its weight could not get out. Commander Riebeeck sent some soldiers with muskets, but the bullets rebounded from its hard wrinkled skin'.

Europeans were familiar with the rhino from a woodcut produced by Albrecht Dürer in 1515. This image was to immortalise the rhino for the next three centuries. The woodcut was clearly that of the armour-plated Indian rhino, with the exception of the artistic licence in the form of an additional horn on the animal's shoulder. The woodcut was based on a rhino that was a gift from Sultan Muzaffar II of Gujarat on the west coast of India, to Afonso de Albuquerque, governor of Portuguese India. Albuquerque, in turn, sent it on to his king, Manuel I 'The Fortunate', who was an aficionado of the unusual. The gift, chained and shackled to the deck of the *Nossa Senhora da Ajuda*, departed from Goa on the west coast of India in January 1515 and arrived in Lisbon on the 20th of May 1515. It was the first rhino in Europe since the fall of the Roman Empire 1,300 years before. In December 1515, Dom Manuel I sent the rhino as a gift to Pope Leo X, from whom he needed some favours. The vessel sank in a storm off the north Italian coast and with it the rhino it conveyed. The carcass eventually washed up on shore. Dürer never saw a living or dead rhino in his lifetime and relied on a brief sketch and an account from an eye witness, who had seen the animal in Portugal.

Imagine the surprise of Van Riebeeck's men reporting the presence of another type of rhino in Africa – with two horns one behind the other, no horn on the shoulder and without the expected armour plating. It took another 162 years before the formal recognition of a second African rhino species appeared when William John Burchell observed the white rhino in the northern Cape, around Kuruman, in 1812.

In September 1685 the governor at the Cape, Simon van der Stel, had a narrow escape when he and his carriage were attacked by a black rhino near Picketberg. Black rhino were plentiful in the Western Cape at the time. Stellenbosch, Paarl, Saldanha Bay and Riebeeck Kasteel all produced stories of incidents with 'the sort of animal that does not go unnoticed or unrecorded'. C. J. Skead records a translation of the carriage attack from an eye witness account by Francois Valentyn:

> an unbelievable large Rhinoceros appeared, coming with great fury and viciousness straight for the centre of our column and from there running along to the rear where His Excellency was in his coach. It made directly for this, His Excellency having barely time enough to get out from the coach. Leaping out with a blunderbuss in his hand and aiming this at the beast which was not six paces distant from him; and he intended to fire, but the blunderbuss misfired, the rear catch striking the forward one. We expected nothing else but that the furious beast would devour his Excellency before our eyes but it ran past him, brushing against his body . . . We believe that this was due to the shot that one of His Excellency's hunters fired at it, whereat it ran from us at great speed. Several others who were on horseback were unable to avoid it, falling from their mounts in great fright, whereby they wounded themselves in many places.

Van der Stel survived and in all governed for 20 years, retiring to his estate, Constantia, which today is famous for its superb wines and beautiful Cape Dutch architecture. Apart from leaving us one of the first-recorded incidents with a rhino, he is noted for having established the town of Stellenbosch – a further memorial to his excellent taste.

The new arrivals brought a weapon that made a very loud noise, filled the air with black smoke and kicked like an ox. In the right hands it was to prove most effective. The San killed only what they needed for many centuries and, armed with a relatively light bow and arrows tipped with poison, the odds were still in the animal's favour. The bantu-speaking people likewise hunted game for their own needs, food, clothing, decoration and medicine. The Khoe pastoralists quickly learnt to use guns to assist their new masters. The arrival of the Dutch in 1652 heralded the beginning of the most wanton slaughter of South

Africa's wildlife, which, while slow to begin with, was to last nearly 250 years. When the first musket shots were fired on the slopes of Table Mountain, and the rhino pricked up its ears, the die was cast.

What is fascinating to historians is that the English arrived in what is now Table Bay in 1601, but made no attempt to establish a base. In spite of two sea captains in 1620 claiming the Cape for James I, the English still failed to take action, leaving it to the Dutch to do so in 1652. The Dutch were in no hurry to allow penetration into the interior, however, for their original intention was the establishment of a victualing station. For the next 150 years, Europeans were largely confined to an area the size of France and England combined, which was known as the Cape Colony. The Cape was the gateway to Africa, but the Dutch authorities were not enthusiastic about their *volk* wandering off into the interior. The terrain was unknown and by all accounts dangerous. What they had not bargained for was the wanderlust of their citizens, many of whom had already drifted north beyond their control. These trekboers were made up of a number of nationalities with Germans accounting for the highest percentage, followed by Dutch and French.

The first expedition into the interior, which used a wagon pulled by oxen, took place in October 1662 and was led by a certain Corporal Cruithoff. They were in search of a river, possibly the Orange, which was believed to be the frontier of Monomotapa. Thus was born the 'ship of the veld' pulled by teams of oxen, which became home, defence, source of provisions and transporter of goods, especially, in time, ivory. It was the forerunner of the 'ship of the American prairies' and was likewise extensively used in Australia and New Zealand. Without these remarkable wood-and-iron vehicles, the great exploration of southern Africa by the likes of Simon van der Stel, who ordered Ensign Olof Berg to seek out the supposed copper mines in the interior, would have been impossible. He set off with 6 wagons and 31 whites, but failed to find the mountain. It would be interesting to know how they handled the oxen or how many wagons fell to pieces. We know he got back because the governor himself set off in 1685 with eight carts, seven wagons, a multitude of oxen, one cannon and one boat to cross the River Esperito Santo in Monomotapa. Their idea of distance was way off, for this in fact is the Limpopo River and they only managed to get to present-day Springbok. They did, however, find the mountain. He abandoned any thought of mining as transport would be difficult. The governor must have known a thing or two about ox-wagon travel for he chose to travel by coach and five horses.

The following people were to use various makes and sizes of the original Cape wagon, which were no doubt refined and strengthened to cope with the tough South African conditions: Carl Thunberg, the father of Cape botany, Andrew Spaarman, who produced the first accurate description of the San and the Khoe, Henry Lichtenstein, who undertook the first serious study of Cape animal life, William John Burchell, David Livingstone, James Chapman, Thomas Baines, William Cotton Oswell and William Charles Baldwin, not to mention missionaries, prospectors, traders, European settlers of varying origin, all the great Dutch hunters, the Great Trek and even the British Army.

By 1690 the musket had already been responsible for the disappearance of the hippo in the Cape and it did not take Simon van der Stel long to complain to Holland that far too many of the colonists were more preoccupied with hunting than farming. By 1720 the elephants in the south-western Cape were written off by hunters, who then proceeded north-east. One can be very certain the black rhino was to give way as well, and while the horn did not have the same value as ivory, both the colonists and their slaves were happy to eat the animal, especially since they had so many mouths to feed.

The question of slavery was to have a profound effect on the subsequent large-scale movement north, which nearly heralded the end of the vast herds of game that once covered the South African veld. To emphasise the point, Alan Cattrick notes that one truculent group of burghers in the town of Graaff-Reinet issued a proclamation in 1789 'that every Bushman [San] and Hottentot (Khoe) shall for life be the lawful property of such burghers as may possess them, and serve in bondage from generation to generation'. Imagine their reaction after the British took control from the Dutch in 1806 and required written authority for anyone intending to conduct an expedition beyond the limit of the colony boundary, which was the Orange River. This was further exacerbated by the emancipation of all slaves by an act of the British parliament in 1834. The fact that the rules came from the English did not help matters, especially in areas pertaining to 'Hottentots and ex-slaves being placed on an equal footing with Christians'.

In the United States of America the abolition of slavery led to a bloody civil war and in South Africa it led to the Great Trek. By 1836, the discontent among the Boers was at its peak. Reports of a land beyond the Orange River teeming with game, largely unpopulated and fertile, was enough to set 7,000 hardy Afrikaners, who were to become known as Voortrekkers, on a journey to the north. Despite the unknown risks they would certainly face, they were very determined to put as much distance between themselves and the hated oppressive British colonial administration as possible. It was a trek into goodness knows where, and the commencement of one of the most momentous events in our history. That story is for others to tell, but before we go any further let us examine how the explorers, traders and hunters made their way into the interior in search of the country's bountiful wildlife, and why the ox wagon was to prove indispensable.

William John Burchell, the son of a prosperous market gardener, was born in Fulham, just outside of London, in 1781. As a child he was fair, of slight build and short in stature. As an adult he was only 1.63 metres tall. William turned out to be brighter than most, taking ancient and modern languages and mathematics. His hobbies included drawing and painting and he played both the flute and the harpsichord. After school he went on to study botany at Kew, distinguishing himself in 1803 by being elected a fellow of the Linnaeus Society – no mean achievement for a young man of 22.

If his father had hoped his son would follow in his footsteps, he was in for a surprise. In 1805, when his parents refused his wishes to be engaged to a young lady, William left England. He took up a post of school teacher with the British East India Company in windswept St

Helena in the Atlantic Ocean, of all places, with the added appointment of 'acting botanist' (why 'acting' it is not known). His parents later relented and gave the young lady their blessing, and she soon followed in William's footsteps. The banns had been called, the lodgings were ready and the big day set – the whole island knew and were most likely all invited. Unfortunately, as can happen on long boat voyages, the young fiancée, Lucian Green, having set sail in 1808, promptly fell in love with the ship's captain. Little William Burchell had waited three years for his bride in the absence of music, art and literature, let alone intellectual inspiration, teaching children and collecting plants on the desolate wastes of St Helena. Imagine the shock he endured when she told him he had waited in vain.

But, as so often in life, when fate deals you such a blow, it is the supposed misfortune that in the end turns out for the best. Certainly for South African travel and exploration we have to be eternally grateful to the fair Lucian for jilting Mr Burchell. He was soon to meet Dr Henry Lichtenstein, who had stopped at St Helena en route to Holland. After meeting and talking to Lichtenstein, his mind was made up to visit what he now believed to be the most abundant floristic kingdom. Nothing like it existed anywhere in the British Isles, and it must have been beyond his wildest imagination. This chance encounter was to set him on a course to the fair Cape where he spent the next ten years of his life, four of which were spent travelling in an ox wagon.

Burchell commissioned the construction of a Cape wagon from one of the colony's wagon builders for the sum of £88, after he had met the new British governor, Lord Caledon, and advised him of his plans to travel and explore the interior of South Africa. The governor was enthusiastic about the expedition, as the motivation was born of science, rather than sport or hunting, and was intended to collect and study the fauna and flora beyond where any European had hitherto travelled.

Burchell spent six months preparing for his expedition and it cost him £800 by the time he was ready to set forth – a not inconsiderable some of money in 1811. This figure included a second wagon and the oxen to pull it. Depending on the load, wagons could be pulled by up to 16 oxen. He did not appear, it seems, to have had much problem with funding, and his list of travel items was considerable. While he is regarded as a collector rather than a hunter, his provisions, which were to become the norm for explorers and more so with hunters, included the following:

6 muskets and powder horns
1 fowling piece and shot belt
1 large rifle that could carry a 2-ounce bullet
2 cases of pistols and belts
1 cutlass
4 barrels of gunpowder
Bags of shot
Bullet moulds, lead and tin bars

In addition to this he took essentials such as wine, rum and brandy as well as 50 books and a vast supply of pens, ink, paints, brushes, writing and drawing paper. The stage was set for the beginning of what may be considered the first great safari.

The so-called Cape wagon measured around 5 metres long and about a metre wide at its tapered floor. The rear wheels stood about 1.7 metres high and the front wheels about 1.5 metres. The upper part of the wagon consisted of a domed bamboo and light wood structure, which was covered in canvas and ran almost the full length of the chassis. To put it in Burchell's words, the Cape wagon's 'principle advantage consists in its sides, bottom, and carriage not being joined together, admitting each part to play freely, to avoid the straining and cracking to which solid-built wagons are subjected'.

He agreed with his oxen that about 20 miles was a full day's work, which he calculated from the fact that the rear wheel of his wagon managed 18 revolutions per minute, which works out to 3 miles, 390 yards per hour. One can only deduce that the oxen were ready to quit after their six daily hours of travel. It is estimated that he rode or walked some 4,500 miles during his four-year sojourn. He clearly enjoyed travel and loved his wagon:

To me every spot on which my wagon stood was home, there was my resting place; there was my abode. Few as were the comforts of such a dwelling, and though they might be such as the luxurious would think very deserving of that name, they were accompanied by health and contentment, and have often afforded greater enjoyment than more splendid accommodation . . . whenever I view my drawing of its interior a thousand agreeable recollections are brought to my mind: and, while indulging in the various, and often opposite, sensations which they create, I am transported back to the Africa scene, unconscious of being in a better land.

Various models were built, including a transport wagon without the upper structure and capable of carrying heavy loads. Of critical importance were the hard, termite-resistant brake blocks, which were operated from the rear of the wagon. These were essential when negotiating steep mountain passes. The wagons could be dismantled and the parts carried individually by oxen over difficult terrain when necessary. This was nevertheless a very hard task as a wagon, even unloaded and taken apart, is a very heavy structure.

By the end of the 17th century, the black rhino was extinct around the Cape Town environs and few were to be seen within the colony. Burchell made the discovery of a second species of rhino near Chue Springs in the vicinity of present-day Kuruman in the Northern Cape. Stoffel Speelman, a hunter and handyman of Khoe descent, shot the first white rhino that Burchell was to classify in 1812. They shot 12 of the species in all. Burchell would have shot specimens of the black rhino as well, for he considered the tongue of the animal the best he had ever eaten.

On his eventual return to Cape Town in 1815 he had amassed over 63,000 specimens. These included approximately 40,000 botanical specimens, 265 bird species and the skins of no less than 120 quadrupeds of 95 species. He was to spend the next six years sorting and classifying his specimens and writing the two volumes of his explorations. *Travels in the Interior of Southern Africa* was published in 1822/3, totalling 500,000 words with 120 drawings, and if you are ever fortunate enough to hold one of these volumes in your hands, you will realise that it is a treasure of priceless value. After ten years of relentless toil, often under very trying conditions, he received only £1,500 for his efforts.

Burchell, while providing the world with an unbelievable treasure trove of collected species, many new to science, was the front runner in what was to become the scramble for Africa's wild game. To his credit he did not kill for profit or pleasure, as did those who were to follow him. He did, however, note that a decline in the once vast array of wildlife was evident.

His English colleagues, in their ignorance of Africa, prompted him to write to his mother before he left St Helena to tell her that should he be so fortunate as to discover the unicorn, he could earn five times the worth of a giraffe skin that had sold in London for £1,500. This was nearly twice what it cost to outfit his entire expedition.

He never married, and returned to England to devote himself to his work and died by his own hand at the age of 82, largely alone and forgotten. He never did discover the unicorn, but what he did discover was far greater. He will forever be remembered for having classified the white rhino.

Following in the wake of Burchell, and right on the heels of the departing Voortrekkers in 1836, came a debonair, striking English officer of the Royal Engineers from Bombay, India. Captain William Cornwallis Harris had been greatly influenced by the writings of Burchell and came to Africa to undertake, in his own words, 'a little shooting and some sketching'. He had been ordered by the army doctors to take two years' leave, to recover from the effects of 'fever'. The journey to Cape Town aboard the *Indiaman* took 11 weeks and during that period Harris persuaded a fellow passenger and English sportsman, William Richardson, to accompany him, 'heart, hand and purse'. One must not forget that they were first and foremost of the gentleman class. Harris had even brought his own teapot, a tent, a barrel of gunpowder (imagine trying to board a ship today with a barrel of gunpowder) and loads of drawing materials. Neither had ever been to Africa before.

On their expedition, Harris discovered the sable antelope (*Hippotragus niger*) in the Magaliesberg. He was the first European to collect a specimen and promptly decided to have it named the 'Harris buck' after himself, although this was later changed to sable antelope. They loaded 18,000 lead bullets onto their wagons and shot no less than 400 animals. A large part of this slaughter was elephants and rhinos, both of which he hunted with ruthless determination. He produced a sensational account of his travels with his refreshingly beautiful illustrations of no less than 30 full-colour plates. *The Wild Sports of Southern Africa* was published in 1838. His delight and description of his various hunts are of particular interest when writing about the white and black rhino, which they encountered in great numbers. When we read the accounts of people such as Harris, are we to excuse them for what we would deem wanton slaughter? Are we to forgive them of their ignorance? Frankly, no. Most were intelligent and well educated, obsessed with collecting, either for personal profit, science, glory or the edification of the 'chase'. In the introduction to his book he wrote:

> Victories gained over the savage tenants of the forest constantly formed the prelude to heroic exploits in war; and the splendid monuments which transmitted to after ages the military achievements of the Emperors of Rome, not infrequently blended with their most celebrated triumphs, the glories of the chase.

It is interesting to note that after encountering the white rhino he noted that 'no quadruped with which naturalists are acquainted would appear to correspond more nearly than the white rhinoceros with the stubborn reem or unicorn of Holy Writ'.

Within the Cashan Mountains (Magaliesberg), he encountered great numbers of rhinos and on one occasion 80 were seen in one day's march alone. On another occasion in the valley of the Limpopo no fewer than 22 were encountered and they were compelled to 'slaughter' (his own word) four of them in self-defence. He described the rhino as 'a meddling officious marplot, perpetually in the way, and always prepared for mischief, wheresoever the rhinoceros was not there was he sure to be'. His colourful way of describing encounters would horrify the modern-day reader, 'It was shortly after we had crossed the Mariqua, [Marico] that the first rhinoceros seen by our party was numbered with the dead'.

In his attempts to shoot a roan antelope (*Hippotragus equinus*) one day, he was repeatedly disturbed by a pair of white rhinos, which he described as 'bullying' in their nature and generally made their lives extremely difficult. Upon encountering the pair again the next morning, he decided to call the belligerent gentlemen to serious account. He and his followers fired a simultaneous broadside of seven lead-and-tin bullets which Harris proudly notes, 'perforated him like a cullender [colander]'.

Harris was even more eloquent in his description of the black rhino, which he was to first encounter on the Molopo River, 'He is a swinish beast, cross-grained, ill-favoured, wallowing brute, with a hide like a rasp, an impudent cock of the chin, a roguish leer from out the corner of his eye, a mud-begrimed exterior and a necklace of ticks and horse flies.' The black rhino was clearly abundant and readily killed by hunters, and he gives it credit for being capable of speed and of determined charges. One is, however, left with the feeling that they did not regard them as capital sport, but rather an animal that could provide a hunting party and the inevitable followers with fresh meat.

So numerous were they that his party would kill two to three black rhino within view of the camp daily. This is an animal that can weigh up to 1,500 kilograms, and the mind simply boggles at the volume of meat they must have consumed. As they advanced each day the species became more and more abundant, and towards the end of his description he refers to one they had shot that was descended upon by famished Baquaina females, more scantily clad than usual, who fell upon the rhino carcass like weird witches, and within a few hours left nothing but a bloody pool to attest to the slaughter.

His description of each species is precise and his pencil and pen drawings are excellent. His illustrations of both species' horns are among the best produced at the time. A keen and observant naturalist and artist, his book was a major contribution of the time and as only 500 were published it must rank as one of the most prized and sought-after works of Africana.

He originally left India on doctor's orders and when he eventually returned his 'fever' caught up with him and he died in Poona in 1848. He was just 41 years old. It can rightfully be said that he was the first of the great white hunters of Africa who was driven by the chase. Unfortunately his book, and Burchell's, were to inspire a new generation of white hunters who sought to close with the 'swinish beast' covered in 'ticks and horse flies'.

Adulphe Delegorgue, a French traveller, naturalist and hunter who also followed in Burchell's wake, arrived in Port Natal in 1839 in the company of the Swedish naturalist J. G. Wahlberg. His travels took him past Thabazimbi at the south-western edge of the Waterberg and ended at the confluence of the Palala and Limpopo rivers. I have chosen to include Delegorgue because he spent time in the very same region that my family has lived and worked in for more than 30 years. Very few conservationists would recognise his name, for a simple reason: his two volumes, *Voyage dans L'Afrique Australe* (Travels in Southern Africa), which were published in 1847, were in French. The volume of interest here, number two, was only published in English in 1997 by the Killie Campbell Africana Library and the University of Natal Press.

The back page of the English edition states that 'he has informed, entertained, charmed and – sometimes – infuriated readers'. He had a sense of humour and his personal observations, if one could forgive his crass behaviour, are of value, even if they are misguided at times. It is possible to overlook his actions and words, some 160 years later, because he realised that the white rhino was becoming scarce, but most of his records leave one in a rage when considering what has since overtaken both African rhino species. He describes the disappearance of *Rhinoceros africanus bicornis,* or black rhino, from the Sisikamma (Tsitsikamma), the country of amaXhosa, amaMpondo and Natal itself, while noting that the country of the amaZulu still held the species *Rhinoceros simus*, or the white rhino. Nowadays one has to look north-east of the Makalisburg (Magaliesberg) to find rhino. He notes in his writings:

> It is not surprising that man has driven this animal from his domains for, apart from the fact that it would be impossible to domesticate it, this swart-rhenoster, as the Boers call it, or chokourou makaley, as it is known to the Makaschlas, is a bad neighbour. The damage it causes in cultivated areas is immense. It frequently scatters the oxen by charging them in a demented fashion, without the least provocation, and even man himself is not safe from its freakish and sanguinary humours. Its flesh, which the Cafres like to eat, and which the Boers find tolerable, is worth killing for, and the skin, strong and translucent when dry, is highly suitable for the making of Chambocks [sjamboks], and so the gentleman hunter is tempted to take a potshot at it, if only for the sake of a dozen sharp and flexible riding-whips.

He describes the flesh of the black rhino as being superior to that of the elephant, not as good as that of the hippo and inferior to that of the white rhino. The fat, which is thinner than that of the white rhino, was quite delicate. The black rhino provided a large quantity of meat for the hunter and his followers. The horn was not regarded as valuable when compared with the ivory of elephants, which imposed far more risk on the hunter. Delegorgue's discussion of the animal's flesh confirms my opinion that it was one of the principal causes of the species' demise in those times.

As for the animal's disposition, he thought it 'noxious' and predicted that it:

> would soon disappear from the region Makalisberg [Magaliesberg], for it had killed numerous men and horses. In spite of this, young men and boys of fourteen or so, armed with powerful guns, have little hesitation

in hunting down a dangerous animal as they are accurate marksmen and have the boldness of children.

His description is accurate for the Boer, as we know, was never far from his *roer* (gun), and youths were taught from an early age to shoot accurately, for they did not have the luxury of unlimited lead and gunpowder.

Delegorgue regarded the rhino as relatively easy to kill, but nevertheless considered the animal dangerous to man and offered the following advice:

> One does not have to take excessive precautions. Leave your dogs behind as they are useless as they are for elephant. Good for lion though. Approach him carefully from downwind by crawling, as you don't want to be detected, select the shoulder joint, and hit him with a ball weighing a sixth or a tenth of a pound, made of two parts lead and two parts of tin.

A muzzleloader in the hands of an experienced marksman can be loaded and fired three times in one minute. What Delegorgue does not record is that not every shot would kill a rhino, especially when considering the many that escaped later hunters. If the animal was hit with the lead-and-tin ball and then came after you, he felt one's chances were slim if you ran downwind, 'A man who is fleet of foot who runs a straight line will outrun the animal for a while but will soon be overtaken'. He describes a man watching over some horses who was surprised by a rhino who did just that. The rhino caught up to him and tossed him repeatedly into the air, as much as 15 feet, as was attested by tattered remains of intestines and hair left hanging in the branches of acacias.

Delegorgue was at a loss to understand the animal's 'horrifying behaviour'. He wondered why a herbivore who was not threatened, and had no need to protect itself, would kill a man. He even considered the possibility that the animal killed for the pleasure of it. He arrived at his conclusion while viewing the dissection of a black rhino. The large number of bot fly larvae (*Gyrostigma rhinocerontis*) found in the animal's gut was, in his opinion, the cause of its implacable fury. He came to this conclusion after discovering that he was himself infected by a tapeworm, which had caused him to 'foam at the mouth'. Whatever the cause of the animal's fury, he believed it was only directed at man and his followers, such as horses, oxen and dogs, and not at other wild animals, which makes his diagnosis even more intriguing.

When reading such accounts is it not surprising that their actions stemmed largely from ignorance? While Delegorgue wrote that the numbers were declining, it never occurred to any of them that they themselves were part of the problem.

The role of the paid professional hunter was to eventually emerge in East Africa in the very early 1900s and the rhino population was to undergo a decline of an entirely different order when poachers began targeting the animal for its horn. By 1900 the black and white rhino were almost extinct from the Cape to the Limpopo River. The Great Trek opened up South Africa to white settlers. Local black peoples were uprooted by the white invasion, which resulted in wars against the various tribes and wars, or rather rebellion, among the Voortrekkers. The scramble for the country was underway and right in its path lay the great herds that populated this once-wild region. As the tide rolled forward, so the rhino, the elephant, the great herds of springbok, the Cape buffalo, the eland and others started to retreat. The destruction was unprecedented.

It was not long before laws were enacted in the Cape to curb the rapid decline of wildlife. But the laws, which would curtail the hunting activities of the early colonists, were not well received. In time, the descendants of these pioneering, hardy people were to take grave exception. In 1858, in the town of Rustenburg, in what would become the Transvaal Republic, laws were going to be enacted to reduce the slaughter of wildlife by limiting the sale of gunpowder and lead. Crenia Bond notes that 23 very irate burghers were quick to respond, by way of a petition to the president in Pretoria, arguing that 'as your Honour knows himself, we must make a living from game alone'.

The 19th century was by no means over, however, and we were yet to be visited by a gallery of some of the most famous names and faces ever to grace the pages of hunting, trading and exploration in South African history. These men were eccentric, bold, zealous, cruel and callous. They were avaricious but also artistic, and wrote books, collected specimens, braved hostile terrain and its occupants, not to mention fever. They went where no other European had trodden before. They often died early, and most had life-threatening encounters with dangerous game – one particular individual met his end under an elephant's foot. Apart from the Boers, only one of these great hunters was born in this country. James Chapman, elephant hunter and trader, was the first person ever to photograph a rhino. The photo is of a black rhino, shot in central Botswana in 1862. He was also the first person to photograph the Victoria Falls. He was friend and travelling companion to Thomas Baines. Before his death at the early age of 40, he was to write his story, as did most, comprising two volumes. All their writings have left us with an incredible insight into travel and the fauna that filled the African landscape from the Cape to the Zambezi. Most eventually wrote books to recover their costs, all shot elephant and rhino and other game that had value. One must not forget that the 19th century was the age of collecting. Ivory was coveted for billiard balls, dice, piano keys, false teeth, bagpipes, cutlery handles and carvings. Ostrich feathers were the craze in Europe's fashion industry, museums were always on the lookout for specimens and rhino-horn goblets were prized. Everything had a value and South Africa was the 'horn of plenty'. It was inevitable that one day it was going to collapse, but when Cornwallis Harris's book came out in 1840, it seemed as if it was just the beginning.

In reality, 1840 was the start of the decline and both species of rhino were in the line of fire. Seeing 80 rhino in a day's march was soon to be a thing of the past, and both species were to come perilously close to extinction.

In 1843 there came upon the scene what was to nearly all, and certainly the Boers, the most outlandish, bizarrely dressed and eccentric individual they had ever seen. A tall, well-built, red-bearded, blue-eyed Scotsman, who was in the habit of wearing a kilt to emphasise to the Boers that he was a 'Berg Scot', believing that 'the Boers are rather partial to Scotchmen although they detest the sight of an Englishman. They have an idea that the Scotch, like themselves, were a nation conquered by the English and that, consequently, we trek in the same yoke as themselves'. He introduced himself to the locals as follows:

> It was the custom in my country when friends meet to pledge one another in a bumper of spirits, at the same time suiting the action to the word, I filled him a brimming glass. This was my invariable practice first meeting a Boer. I found it a never-failing method of gaining his goodwill and he always replied that the Scotch were the best people in the world.

The spirit was neat gin.

Educated at Eton, Roualeyn Gordon Cumming of Altyre, Scotland, was a cavalry officer, a lieutenant of the Cape Mounted Rifles and was later to become a trader and a renowned elephant hunter. South Africa had never seen his like before or since. Reckless, conceited and boastful, he lived to shoot and the five years he spent in South Africa between 1843 and 1849 must rank as one of the most destructive trails of the death of wildlife ever undertaken. In his much publicised book, *A Hunter's Life in South Africa*, which was published in 1857 by John Murray, he offered his impressions of both species of rhino and recorded a number of hair-raising encounters. Both species were clearly still reasonably abundant and he took full advantage of this fact to run them down on horseback, although he had his fair share of adventures on foot. He killed rhino after rhino, merely to take the horns.

He was fearless and thought nothing of charging full tilt into his quarry, firing off the back of his various mounts into herds of elephant or rhino, buffalo and giraffe. He succeeded in losing 45 saddle horses and 70 oxen to lions, tsetse fly and accidents, and 70 dogs to lions, crocodiles, leopards or being trampled by buffalo. These losses included his best dog, favourite horse and his most-trusted wagon driver, Hendrick, who was snatched by a lion from beside the fire and devoured within hearing. All that remained were both legs below the knee with one shoe still attached.

The man was without remorse or feelings concerning his prey and never seemed to have tired from dawn to dusk. He particularly enjoyed setting up a hide near a waterhole and would spend the entire night blasting away, at point-blank range, at anything that came near the blind. On one evening, suitably fortified in his waterhole hide, he killed one kudu, two white rhinos, one black rhino bull and wounded two others. In his book he notes that 'three other rhinoceroses came up, but I was too drowsy to watch any longer and fell asleep'. It is not surprising that the rhino was most certainly not going to make it into the 20th century.

Over a period of two years, from 1846 to 1848, which were to be his last in Africa, he hunted extensively in Bechuana country. I have worked in this region, which stretches up to the Motloutse River in what is now eastern Botswana. He was among the first white men to travel to its junction with the Limpopo River and into what today is the Limpopo province.

His bag over four years amounted to some 800 antelope, 105 elephants, 80 lions, 60 hippos, 45 rhinos and more than 30 giraffe. This is an appalling loss of life and one shudders to think how many animals he wounded and left to die. His arsenal included three heavy double-barrelled rifles, one heavy single-barrelled German rifle and a further three 'stout double-barrelled guns for rough work'. The Boers by contrast were far more conservative in their choice of weapons, not having the luxury or the means to possess such heavy weapons as the English. They generally hunted with long, heavy, single-barrelled muzzle-loaders known as *roers*. Each ball fired had to count as they could not afford to be wasteful, something that never occurred to Cumming. His wagons carried 3 hundredweights of lead for moulding bullets and 50 pounds of pewter to harden them, along with 10,000 prepared lead bullets, 300 pounds of coarse gunpowder, 100 pounds of fine sporting gunpowder, 50,000 percussion caps and 2,000 gun flints. He certainly had no intention of running short.

Dr David Livingstone, who had assisted Cumming on an occasion when he lost all his oxen, was wrongly accused by the Boers of supplying muskets to Matabele tribesmen, who used them against the Voortrekkers, and burnt his mission down in reprisal. In reality the Matabele acquired most of these weapons in raids against the Bechuana tribes. Cumming regarded himself as being liked by the Boers who were more inclined to place the blame of what they considered a betrayal on poor old Livingstone whom they distrusted intensely.

Cumming considered muskets as a trade item and he mentions 'a number of common muskets which represented to me as being the most available articles to barter for ivory with the tribes in the interior'. A case of 20 muskets cost him £16. At 16 shillings a musket, it is anyone's guess what quality of weapon it must have been, which was probably of little or no concern to him as his intention was to acquire as much profit as possible by bartering them for ivory. 'I demanded for each firelock ivory to the value of upwards of £30, being about 3,000 per cent, which I am informed is reckoned among mercantile men to be a fair profit,' he said.

When he finally departed South Africa in 1848 it took nine wagons to convey his massive collection and piles of ivory to the coast, the like of which had not been seen before in Britain. He would have sold most of his ivory in Grahamstown before sailing. Apart from the ivory of the 105 elephants he shot, he would have bartered beads and trinkets for more ivory, which would have brought him at least £5,000, not to mention the ostrich feathers, rhino horns, lion and leopard skins and various assorted items one would expect after travelling in the interior for as long as he did.

How he ever survived so long is a mystery for he had more than his fair share of danger and adventure and the loss of so many horses and dogs tells one something of his insatiable desire to close with his quarry be it lion, elephant, rhino, buffalo or hippo. His rifle once exploded in his face and he, along with all those 19th-century hunters and traders, suffered from malaria and dysentery and existed on an appalling diet.

Upon his return to London he was, for a time, the talk of the capital and was most likely wined and dined till he dropped. Or perhaps, in his case, not for he clearly had the constitution of a buffalo. In the end, however, it did get to him. It is reputed that he took to the bottle and in failing health anticipated his own death in 1866 by ordering the coffin that he was shortly to occupy. He was 47.

All 63 rhino horns, and several rhino-horn walking sticks, were sold at an auction held not long after his death. Most pairs sold for less than £3, with the highest selling for £7. Among the trophies he took back to England were two white rhino horns measuring 1.58 metres and 1.32 metres (one weighing 19 kg!), which were housed along with his collection at Inverness in Scotland. Both horns were stolen in October 1988 from the family's stately Scottish home and never recovered.

William Cotton Oswell arrived in Africa in 1845. Like his contemporaries he was a product of India, but not of the military. He suffered from severe attacks of malaria, which resulted in his departure to the Cape. On his very first expedition into Bechuanaland (Botswana) he and a companion, Mungo Murray, killed 89 rhinos, six of which were killed with single shots. He was to survive two serious charges by rhino. The first tossed both him and his horse, and although he escaped unharmed, his favourite horse was killed. His horse survived the second incident, but Oswell was badly gored in the right thigh – an 8-inch flesh wound that reached down to the bone and stopped close to the femoral artery.

While perfectly content to shoot every rhino he came across at the time, Oswell was struck with remorse 50 years later, as is evident in his writing:

> one species of rhinoceros, the Mahoho [white rhino] is extinct! I am very sorry. He was never found north of the Zambezi, but between that river and the Malopo . . . he was formerly in great force. Poor old stupid fellow, too quiet as a rule, though when thoroughly upset (like

a good natured man in a passion) reckless, he was just the very thing for young gunners to try their prentice hand on and once the kafirs got muskets he was bound to go; though considering the numbers there used to be, I hoped he would last a little longer.

Unlike their English counterparts, hunting was a way of life for the Boers, and in those early days often a matter of survival. With the advent of the Great Trek, they were on the move, trekking for years on end. During this time hunting provided them with a source of food and skins for shoes, thongs, karosses and various other leather goods. Meat was salted and dried and lasted a long time. It fed their slaves and followers. Elephants, and their ivory, soon became their main hunting focus, however. They could shoot from the back of a steady horse, which is no mean feat given the kick of the weapon and the ensuing cloud of black smoke. It must have taken a great deal of skill to hunt an elephant from a horse; if the first shot did not kill it, the hunter would have to chase after the brute while reloading.

Although none of the Boer hunters wrote books or kept records, two names stand out among many: Petrus Jacobs and Jan Viljoen. They were both fearless and were good friends. Elephant hunting was a way of life and a business for them. These men took their wives and children with them and would set up camp near a supply of good water and hunt from their base going after the elephant until they had virtually cleaned them out and then moved to new territory. We know that Jacobs shot upwards of 750 elephants and 110 lions. In one season they took 210 elephants between them.

The English-speaking hunters were not always complimentary about the Boer hunters in their writings. They were especially critical of their cruel method of anchoring an elephant by shooting the animal in the knee, and then returning later to finish it off at the end of the hunt. Apart from elephant, however, which they regarded as a source of income, the Boers' approach to hunting was a means of survival and they were, as a result, somewhat contemptuous of visiting sportsmen.

The Boers and foreign hunters came from entirely different worlds and hunted game for different reasons, except when it came to elephant. At 4 shillings and 6 pence a pound, the one paid for the pleasure of hunting and the other to provide for the daily needs of his family.

No story about the African veld would be complete without a mention of William Charles Baldwin, who arrived in Natal in 1852. He was largely influenced by the writings of Gordon Cumming in *The Lion Hunter of South Africa*. This set him on the path to adventure which lasted from 1852 to 1860. Upon arrival he was by no means a wealthy or eccentric individual, as was the case with his predecessors. He started out with, in his own words, 'my little all', which largely consisted of his weapons, saddles and seven deerhounds. He was anxious to join up with 'Elephant White', who had the reputation of being a great elephant hunter and was making preparations for a journey into Zulu territory. Within three weeks of landing, Baldwin and White set off with three wagons, seven whites and a large number of native staff.

Their first big-game encounter was with a large bull elephant, which they eventually killed after expending vast amounts of lead and energy. They immediately cut off a 'rasher' and fried it on the spot, but complained that it was as tough as a halter. When they eventually made it back to the wagons, they had the elephant's heart for supper, which was 'very tender and good' and for breakfast the next morning ate one of the feet baked in a large hole in the ground. Baldwin noted that it was 'very glutinous and not unlike brawn'. Their trip was largely focused on hunting hippo and ended in disaster as eight of the party died of fever. Baldwin and two companions were lucky to make it back to Durban, more dead than alive.

In 1854 he travelled as far as the Pongola River near the border of Mozambique and encountered numerous rhino of both species. He notes that he 'had three shots at a white rhinoceros with remarkably fine horns. I saw a good number, but they were in the open, and though they are stupid things, and easy to approach, if met with alone, they generally keep near quaggas, wildebeests, or buffaloes, who give them the alarm'. He made three trips into 'Zulu country' and then turned his eyes to the north and ventured as far afield as present-day Zambia, Botswana and Zimbabwe. He was to lead a most extraordinary life and later write his experiences in a book entitled *African Hunting and Adventure*.

Baldwin's pursuit of elephant knew no bounds, for that was how he funded his travels. On his final return to Natal and his departure for England his wagons carried 5,000 pounds of ivory. On his last expedition to the Zambezi he shot 61 elephants and 23 rhinos by himself. It is anyone's guess what the total figure was during his eight-year sojourn.

By now you may be punch drunk from what seems like wanton slaughter, and you would be right to think so. These records are from those who wrote of their adventures, and there were many more who did not. One can safely assume that their motive was not natural history or country rambling, but profit. At the expense of displeasing you I feel one should record the travels of one Swedish explorer, Charles John Andersson who made a number of interesting observations on rhino in his book, *Lake Ngami*, which was published in 1856.

The first was on the flesh of both species of rhino, which clearly indicates why these animals were pursued with such vigour:

> The flesh of the rhinoceros varies greatly in quality. That of the 'black' species, from its leanness, and the animal feeding on the 'wait-a-bit' thorn-bushes, which gives it an acrid and bitter flavour, is not over esteemed. That of the white, on the other hand, whose sustenance consists of grass, which imparts to it an agreeable taste, coupled with its usual fatness, is greatly sought after by natives and colonists. Indeed, the flesh of this animal seems always to have been in repute in the Cape Colony.

He goes on to say that 'the number of rhinoceroses destroyed annually in South Africa is very considerable'. The fact that he considered it relatively easy to kill, providing one was at least 30 to 40 paces away, may account for the following encounter. He had gone in search of a white rhino he had shot and came upon a female rhino. He was not satisfied with the angle at which she was standing and hurled a stone at her with all his force, hoping that she would alter her position and enable him to get a better shot. The reaction he got was not quite what he expected and nearly cost him his life:

> snorting horribly, erecting her tail, keeping her head close to the ground, and raising clouds of dust by her feet, she rushed at me with fearful fury. I had only just time to level my rifle before she was upon me; and the next instant, whilst instinctively turning round for the purpose of retreating, she laid me prostrate.

Andersson was very lucky to have survived.

Fredrick Courteney Selous arrived in Algoa Bay in 1871 when he was just 19 years old, 11 years after Baldwin had departed. Determined to follow in the footsteps of the man who had influenced him immensely, he was to lead an astonishing life. He was killed at the age of 65, not by an enraged elephant, but by a bullet during the First World War in a miserable engagement in 1917 at a place named Beho Beho in Tanzania. He was a captain in the British army. He died, and was buried, in Africa, a continent he loved greatly. An outstanding naturalist, hunter and author, he lies in the world's largest game reserve, The Selous, which is named after him. Just as he was influenced by the 19th-century hunters who wrote accounts of their exploits, so too were many of us who held him in high regard.

Before setting off from Kimberley after a four-month wagon trip from the coast, he had his double-barrelled rifle stolen, which left him no choice but to purchase two 12.5-pound single-barrelled, smooth-bore, muzzle-loading weapons – the type used by the hardy Boer hunters – for £12 each. They were sturdy and, if a little crude, they could get the job done and clearly Selous was not going to be put off by his loss, even if he described them as being 'of the commonest make'. They were in fact made by Isaac Hollis and were as strong as small cannons. Selous notes in his writings that 'they kicked frightfully and in my case the punishment I received from these guns so affected my nerves as to have materially affected my shooting ever since and I am sorry I ever had anything to do with them'.

They fired a 4-ounce bullet and he succeeded in killing no less than 78 elephant with these 'frightful' cannons. Selous was advised by Jan Viljoen, the contemporary of Piet Jacobs, to seek the permission of King Lobengula of the Matabele before hunting in his territory. The king asked Selous if he had ever seen an elephant, and Selous replied that he had not. 'They will drive you out of the country,' was the king's reply. 'Go, you have my permission to shoot.'

In the preface to his book, *A Hunter's Wanderings in Africa*, Selous writes, 'Some people may consider it a dreadful record of slaughter, but it must be remembered by these, that I was often accompanied by a crowd of hungry savages'. Selous was an elephant hunter, first and foremost, and generally refrained from shooting in order not to disturb his quarry. 'Personally I find it impossible to believe, nor does it seem implied, that any great danger attended this oft-repeated and senseless slaughter of animals, which are attracted to the wagons by nothing more reprehensible than inquisitiveness.'

Selous felt very strongly that the reputation of the black rhino was overrated from his own personal experience: 'I have always found it very difficult to credit the vast majority of these stupidly inquisitive but dull-sighted brutes with the vindictiveness and ferocity of disposition that has so often been attributed to the whole race'. He had never heard of a Boer hunter having been killed by a rhino and was not aware of any one of the 'white hunters' being killed either.

The records reveal that the black rhino occurred in great numbers from the Cape to the Zambezi, but there is no record of the exploits of the Boer hunters or the early tribesmen who came to be armed in a variety of ways: skirmishes, war, trade, barter and European hunters who required assistance. The Boers could not be held to account in this respect for they viewed the practice in a most serious light as it posed a threat to their very own safety. Although the black rhino hung on in the Kaokoveld of Namibia, parts of Zimbabwe, Zambia and Mozambique, extinction was a real possibility by the turn of the 19th century. The white rhino had a more restricted range, but was nevertheless present in large numbers right up to the Zambezi. That even a pocket of white and black rhino survived in the wilderness of Zululand was due to the tsetse fly and the action taken by a handful of men, which afforded both species the protection they so desperately needed.

In 1894 six white rhino were shot by hunters between the Black and the White Umfolozi rivers in Zululand. This so stirred the authorities that it led to the proclamation of a number of reserves in 1897 in an effort to save the last of the species. Selous himself lamented the disappearance of the animal after shooting the last two he ever saw:

> To the best of my belief, the great white or square-lipped rhinoceros will in the course of the next few years become absolutely extinct . . . some few white rhinoceros no doubt will survive, but it is not too much to say that long before the close of this century, the white rhinoceros will have vanished from the face of the earth.

In the case of all these visiting sportsmen, the words of the American poet and writer Henry David Thoreau have meaning, 'How vain it is to sit down to write when you have never stood up to live'. For a while they all certainly stood up and lived and then sat down and wrote.

My story is not intended to be about the great hunters of the 19th century, but there were many who witnessed and recorded the once widespread number of rhino that inhabited southern Africa. Each of the individuals mentioned left us an excellent account of their journeys and their encounters with the white and black rhino. The reader may be forgiven for being horrified at what, at times, appears to be nothing but wilful slaughter committed by supposedly civilised human beings. Today it would be unacceptable and we have laws to prevent such behaviour, which did not exist then. However, laws and better-educated people are no guarantee of species conservation or survival in the 21st century. *Homo sapiens* has, unfortunately, become a master of killing things in far more insidious and masterful ways.

CHAPTER 5

Valley of
the Rhino

. . . yet nothing but breathing the air of Africa, and actually walking
through it and beholding its living inhabitants in all the peculiarities of
their movements and manners, can communicate those gratifying and
literally indescribable sensations, which every . . . traveller of feeling
will experience.

William John Burchell, *Travels in the Interior of Southern Africa*

EARLY ONE MORNING IN JANUARY of 1960 I was aboard the *Warwick Castle*, a liner of the old Union Castle Line, gazing intently ahead as she moved ever so slowly into a heart-stopping Mombasa harbour. The walls of Fort Jesus, the 16th century Portuguese stronghold, were gleaming in the tropical sun. Waving palms, ancient baobab trees and scores of white-clothed figures were scrambling all along the old harbour wall. Dhows anchored in the roadway from various ports in the Arabian Gulf wallowed against the ship's gentle wake.

The earliest written account of the coastal region of East Africa, *Periplus of the Erythraean Sea*, comes from the 1st century and was most likely written by a Greek merchant. His writings reveal that a lively trade already existed between Arabia and the countries stretching from Somalia to Tanzania. Trade items included cloth, olive oil, ironwork and an assortment of other items, such as beads used in exchange for cinnamon, ivory, rhino horn and slaves. Mombasa was but one of a number of trading ports, and over the centuries, both Arab and Chinese merchants sailed with the north-east monsoon to East Africa and returned with the monsoon from the south-west. The Arabs had the greatest influence in the region until their fall after the invasion of the Omanis in 1698. Prior to the arrival of the Portuguese at the end of the 16th century, the population was a mixture of Africans and Arabs, speaking a language which is the lingua franca of the country to this very day: Swahili.

Mombasa is the main port of Kenya today and the gateway to some of the most spectacular game reserves in Africa. I set sail from London three weeks earlier, bound for the Mediterranean, Suez and Aden. I managed to persuade four fellow passengers – two British girls, one South African and a Northern Rhodesian tobacco farmer – to join me on a self-drive safari to Tsavo National Park, Kenya's largest at 20,800 square kilometres. Our arrival in 1960 was the realisation of a long-held wish of mine to visit Tsavo, and in particular to set eyes on Kilimanjaro located across the border in Tanzania. The Masai call Kilimanjaro *Oldinyo Oibor*, the 'White Mountain', which at 5,895 metres is the highest mountain in Africa.

At the time Africa's elephant population numbered in excess of 1.2 million. From the number of elephant one saw carrying impressive ivory one never gave a thought to what would befall these animals. The number of black rhino was of less interest to me at the time, largely because their numbers were so low in South Africa and they were confined to a few reserves in Zululand.

I knew of the white rhino, for I had been to school in Natal with Christopher Goldsbury, the stepbrother of Ian Player, who was one class ahead of me. Our contact was largely limited to our joint train journeys to and from Johannesburg, which was home for both of us. We separated after junior school, but maintained contact, and in 1952 he told me that Ian had secured a position in the Natal Parks Board as a junior ranger. The idea of this appealed to me greatly. Ian had served up north in the western desert during the Second World War and then worked on the gold mines before landing this job. Little did he or I know the paths our lives were to take, and it would be 20 years before we met. Before I left for England in 1959, Christopher gave me a number of pictures of Parks Board rangers rescuing a white rhino that was horribly stuck in a mud hole. I filed them away and only learnt the story of the rhino in the mud 52 years later.

We spent three days driving the park roads and would spend lunch up on Poacher's Lookout where we used the mounted telescope to locate the many rhino on the plains below. Unlike South Africa, East African parks are not fenced. Poaching was not new in these parts and was most often undertaken by the Waata tribesman, generally known as Liangulu, who were master bushcraftsmen and lived in settlements in and about the park. They used large bows with a draw weight of more than 60 kilograms and arrows tipped with the poison from the Acokanthera tree (*Acokanthera* spp.), mainly in pursuit of elephant. The poison enters the bloodstream very rapidly and causes heart failure. The Liangulu knew every square inch of the park and did their best to avoid David Sheldrick, the chief game warden, and his men.

At the time of our visit the population of black rhino from the Sudan to Zululand was in all probability nearly 100,000 animals. This figure stood in stark contrast to South Africa, which had seen virtually all its black rhinos vanish by the turn of the 19th century. Kenya's black rhino population, most likely, numbered 20,000 at the time, so why would anybody worry about them? Africa still had large populations of black rhinos in spite of centuries of poaching, but that was about to change. The five of us never gave this a thought as we had lunch on our last day at Mudando Rock, which overlooks a lovely waterhole that attracts great numbers of elephants and masses of plains game in the heat of day. While no black rhino came to drink, we knew they were there. The park's black rhino population topped the 9,000 mark, which is more than double Africa's current total. We all returned to Mombasa elated. I had gone to see the mountain and the elephants, not rhinos. I was not to know it, but my life, and that of my eventual family, was to become very intertwined in the destiny of this strange animal.

I was not to return to Kenya for the next 20 years, largely because of the apartheid policies of South Africa. We were not welcome in most countries, and Kenya was no exception. What had, however, commenced in 1970 was a drought of horrific proportions and some 1,000 black rhino, and countless more elephant, died in Tsavo. The amount of ivory and rhino horn lying out in the bush proved to be too much of a temptation for the poachers. Northern African countries were awash with AK-47s due to internal strife and civil war, and it wasn't long before traditional weapons were replaced with these automatic weapons and a new breed of poacher arose. With trade routes in place for eons, all that was needed was the supply, and Tsavo had plenty of rhino horn and ivory and poachers skilled in the art of killing. The stage was set for the most frightening collapse of a species.

White Rhino

The white rhino saga, by contrast, had its origins in the tsetse fly- and malaria-infested bush of Zululand. In 1890, when the plight of the species was first recognised, a law was passed that required permission to shoot the rhino, which was only grantable by the governor. The white rhino was down-listed in 1893, however, which allowed for restricted hunting. In 1894 hunters killed six white rhino on the Umfolozi River. This news caused great concern among those who were distressed at the very low rhino numbers. In February 1895 a well-known sportsman, C. D. Guise, 'pressed for greater preservation measures for game in general and the white rhino in particular'. He wrote a letter, which ended up on the desk of the governor, Sir Walter Hely-Hutchinson, suggesting that no more permits be issued to hunt rhino and that 'a reserve be created to protect their habitat'. If the white rhino had not been declared 'royal game' in 1895, along with the black rhino, and had it not been for the proclamation of reserved areas for game, including the Umfolozi and Hluhluwe game reserves in April of the same year, its demise would have been certain.

Ian Player wrote a book in 1972, *The White Rhino Saga*, and saga it most certainly was. Player and the field staff of those reserves will forever be recognised as the men on the ground who risked life and limb in the struggle to ensure the species' survival. When it was believed that

fewer than 50 still hung on, men such as Vaughan Kirby (first game conservator in Zululand), Sir Charles Saunders, William Foster and Captain H. B. Potter took on the task of protecting the white rhino from poachers, and formed the core of what was to become the Natal Parks Board. It is of great importance to remember their role, which is sadly often forgotten and overlooked.

In his foreword to the Endangered Wildlife Trust's booklet published in 2011, *Rhino Security*, Ian Player states that 'in 1953 we conducted the very first aerial count of the white rhino with ranger Hendrick van Schoor and pilot Des van der Westhuizen who worked in the Nagana (tsetse fly) campaign'. They counted 437 white rhinos. By 1960, under careful protection, the population had risen to 600 and Ian had risen to the position of senior ranger of the Umfolozi Game Reserve. In the same year, the Natal Parks Board decided that it was vital for the long-term survival of the species to re-establish populations in Natal, the Orange Free State and the Kruger National Park, thereby reducing the risks of having only a single breeding population of white rhino. This was the first-ever operation of this magnitude and Ian was given the task of mounting and organising 'Operation Rhino'. With the assistance of Dr Toni Harthoorn from Kenya, and by using a variety of drugs on a trial-and-error basis, they finally found the most suitable drug for sedating rhino, but not before many horses were gored and men and equipment were damaged. Etorphine hydrochloride, a synthesised morphine, more commonly known as M99, turned out to be a wonder drug. The original capture team comprised Ian Player, Nick Steele, Owen Letley, John Clark and Magqubu Ntombela. The operation was unique and was, in Player's words, 'due to the dedication of both black and white rangers whose task it was to work with these large animals'.

Under careful and watchful anti-poaching measures, the white rhino continued to increase to the degree that the decision was taken to offer animals for sale to private landowners, in the full knowledge that they would eventually, in some instances, become available for trophy hunting. This may be anathema to many, but rhinos were to become very valuable in what was heralded as a major step forward by the private sector in developing the game industry as we know it today.

Landowners started to invest in the game industry in a very big way. We were to become involved ourselves in 1981 when we played a part in the return of white and black rhinos to the Waterberg of Limpopo after an absence of 150 years. In 1970 Ian Player set off on a journey that was to take him to the open zoos of the world to offer them live white rhinos as part of their exhibits. This was a world first, which resulted in further, and much-needed, revenue for the Natal Parks Board.

The conservation world was to applaud the Parks Board and its staff for the sound recovery of the white rhino, but what about the last of South Africa's black rhino who shared the same area? What happened to them? All too often we only hear of the white rhino, but do not forget that it was the plight and concern for the white rhino that led to the survival of the black rhino, and in the end a host of other species. In the years to follow the white rhino was reintroduced into Mozambique, Angola, Botswana and Namibia. Today they are to be found as far afield as Kenya, Zambia, Swaziland and Zimbabwe. Both Mozambique and Angola were to lose their introduced rhino as a result of civil war. Botswana almost went the same way and the last surviving rhinos were saved in the nick of time. In spite of great strides in our knowledge and management of the animal, they continue to remain under threat, as are all rhinos.

I met Ian Player for the first time in 1972 after attending a wilderness trail in the Umfolozi Game Reserve. The threads of our lives were about to come together and there was no turning back for me. But let me start at the beginning. . .

In 1963 I met Michael Brett, a man who shared my love of wildlife, in Johannesburg. He and his wife loved deep-sea fishing in what was then Portuguese East Africa, and I was familiar with the country from my hunting days when I pursued elephants for their tusks. Over the years we shared many adventures, not least when they visited me at my lonely ranger station in the Tuli Block of Bechuanaland. We continued our friendship after I married Conita and moved to Johannesburg to enter the world of art and advertising – my ranger post did not provide enough for the proper care of a wife. At about this time I started to concentrate on painting wildlife with the encouragement of firstly W. H. Coetzer, a doyen of landscape and still-life painting, who was to open my very first exhibition, and secondly the late Cecil Skotnes, the founder of the Polly Street Art Centre in downtown Johannesburg. Skotnes told me not to be in a hurry to have an exhibition, as animal art was in its infancy in South Africa. He suggested that I should rather gain as much experience in observing animals in the wild as possible. I was, in fact, about to embark on that very advice when Michael called to tell me he had booked us on a wilderness trail in the Umfolozi Game Reserve. I had no idea that, apart from gaining my first glimpse of white rhino on foot, it was to become the second-most important step of my life after marrying Conita.

The idea of wilderness areas in big game country in South Africa had its origin in the Umfolozi Game Reserve. The concept was first brought to Ian Player's attention by Jim Feely, a friend and colleague who was familiar with American conservation literature on the subject. In the park's planning it was agreed to set aside an area of 37,000 hectares, nearly half of the reserve's total size, as wilderness. The area was to have no roads or any man-made structures and was to remain untouched by any form of human intervention. The Natal Parks Board led the way in developing walking trails, which later prompted Ian to establish the Wilderness Leadership School, a not-for-profit organisation with its headquarters in Durban, in 1969. Barry Clements, a former trails leader from the Parks Board, was the school's first director and worked with a team comprising Don Richards, Jim Feely and the late Hugh Dent, who were all former game rangers with wide experience. The Umfolozi wilderness was the first area in South Africa, and the world, where school children and adults could undertake a trail in an area with both species of rhino. It was with this organisation, in 1972, that Michael and I were to spend five days walking and camping in what was once the last stronghold of the white rhino.

We flew to Durban where we overnighted and were collected at 7 a.m. by Don Richards. He was a former school master, and his job would be to guide and teach eight of us about the value of wilderness, and hopefully return us alive as better informed citizens. He managed to do exactly that and revealed to us that there is no experience quite like walking in wild country. It is precisely what Ian Player felt so passionate about and ultimately led to a wide movement, which has since been replicated in the Kruger National Park and elsewhere. The experience led Michael, Conita and me to establish and conduct, for nigh on 20 years, our own trails organisation, Educational Wildlife Expeditions. The only difference was the absence of rhino, which had long ago been driven to extinction in our area. No one needs a Don Richards to go walking, but when it comes to dangerous game you need an experienced guide, and Umfolozi had its fair share of lion, buffalo and white and black rhino. The elephant had long been shot out, but they have since been re-introduced from the Kruger National Park.

Upon arrival at the base camp, high up on a hill overlooking the wilderness, Don explained that each person should pack a kit bag with supplies for three nights, including liquid refreshments. This amounted to six beers each, as we were told we were undertaking a wilderness, rather than a drinking, experience. Fortunately we did not have to carry much ourselves, other than our cameras and binoculars, as the school used donkeys to convey our personal gear and the food we needed for the journey. They would take a shorter route and be at our first base camp when we arrived sometime much later in the afternoon. We all breathed a sigh of relief; from where we stood the bottom of the valley was way off in the distance.

We were soon all on first-name terms and anxious to be away, but before we set off Don gave us a pep talk. He introduced us to his Zulu game scout, Johannes, who was armed and neatly turned out, especially when compared with us in our running shorts, floppy hats and golf shirts. We had been advised in advance, to wear nothing white. Don told us that we had to walk in single file with no talking until he, or Johannes, found something of interest – and even then only in low tones. We were reminded that lions abounded in the park, as did buffalo; that white rhinos were not really a problem to trailists, provided we paid attention to his instructions; and what could happen in the event of surprising a black rhino.

Most people quiver at the mere mention of its name, because it has acquired, rightly or wrongly, a very bad reputation. Don did not ease the tension when he told us that we needed to get up a tree, any tree, as quickly as was humanly possible, in the unlikely event of a charge. Not *behind* the tree, but *up* the tree. Most, I hasten to add, are thorn trees. He then advised us that he carried a first-aid kit and was trained to deal with most emergencies. Very encouraging, I thought, when the only way in or out was by helicopter. Why worry, we all agreed, as none of us had experience of what a black rhino looked like at 20 paces on foot.

We duly set off at 2 p.m. with Don in the lead and Johannes bringing up the rear. This is important for two reasons. Firstly, if an animal is lying down or obscured, then the lead may not spot it and the tail end then has a chance to alert the leader if the animal moves. Secondly, it keeps the group bunched, rather than spread out. We could pick out the White Umfolozi River[1] winding its way in great lazy curves through the wilderness in the early afternoon haze. Trails are not just about seeing game. They are about experiencing the natural world at ground level, which we were to experience later that evening around the camp fire.

Before the floods of 1982, both the White and the Black Umfolozi riverbanks were crowned with the most spectacular riverine vegetation – towering Sycamore fig trees (*Ficus sycamorus*) and the heavy, dark-leaved Natal mahogany (*Trichilia emetica*) or *umKhuhlu* in Zulu – and this is where we had our first night's camp. Crystal-clear water flowed close to the bank and it didn't take us long to strip down and settle our tired bodies in the cool water. The beer had spent the afternoon on a donkey's back, but that mattered not. A little while later, refreshed, we all sat around the fire as Don prepared supper, and warm beer has never tasted better. We were to learn that each one of us was to sit

---

1 In Zulu it is called the *iMfolozi*, 'the river of fibres', which is taken from the stinging nettle tree (*Urera tenax*), whose fibres are used in the making of mats and married women's headdresses.

watch for an hour from 9 p.m. to 6 a.m. and we all drew straws, or sticks rather. The idea was firstly to keep watch over the group and secondly to contemplate why we were here and what our motives were in coming along in the first place. Our groundsheets were sacks from the donkeys' backs and we were laid out in a tight row in sleeping bags with Don at one end and Johannes at the other.

Whoever stood watch had to sit at the fire and not in their sleeping bag to stay awake and to make sure that the fire did not go out. Lions can be fairly active at night, as are rhinos, which certainly added to our alertness. Nothing arrests the mind more acutely than the far-off moan of a lion at 2 a.m., especially when the donkeys become aware of their proximity. Shadows take on strange shapes and you soon ask yourself what might be out there staring back at you. You remind yourself that it is only your imagination as you happily hand over the watch.

Few things are more beautiful than early dawn along this river, as the mist starts to rise and the calls of the hadeda ibis draw closer as they fly upstream. Trumpeter hornbills zigzag back and forth across the river, emitting that crazy, crying, spanked-child-like sound as we were roused by Don who stood the last watch. This, Michael and I told each other, would be 'the day of the rhino'. It was to be a full-day's outing and we were not to reach camp much before 4 p.m. Each of us took turns in carrying a rucksack, which contained lunch, a kettle and iron mugs. We would get water for tea from the river, not that boiling the water was necessary for health reasons as the river water was drinkable. At the time of our trail the total South African population was some 21 million. Today the population of KwaZulu-Natal alone is almost half that figure. It's no surprise then that 84 per cent of our rivers are critically endangered or vulnerable. I seriously wonder if anyone drinks from the Umfolozi when on a trail today. Staying close to the river bank, it was not long before we came across three white rhinos grazing the short grass in an open area. To view these animals on foot for the first time was a telling experience and we sat down under some shade and watched them for more than half an hour. White rhinos are large animals and, when not disturbed, they move along cropping the grass like large lawnmowers. They were completely unaware of our presence and I realised, as a former hunter, how easy they would be to kill. No wonder they nearly disappeared. Mounted on a good horse, the odds were most certainly in the hunter's favour, even if the weapon was a smooth bore muzzle-loader.

We eventually left them and moved away from the river, which we would pick up later, and entered the partly open thornveld. A loud crash had everyone hastily searching for a suitable tree – it's amazing how one's first thoughts are for oneself in times like this. Most people have an innate fear of black rhinos, and we were all well aware that we were invading their territory and that this could well provoke a response. We all felt slightly let down, however, when Don told us that it was only a kudu. They were most certainly lying down by 10 a.m., he reminded us, and advised us all to keep a good eye out for any dark image under a tree. At first that is exactly what we all did, but our interest was soon diverted and our gaze settled back down to our feet so that we would not fall or trip over any obstacle.

When a second, louder, crash came, followed by the most electrifying sound of air being expelled with great force, we knew in an instant exactly what it was – and believe you me it was not a case of women and children first. Only Johannes had seen the black rhino as it hightailed through the undergrowth away from our group. It took a while to locate everyone after the encounter and we all agreed that it was time for tea. We had at last had our black rhino experience, even though none of us had even had the faintest glimpse of it.

That evening around the campfire, Don told us about Jim Feely's experience when leading a trail of high-school girls and their chaperone. (Girls had to be accompanied by a chaperone as the school staff in those days were all men.) At some unearthly hour of the night, Jim, who was asleep at one end of the group, awoke to discover that the watch had fallen asleep. What he then noticed, which no doubt riveted his attention, was a black rhino standing motionless at the opposite end of the sleeping group. Leaping out of his sleeping bag, rifle in hand, he fired a shot over the animal's head. It is anyone's guess what transpired next, but suffice it to say the shot had the desired effect and the rhino vanished before anyone other than Jim knew what it was. It seems, however, that everyone noticed that their guide was not in the habit of sleeping with any nightwear on.

On our last morning, when we emerged from the depths of the Umfolozi bush, we were treated to a talk by two Parks Board staff – Derek Potter and Peter Hitchins. It all had to do with veld management and the importance of understanding how it functioned. Michael and I found it rather boring; the serious, scrawny little guy was not exactly friendly and seemed to be at the talk under sufferance. Game rangers I knew had the reputation of not always being the best PR material, often preferring their own company, and he seemed to fit that description. We were probably a nuisance and we felt it. It was to take a number of years before I learned that Peter understood black rhinos better than most.[2]

There is something very special about this place that, along with Hluhluwe Game Reserve to the immediate north, and a further block in between known as the Corridor, forms part of one system today. Once the royal hunting grounds of the former Zulu kings, it was to become the last stand of the rhino, especially the white rhino whose range was more restricted and was certainly on the brink of extinction. Thousands of students and adults have walked these wilderness trails through the years with a succession of great guides. It was exactly as Ian Player had always hoped it would be: people were getting to experience the meaning of wilderness on foot. We never came face to face with a black rhino on our first walk, but the experience made me realise how effectively, and profoundly, wilderness trails could get to the heart and soul of people. I still hoped to one day have the opportunity of coming face to face with Africa's most misunderstood, feared and elusive beast.

On our return to Durban, and before our departure to Johannesburg,

---

2 Peter Hitchins's project to determine the home ranges of black rhinos in South Africa, for example, was one of the first of its kind. This was at a time when radio telemetry was in its infancy, and proved to be a matter of trial and error in many respects. A transmitter is housed in a cavity drilled into the base of the horn, and an aerial is housed in a cavity drilled into the length of the horn. Dental acrylic resin (or similar material) is commonly used to keep the transmitter in place. The receiver's antenna is directional, so a signal in the form of a beep indicates that a rhino is in line with the receiver. The closer you get to the transmitter, and therefore the rhino, the more frequent and intense the beep. Each transmitter emits a unique frequency, so the individual animals can be identified.

we met Ian Player. I was, at last, to meet my old school chum's stepbrother. I was not about to tell him that I had two pictures of him – one of him riding a horse looking back over the wilderness that we had emerged from earlier, and the other of a white rhino stuck in the mud. It took another 40 years before I sat down with him one winter morning at his home and told him how I came to acquire them and he in turn related to me those long past events.

High above the Atlantic Ocean, aboard a Varig Brazilian Airlines Boeing 707, Conita and I were en-route to Rio de Janeiro. It was the shortest way to get to the city of San Antonio in Texas from Johannesburg. My reading material for the journey was *The White Rhino Saga*, which was appropriate reading material as we were to attend a hunters' convention and art exhibition of Game Conservation International (Gamecoin). I understand that it no longer exists, but back in 1973 it was a big event, big enough to attract the likes of British artists David Shepherd and Jonathan Kenworthy. From Kenya came Terry Matthews, hunter turned sculptor of note, and Americans Guy Coheleach and Bob Kuhn, among the best of a bevy of wildlife artists from the US and the UK. I had only just begun to emerge as a wildlife painter in South Africa, but had applied to the organisers to exhibit and for Conita and me to attend the week-long convention. We had to pay our own way and donate an oil painting for the auction. The organisation was a great supporter of the Wilderness Leadership School's student programme, which is how I learned about the event. Both Ian Player and Barry Clements, the school's director, were also in attendance.

Hunters' conventions frequently promote wildlife art, along with hunting safaris, hunting equipment, hunting books and donated safaris, and are a great opportunity for the industry to meet and showcase itself. They have a great carnival atmosphere and allow one the opportunity to meet fellow hunters and conservationists, who are often the invited speakers, and those selling everything from handmade knives to elephant guns. Hunters seem to project a slight guilt complex on these occasions. One gets the impression that they are conscious of the anti-hunting lobby that is always out to knock them. One only has to look at our own track record to realise from where the sensitivity arises. To be perfectly fair, the modern-day hunter who sticks by the codes of conduct laid down by these organisations is the last person who wants to see his sport disappear, and the industry both in South Africa and the US bears testimony to this. There is more wildlife on private land in South Africa today than at the turn of the 19th century and the hunter has had a lot to do with that. Unfortunately a dark cloud has drifted over the South African scene, which will be discussed in a later chapter.

My donated painting was of a black rhino that I had seen first-hand the previous year when Michael and I had again ventured into the wilderness of Umfolozi. We had selected Don as our guide again, and on this occasion we knew our whole group, which included Michael's brother Morris. A black rhino paid us a great deal of attention on one particular day. The animal had been lying asleep in a sand bath and had not detected our silent approach. Our scout saw the animal first and clicked his fingers, which got Don's attention very quickly. When the rhino became aware of our group, it was on its feet in seconds. This time it came straight at us. We needed no invitation to take off and everyone sought trees. Before either of our minders could take any action, however, our rhino had a rethink and spun off at 90 degrees and vanished. It took a while to gather everyone together. I tried to capture the scene in my painting, but no painting compares with the charge of one of these creatures. I was nevertheless delighted when it fetched a good sum at the auction, and it now hangs on a wall somewhere in Texas.

David Shepherd had painted a picture of a Bengal tiger, and he was exhibiting it along with the limited-edition prints, which I recall were about US$100 each. The sale of the prints raised a tidy sum of money for 'Operation Tiger', which we were told, in 1973, was in serious threat of extinction. Upon our return to South Africa I realised that David's prints had great merit and I decided to borrow the idea as a way to make some contribution to wildlife through my own art.

I have always been fond of the cheetah; in my early ranger days a farmer near the border post had a tame one. The mother had been shot in the Transvaal and the cub had been hand-raised. They were considered a pest by the local farmers, and on subsequent visits to the Africana Library in downtown Johannesburg, I saw both cheetah and leopard skins hanging up in a 'muti' shop in Diagonal Street. It was still fashionable to see coats of spotted cats, but protests were emerging over exploitation.

I set about painting a watercolour of a pair of cheetahs and had 300 prints run-off in a signed, limited edition. I met Neville Anderson, a previous participant in the Wilderness Leadership School trails, through a local newspaper journalist, Suzan Fox. Neville had offices in Braamfontein and kindly consented to the use of his premises and postal address. Suzan wrote a story for her newspaper and, surprise of surprises, we sold out the entire edition in two weeks. We thought of donating the funds to the Wildlife Society of South Africa, but changed our minds as we felt the cheetah was not high enough on their agenda. Shortly thereafter, while attending a conservation symposium at the University of Pretoria, I found myself sitting next to the head of the Eugene Marais Chair of Wildlife management, Prof. Kobus 'Koos' Bothma. In due course we shared a lunch table and I realised that his Chair could be the body to carry out a survey on the status of the cheetah in South Africa. It had legitimacy and it had access to students. He was more than delighted to agree, for it provided students with higher degree options. Neville agreed, and it occurred to me that there must be more creatures in the threatened category. The idea dawned on me to create an organisation dedicated specifically to protecting endangered species. A lawyer friend, David Botha, advised me to form a trust. It would need a name and a logo, so I chose the cheetah spoor and called it the Endangered Wildlife Trust (EWT).

Neville agreed to become a trustee, as did James Clarke, a friend of his who happened to be an environmental journalist. Between the three of us we donated the funds to the university to undertake a survey on the status of cheetah. It certainly helped having South Africa's leading environmental reporter cover issues, even if we operated from a tiny office in Braamfontein. We did not stop there. My idea was to exploit the talent of other emerging South African wildlife painters. The response from the public was amazing and there was a basket full of species in need of help.

The whole story of the EWT belongs elsewhere, but suffice it to say that it was not too long before the black rhino came to my attention and remained there for the 13 years that I was first chairman and then director. It was none other than Peter Hitchins, the man I had met after the first trail I attended in Umfolozi in 1972, who first brought it to our attention via a paper entitled, 'The Status of the Black Rhinoceros in Zululand Game and Nature Reserves'. He presented it at the very first symposium staged by the EWT, at the University of Pretoria, in 1976. Soon after, the EWT was to attract the attention of another person with an interest in both rhinos and elephants, Dr Anthony Hall-Martin, who was a research scientist in the Addo Elephant National Park. He had applied for funding for a study on the endangered flightless dung beetle and the beetle's preoccupation with elephant and rhino dung. Dung beetles and faeces don't make for good fundraising, but throw in elephants or kids with haunted eyes, and things change. People give money from an inner compassion that appeals to their conscience.

Both Peter and Anthony were to become advisers to the EWT as the organisation became more and more involved with the rhino, and our relationship has spanned more than 35 years. Once bound up in the destiny of these animals, one is, in a sense, tied forever. They were also both to assist in the work that the EWT was to undertake in Namibia's Kaokoveld, concerning the decline of both rhinos and elephants, and together we were to establish the Rhino & Elephant Foundation (REF) in 1987, which was to undertake considerable fundraising and conservation work during the 'rhino wars'.

In 1980 Anthony and I flew to Kenya to attend an IUCN conference held in the Tsavo National Park. If one is going to have a conference on wildlife, then no place is better than the Kilaguni Lodge in Tsavo with its distant views of Kilimanjaro. Anthony held both the position of rhino and elephant specialist and attended both sessions, running between rooms. I was there on behalf of the IUCN African Elephant Specialist Group, raising issues on the uncontrolled trade in ivory taking place in South Africa at the time. Both the Elephant Specialist Group and the Rhino Specialist Group were relatively new and had arisen over the serious poaching of both species throughout Africa. The situation was extremely serious, attested to by the attendance of no less a person than Sir Peter Scott.

It had been 20 years since I last set foot in this park and much had changed. Much, that is, in terms of the number of black rhino. From almost 100,000 on my last visit, the species' continental population had plunged so dramatically that there was now cause for grave concern. There were, we were told, less than 15,000 surviving in Africa. I did not sit in on the rhino meetings as I was not sufficiently knowledgeable about the species, but Anthony kept me well informed. The situation did not look good for the black rhino at all. It had been wiped out in South Sudan, Uganda, Ethiopia and Somalia. Kenya was fighting a major battle, and this very park, which once had a population of between 6,000 and 9,000 black rhinos, was down to less than 200. Anthony flew over the park with the warden, Bill Woodley, in a Piper Super Cub and actually saw a few of the survivors.

The South African delegation, both from the Rhino and Elephant specialist groups, was present on special visas arranged between the attorney general of Kenya, Charles Njonjo, and the South African minister of foreign affairs, Pik Botha. South Africa at the time was largely the hyena of the world, because of its abhorrent apartheid policy. In addition to that, we weren't exactly welcomed because of the country's culling methods and their utilisation of ivory. East Africa has always had opposing views in this regard. Representing the EWT, we were very concerned at the lack of controls on the movement of ivory from within the borders of our neighbours who shared a customs union agreement. Our view was that South Africa was a convenient clearing house for other countries' dirty ivory.

When it came to funding, we were often looked upon as being wealthy enough as a country to pay for our own efforts, which was very frustrating. In addition to this, the EWT was considered by many prominent organisations in South Africa as an upstart NGO, who would have preferred it if we quietly went away. I was personally regarded with deep suspicion by certain state institutions, which included the military, and I often found myself, and the EWT, crossing people on a number of controversial wildlife conservation issues. I was regarded by some as a maverick who lacked background, yet dared to argue with them on topics in their own field. I upset not a few, irritated some and infuriated others, and at the same time, rather pleasingly, earned the approbation of many. The conservation world, despite its aura of altruism, is by no means free of petty jealousies, back biting and glory-seeking – a label frequently used in reference to me. At the end of the day it all comes down to a matter of competition for publicity and funds. After nearly 40 years, the organisation is still here and has earned its place in the annals of conservation, even if it still irritates some. The EWT today is still not afraid to stick its head above the crowd.

During one of the breaks, Anthony and I borrowed Iain Douglas-Hamilton's Land Cruiser and took off for the morning, after an early breakfast, to Tsavo East. Arriving at the park headquarters, Anthony and I sought permission to view the jaw bones of rhinos and elephants killed in the drought and those recovered from poaching incidents. We walked in stunned silence in what was, in fact, a rhino and elephant cemetery. By 1979 Kamba and Somali poachers had wiped out 96 per cent of the park's rhino population in just four years. To put the price of rhino horn in 1979 into perspective, the poacher was getting around US$135 per kilogram from the middleman. If you fast-track that figure to South Africa today, the price of rhino horn can earn the poacher as much as US$5,000 per kilogram.

In the end, the poachers killed every single rhino in both Tsavo East and Tsavo West. The bloody war was to turn to southern Tanzania, as the northern areas had already lost more than half the country's rhino population by the mid-1970s. The target was then the 3,000 or so rhino still in the Selous Game Reserve and eventually the next in line would be the Luangwa Valley in Zambia, which contained an estimated 4,000–8,000 black rhino.

The scourge was to move steadily south. What had taken place in South Africa during the 19th century was now taking place in the rest of Africa. Instead of muzzle-loaders the poachers were now armed with a modern weapon, which could easily be purchased in the back alleys of way-out places.

The rhino war was heading south.

CHAPTER 6

Silent Desert

Elsewhere the darkness was impenetrable. Silence, like that of the sepulchre, reigned in this remote solitude, relieved at long intervals by the hyaena and the jackal lapping the water, and the distant grunting of the rhinoceros.

Charles John Andersson, *Lake Ngami*

THE SO-CALLED DESERT RHINOS of the Kaokoveld are regarded as belonging to the nominate subspecies *Diceros bicornis bicornis*, the original form described from the Cape of Good Hope by Carl Linnaeus in 1758. Rhinos were distributed continuously from the Cape up the escarpment zone to the Kunene River and further into southern Angola. The original Cape rhino is known today only from the records and from seven skulls in museums. The skulls are considerably larger than those of other rhinos, and the closest in size to them are the black rhinos of the Kaokoveld. The desert rhino appears slightly larger in build and carries larger horns, with the posterior horn often longer than the anterior horn. Dr Anthony Hall-Martin notes, 'That these rhino can survive in a region with less than 100 mm mean annual rainfall is astonishing and appear capable of going for a number of days without drinking'.

Elephants and rhinos have worn a track across the rock desert in the far north-west of Namibia's Kaokoveld. Thousands of heavy feet over thousands of years have polished the stone as they have marched for kilometres out over the plains to a distant fountain. Every winter, as the last pools disappear from the rivers, the elephants and the rhinos follow this road to water, travelling in the hours of darkness, drinking, then trekking back over the gravel flats. Nobody will ever know when the first rhinos began to rub a shine on the Kaokoveld rock with their steady plod back and forth, but in 1970 the total western desert-living elephant population of the region was about 300–400 and declining rapidly, and the black rhino numbers were far worse. We were uncomfortably close to seeing the last of both the rhino and elephant in their forbidding desert environment.

We heard all of this over lunch in the dining room at the University of Pretoria from Prof. Fritz Eloff and Prof. Koos Bothma, my hosts. I had travelled with both men on a previous occasion to view a project that the EWT was funding in the Kalahari National Park. Fritz was researching lions and Koos had a master's student, Gus Mills, working on the brown hyena, which was the object of my interest at the time. Fritz and Koos invited me to join them a few months later, as they had completed a major study of the Kaokoveld, which they had been working on for the past two and a half years, and were going to present it to the South African government. The invitation was not intended as a holiday; without some form of intervention both the rhino and elephant were in serious danger of being poached out of existence.

The fact that both elephants and rhinos could survive in such a remarkable desert environment was of great interest. Fritz insisted that 'they represent a new dimension in the animal kingdom, and deserve the highest conservation priority'. He knew exactly what he was talking about, for both men had witnessed the decline in the species' numbers. It was clearly difficult for the university to get involved as they were a state institution and the project had been funded by the Department of Bantu Administration. What made it more difficult was the fact that only government officials could gain access to the region and, as a consequence, no member of the public had any idea what went on there. Most people in South Africa had never heard the name Kaokoveld.

It was 1977 and Namibia was still known as South West Africa and was effectively under the control of South Africa, which was involved in a high-intensity conflict across the border into Angola. The board of the EWT was less than enthusiastic about yet another elephant project, particularly one in a potential war zone, even if it was linked to rhinos, and told me so. I, however, was convinced that this was a project of considerable merit, so I accepted the invitation and funded myself; the university would provide everything I would need once I arrived. I knew, of course, that the poaching of large game species was rife. I looked upon the trip as a fact-finding mission, which, depending on the findings, I would present to the EWT board.

I obtained special clearance from the Department of Bantu Administration as a member of the university team that had preceded me by road, ten days prior to my departure for Windhoek on the 7th of September. I was to be picked up by a private pilot in Windhoek. Neither he nor I had ever been to the Namibia–Angola border, and the only thing we were sure of was that if we crossed the Kunene River we had gone too far and would be in serious trouble. We didn't have the benefit of GPS in those days and Namibia is a very large country. The Kaokoveld alone covers about 9 million hectares and is very sparsely populated. My pilot made sure we had 20 litres of water on-board before we headed north in the Cessna 182. Other than the Spitzkoppe and Brandberg, which rose up high to our west, the area we flew over was quite flat. We refuelled at a military-cum-civilian airfield halfway to the border and pressed on to our destination. The Marienfluss Valley is bounded by a chain of high mountains, the Otjihipa, in the east, the Hartmann mountains in the west and the banks of the Kunene River in the north. It is about 700 kilometres from Windhoek, and about 80 kilometres long, and my pilot didn't think we'd miss it, which was encouraging. If we did, and overshot the river, we were to make an immediate about-turn. Now, the Marienfluss Valley is not much more than a flat piece of desert, and we were supposed to easily pick up two F250 Fords and a radio-equipped, mine-proof army vehicle. Our arrival party was made up of a driver and radio operator who were doing their national service; they were assigned to take care of us if we got lost or ran into trouble. Our military escort had to radio in our progress every evening, but otherwise it was more of a holiday for the two of them, and frankly far safer than being on the border. The South African Defence Force invaded Angola in 1975 in support of UNITA at the outbreak of civil war when the Portuguese departed that country. This resulted in a protracted war, which explains our military backup.

We had not yet landed and knew nothing about these arrangements. We just strained our eyes in the desert haze to find the 'airfield', which turned out to be one long flat valley. In the far distance we finally made out a row of fuel drums and alongside that the welcome party and the escort. I was delighted to get onto the ground. I bid my young pilot a hasty goodbye and he turned around and was soon lost in the vast landscape. My new companions told me that the desert is so quiet that they could hear the aircraft for a long time before they actually spotted us. My Kaokoveld journey was about to begin and I had no idea what it would lead to. We turned south and put as much distance between ourselves and the border as possible before making camp out on the desert flats.

We travelled for 14 days into the heart of the Kaokoveld desert. Stretching as far as the eye could see, rock upon rock littered the plains and crawled up the mountains to their summits like edge-to-edge carpeting in pale shades of mauve and red. Damaraland and Kaokoland, which comprised the Kaokoveld (now the Kunene), were lost worlds into which few had been privileged to venture. These combined areas run parallel to the famed Skeleton Coast and reach north to the Kunene River and the border of Angola.

The Kaokoveld is home to fascinating plant life that is found nowhere else in Africa, waterless gravel plains stretching to eternity and a host of large mammal species including elephants, giraffes, black rhinos, lions and antelope, which are depicted in 6,000-year-old rock engravings at Twyfelfontein – the 'Fountain of Disbelief' or 'Uncertain Fountain'. Some 2,500 rock engravings occur at this site, which is located in the Huab River Valley in southern Damaraland. 'Fountain of Disbelief' is an apt description because it was eight days before we saw an elephant. It was dead and its ivory had been hacked out. The same day we found the carcass of a black rhino on a well-used game trail. It had been shot on its way to drink.

By this time two of our party, Koos Bothma and Stoffel Le Riche, warden of the Kalahari National Park, had left us due to vehicle trouble. Fritz, myself and Slang Viljoen, a master's student who was undertaking a study funded by the South African Nature Foundation (SANF), occupied one vehicle. The foundation was the equivalent of the World Wide Fund for Nature (WWF), but could not operate under that name due to our political isolation. No one lives out in these remote areas, and we never saw another soul for two weeks. Every late afternoon we would find a place to camp and lay out our sleeping bags on large tarpaulins with a vehicle at each end and a fire in front with five deck chairs.

When we finally reached the Hoanib River, the border between the two regions of Damaraland and Kaokoland, we saw our first living elephants, who fled at our intrusion. Slang stopped the vehicle and Fritz and I sprinted up a steep dune to get a shot of them running over the black gravel and pale, sandy desert floor. I had never witnessed elephants in such a lunar-like landscape. It was positively surreal. We never found a single living rhino.

To place these events into context, 2,000–3,000 automatic rifles and 200,000 rounds of ammunition were issued to selected residents of Kaokoland, ostensibly to protect themselves against insurgents. But there was nothing to prevent these weapons from being used against game. Poaching was already widespread in the region and a variety of snares were used to trap animals, largely as a food source. One popular method was the use of the lid of a 200-litre drum, cut into wedges from the rim inwards. The lid is placed over a hole dug into the ground and the weight of a heavy animal will press through the splines, trapping the animal in the most fearful manner. These snares were responsible for the deaths of many large animals, including rhinos. The demand for ivory and rhino horn was also increasing at the time and the price was climbing accordingly. All the complex events of the mid-1970s were seemingly channelled by a malevolent fate to work against the survival of wildlife in the Kaokoveld.

The final act in the unfolding destruction of the wildlife of the Kaokoveld was played out from about 1977 to 1981. The worst drought on record occurred during this period and wildlife and livestock died in their thousands. Elephants, giraffes and rhinos could cope more easily with the drought conditions, but in some instances rhinos did perish. Many people lost cattle – their very livelihood – and turned to hunting as a means of subsistence. The intensity of hunting increased and it seemed likely that the final stage leading to the extinction of the rhino and elephant would soon be reached.

In July of the year of my visit, a press investigation focused on the illegal hunting that had been taking place in Kaokoland. This was followed by my report in 1978 to the IUCN, the South African government and the South African Defence Force. My report drew the attention of the authorities to the rapidly deteriorating state of affairs. It was not long thereafter that I was visited by a military intelligence officer who was most interested to know how I came by my information. Both military and state officials were implicit in the poaching. The Kaokoveld had been cloaked in secrecy for far too long. Fortunately this had a good outcome with the military in the long term, as they were later to work closely with the EWT in their areas of operation.

By June 1979 the SANF provided funding to the Eugene Marais Chair of Wildlife Management under Koos Bothma, which enabled Slang to carry out an urgent field study on the elephants, rhinos and giraffes of the region. Having spent the past two and a half years on the general ecology of Kaokoland, he concluded that the populations of elephants, rhinos and giraffes in the western parts were critically low and locally endangered and their extinction would be irreplaceable. The EWT was in the forefront of media campaigns to alert the authorities and the public and the board was by now fully convinced of the importance and urgency surrounding the situation. Our contribution was the provision of an aircraft, fuel and counters for an extended series of aerial surveys commencing in 1980, which we hoped would assist Slang in determining how many elephants, rhinos and giraffes still existed in this silent desert.

Koos had, in the meantime, been put in touch with Colin and Ina

Britz, a couple who were stationed at a place in Damaraland known as Wereldsend (World's End). Colin was a geologist with Consolidated Diamond Mines who generously made the base available to the university and the EWT by way of a contribution. The entire camp consisted of two caravans under canvas awnings and three tin Nissen huts for visitors and a few longdrops / bathrooms. The main feature was a gravel airfield, which rolled right up to the camp. One literally landed and walked no more than 50 metres to the camp.

Peter Joffe, one of the EWT trustees, owned a four-seater Mooney aircraft, which was both economical and powerful. It was easily able to get in and out of canyons and steep mountain sides while dealing with what were, at times, very strong winds. Displaying the hospitality that is typical of the country, Colin and Ina were indispensable to the operation, providing beds and meals to keep the aircrew functioning. The camp and aircraft became our workplace over the next four years while we carried out low-level surveys counting elephants, rhinos and giraffes, with Peter as pilot, Slang as navigator and Koos and myself as observers. Koos could not always make the long trip from Lanseria, and this afforded me the opportunity of inviting various advisers and board members along as observers. The EWT was a hands-on organisation in those early days, which enabled board members to experience first-hand the work of the organisation.

The aerial surveys clearly revealed the extent of the poaching and confirmed the urgent need for action to save both the elephant and the black rhino, which was the most critical. As the days passed we came across more dead than living elephants and rhinos, which left us with a feeling of hopelessness. When we did find a rhino, it was often out in the middle of nowhere and one marvelled at their ability to survive in such a landscape. By 1982 the aerial and ground surveys had discovered a total of 55 black rhinos for the entire Kaokaland and 29 carcasses, most of which had been poached in the preceding three years.

In the same year, Ina and Blythe, who was married to Rudi Loutit, the conservator of the Skeleton Coast Park, came up with the idea of forming a locally based NGO, which they named the Namibian

Wildlife Trust (NWT). This was a good move politically because the EWT, and me in particular, was by now regarded with a jaundiced eye. Even though the Directorate of Nature Conservation, the official conservation agency, was not directly responsible for the Kaokoveld, the attendant bad publicity was not to their liking.

By this stage the world had woken up to the uniqueness of this amazing region and support was flowing in. With the promise of financial assistance from the EWT, the fledgling NWT was able to offer a position to Garth Owen-Smith, who was a ranger in the Etosha National Park. Formerly an agricultural officer between 1968 and 1970, he was the first person to sound a public warning about the territory's wildlife in 1971. Garth knew more about the Kaokoveld and its wildlife than anyone. Peter, Ina and I flew to Etosha where we offered him a position with the guarantee of a salary for two years from the EWT. He accepted the post as it enabled him to return to the Kaokoveld where his heart was. His contribution over the years was a major reason for the recovery of the territory's wildlife. Garth went on to lay the groundbreaking work for the establishment of community-based conservation.[3] He also established a conservation network of auxiliary game guards from among the local people and this was to prove invaluable in the fight against poaching. By 1983 much of the poaching had been brought under control, but the efforts that had gone into the struggle could by no means be abandoned.

Conita and I flew to the US in 1982 to attend a fundraising benefit, where I was one of the speakers, at the Explorer's Club in New York. The benefit was attended by members of the South African consulate and the friends and colleagues of two amazing American women, Ingrid Schroeder and Babette Alfieri. After visiting Africa's game reserves, and subsequently meeting me in Johannesburg, they were committed to assisting the EWT. The gala benefit raised US$5,000 to purchase Garth a new Land Rover, and they arranged for me to be interviewed the next morning on 'Good Morning America'. The world was suddenly aware of the plight of the rhinos and elephants in the place with the

---

3 To read more about this remarkable individual, and to better understand the story of the Kaokoveld, one should read his memoir, *An Arid Eden*, which was published in 2011.

unpronounceable name halfway around the world. Most were aghast that anything that size could live in what appeared to be so hostile an environment.

Ingrid and Babette went on, not unlike Blythe and Ina, to form an organisation they called Save Africa's Endangered Wildlife (SAVE), and eventually made a major contribution to 'Operation Rhino' in Zimbabwe. Our world is the better for their efforts and those of us in the conservation movement owe them a huge debt of gratitude. So often one never hears of these people, but without their concern and effort, Africa's rhino would be the poorer.

In June of 1984 I was back at Wereldsend with Dr Anthony Hall-Martin and Peter Hitchins, who were both advisers to the EWT. Our mission was to determine our future role in the Kaokoveld and to meet with the Directorate of Nature Conservation, who was going to take over control of wildlife-related matters in the region. The intention was to first pay a visit to Wereldsend to see old colleagues and then to call on the conservation agency on our way out. Blythe had by now founded the Save the Rhino Trust (SRT) and came across from her base at the mouth of the Ugab River. She showed us around and we learned about the impressive programme that employed local trackers to monitor every known rhino in the area. The SRT had also established an identification file, which had photographs of every monitored rhino. Trackers to this day patrol a huge area of some 25,000 square kilometres by vehicle, camel, donkey and on foot from their base at Palmwag. The David Shepherd Wildlife Foundation (DSWF), under the leadership of David's daughter, Melanie, provides ongoing support in this vitally important operation, from its base in Cranleigh, Surrey, in the UK.

We set off from Wereldsend in Garth's Land Rover, hoping to see a live rhino now that the situation had improved. Anthony sat upfront with Blythe, who was behind the wheel, and Peter and I sat in the back. We scanned the golden stubby grassland that merged into the rock landscape and eventually disappeared up to the steep mountain rim.

By mid-morning we found fresh tracks of a rhino that Blythe thought was one of their study animals. Large clusters of *Euphorbia damarana* shrubs, Namibia's most toxic plant, were dotted about the landscape, showing up bright green against the grassland. Rhinos are known to lie up in the plants' abundant long stems, which grow two to three metres high and have a diameter of about four metres. Of the 103 plant species that Blythe had identified in her field studies, 74 were utilised by rhino. One of these was the *Euphorbia virosa*, or gifboom, which is covered in formidable spines. This highly toxic plant is a favourite of rhinos even though it has a virulent sap that can cause severe skin irritation in humans.

We came upon a lone rhino sleeping contentedly beside a water course. It was lying under the only tree in the area, about 300 metres from the rough track we were travelling along. Blythe carefully drove closer in order to photograph, and hopefully ID, the animal. When we were about 150 metres away, she cut the motor and the rhino suddenly sprang to its feet and faced us with its characteristic raised head and peered at our intrusion. It was midday and we now had an annoyed, irritated or confused rhino staring us down.

Anthony alighted from the vehicle, camera-motor winding, when the rhino decided that enough was enough; he came straight for us, giving a sharp blast through his nostrils. There is absolutely no way he could have smelled us because the wind was blowing from him to us. I believe he acted on sound and, having been rudely awakened, had responded in a defensive manner. Garth had requested that his Land Rover not come to any harm and that possibility now seemed reasonably certain. Weighing up to 1,500 kilograms, and travelling at speeds of up to 50 kilometres per hour, there is no question about a black rhino's ability to cause considerable damage. From the back of the vehicle, Peter and I had the most stunning view of this animal bearing down on us. By this stage Anthony had leaped aboard and Blythe had started the engine and was on the point of speeding off. At 40 metres the rhino abruptly turned about and rushed headlong back to its starting point and faced us for a few seconds, broadside, before taking off at high speed into the distant haze.

As it transpired, Blythe did not know the animal, which turned out to be a bull. Anthony's stunning images confirmed the new find and he was named Andy CAP (Clive, Anthony and Peter). Sadly, the bull was to disappear and was presumed poached or possibly killed by another bull trying to occupy new territory. His carcass was never found. He was, however, to become the symbol in a rhino telethon, which raised over R1.5 million in the most successful fundraising campaign for rhino conservation at the time. Part of the funds went towards supporting Blythe's work.

A few days later we flew to Windhoek and headed for our interview with the Directorate of Nature Conservation. They politely advised the three of us that a new order was taking over and that in their opinion our 'survey' work had come to an end. They argued that we had done our job and that there were now Namibian NGOs in place that were doing great work. The truth was a little deeper than that. The fact that we had contributed towards exposing the extent of the poaching with all the attendant publicity irked them considerably. The EWT had become more than an irritant and had caused more than enough embarrassment. Rumours circulated that I could be declared an 'undesirable'. The Directorate of Nature Conservation could hardly wait for our departure.

At the end of 1984 I announced my intention to step down as director of the EWT and to hand over the reins to Dr John Ledger, a trustee of the organisation and chairman of the Vulture Study Group. John went on to play a major role in support of a new initiative in Namibia. Anthony, Peter and I were to return one day, although at the time of our departure this seemed a very remote possibility.

My journey back to Damaraland, in June 2003, was a pilgrimage for me, in more ways than one. As a member of the Southern African Development Community Rhino Management Group (SADC RMG), I was heading out to a remote desert oasis named Palmwag Lodge on the edge of the Uniab River. Palmwag was a natural choice as it was situated in the heart of the Kunene region and was the field headquarters of the SRT. The group was to spend the next five days discussing the progress of the black rhino situation in southern Africa.

The meeting took place frequently to share information and receive updates on the status of the species.

It was a special occasion for me because it had been more than two decades since I had travelled in the region. The visit was accompanied by a real sense of joy thanks to the achievements of the EWT, NWT, SRT, DSWF and others, that had turned a hopeless situation around and achieved what many thought was impossible. The position back in 1980, for the elephant and rhino, was one of utter despair, but in 2003 it was one of guarded optimism.

There are many individuals that deserve mention when it comes to the Kaokoveld, and these have been recorded in the acknowledgements. A few, however, deserve a special mention here. The first two are Ina Brits and Blythe Loutit. They both plunged themselves into the struggle in 1982 when most timid souls would have vanished into thin air. No one escaped their relentless drive to save the desert wildlife, which led to the founding of the NWT. Sadly, Ina, who had supported the EWT from the outset of the aerial surveys in 1980, passed away before she realised the fruits of her labours. Blythe passed away in 2005 after a long illness and lies buried in her beloved desert nearby the SRT base. The desert rhinos were her very life and she witnessed the hopelessness of the rhino's position turn around to the extent that people could actually be taken out into the desert landscape to view these extraordinary animals. Her legacy lives on.

David Shepherd and the late Paul Bosman, who both painted stunning pictures of the desert elephants, deserve special mention. The limited editions of their artworks raised hundreds of thousands of rands for rhinos, elephants and the community game guard programmes, which ultimately led to much of the success in the recovery of the desert wildlife. Through their generous spirit, these two artists brought the Namibian wilderness into the living rooms of countless supporters.

Lucky Mavrandonis, the managing director of a Johannesburg-based pharmaceutical company, was always a great supporter of the

EWT. He was a concerned individual who was deeply moved by the plight of these animals. He sponsored the trip to the Kaokoveld to give David Shepherd a first-hand impression of the desert environment. It also allowed him to meet Garth and Blythe, but most importantly it gave him the opportunity of actually seeing elephants and rhinos. Lucky suggested that David create an edition of 850 signed and numbered prints of one of his paintings, film the expedition and eventually flight the programme on SABC's *50/50* in the hopes that viewers would support the appeal. The beneficiaries would be the EWT, REF and NWT, and the proceeds would go to their various projects in the Kaokoveld. The project was a massive success and 600 of the 850 tickets were sold before David had even painted the picture, realising R360,000 for the various projects and cementing the relationship with the SRT. The David Shepherd Wildlife Foundation remains to this day an outstanding example of how the sensible application of private-sector funding, as has been the case throughout this area's history, can reverse the decline of a species.

In the meantime the rumble of a distant drum was beginning to be heard elsewhere in southern Africa.

CHAPTER 7

The Rhino Wars

Guns and rhinos go together.
Clive Walker

THE IDEA FIRST MATERIALISED on the back of a Land Rover in the Damaraland desert in Namibia in 1984. Dr Anthony Hall-Martin and Peter Hitchins were concerned that whoever took over from me as director of the EWT would not have the same interest in rhinos and elephants. Peter felt very strongly that a major threat was on its way because Zambia's Luangwa Valley was embroiled in massive rhino and elephant poaching. The situation was so bad that in 1980 Norman Carr, and others concerned with the area, initiated the formation of the Save the Rhino Trust (SRT), an anti-poaching organisation, to assist in combating the problem.

Historically, an enormous number of black rhinos were to be found in the Luangwa basin of south-east Zambia. In 1931, Captain Charles Robert Senhouse Pitman, a game warden in Uganda, had been seconded to Northern Rhodesia to undertake game surveys. His recommendations led to the proclamation of South Luangwa, North Luangwa and Lukusuzi national parks in 1938. He clearly realised that the areas had enormous value, especially due to the prevalence of black rhinos. He produced a comprehensive and far-sighted report, which suggested the establishment of a number of reserves and setting up an elephant control department. Norman Carr, who was appointed in 1939, was one of the men employed to control the elephant populations. He was later joined by Bertie Schultz and they remained the only two senior men in this entire region up to Norman's departure for the war in 1940.

Norman became something of a legend in his own lifetime and by 1972, together with his colleagues, had established national parks in Zambia collectively covering an area of 16,400 square kilometres. At the time of proclamation they had an estimated population of 100,000 elephants and 8,000–12,000 black rhinos. In spite of their best efforts, with support from various international conservation organisations including the SRT, Norman and his colleagues could not stem the tide of poaching. The black rhino numbers dropped from around 8,000 in the early 1970s to less than 100 in the mid-1980s. In the end the poachers killed them all. Zambia lost every single rhino.

Norman was to retire in 1961 and went on to establish the first hunting operations, and then the first-ever walking safaris, in Africa. We were to meet in London in 1962 at the Courtfield Gardens Hotel where I was the assistant manager of the hotel group. He was in London promoting his book about the rearing of two lions, Big Boy and Little Boy. My interest in Norman stemmed from the fact that he knew my mentor, Hans Bufe, who was a frequent elephant hunter to the Luangwa Valley in the 1950s. The cost to take a rhino on licence at the time was £100.

I travelled to the South Luangwa National Park in 1994 and had the pleasure of dining with Phil Berry, who was at one stage the head of the task force fighting to protect the rhino. The following day I met a gentleman employed by an aid organisation involved with the park. I asked him, knowing that he worked with the local communities, about the loss of all the park's rhino. He lowered his voice and said that 'the promises made by government to the people living alongside this great system, have never been forthcoming'. If all that stood between you and starvation was a well-stocked game reserve with an especially

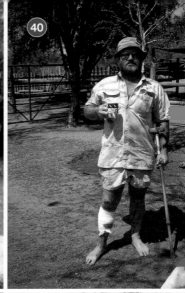

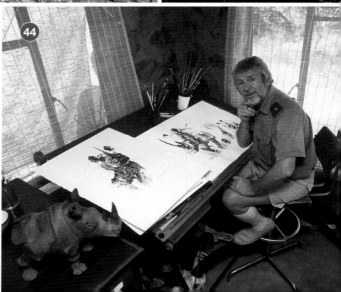

valuable animal such as a rhino, would you consider becoming a poacher? Of course the answer has to be yes. By 1984 poaching began in Zimbabwe, because by then Zambia's dwindling rhino population was becoming increasingly difficult to locate. The SRT did incredible work, and enormous funds were raised by well-meaning people, but in the end they lost the battle.

One only has to consider the Kruger National Park, which, at nearly 20,000 square kilometres, and in spite of a military presence, lost more than 250 rhino in 2011 alone. The May 2012 figures were: Kruger 129; South Africa 217. We know today that the cost of effectively covering large areas is prohibitive. Even though the Kruger is regarded as one of the best-equipped parks in Africa, it still seems incapable, at this point, to stem the tide. Luangwa, which is almost the size of Sri Lanka, must have been impossible to patrol; the rhino are spread out, staff and equipment are limited, the heat is unbearable, the tsetse flies and mosquitoes are relentless, and to top it all one is up against armed and dangerous men. Governments have either been powerless to intervene or, as has been the case in some instances, elements within government have been complicit themselves. The same scenario was simply repeating itself, from Uganda down, and the spiral was working its way inexorably south. South Africa, which had seen virtually all its rhino wiped out by the turn of the 19th century, and had managed to recover, now had only Zimbabwe as a buffer. Would it be our turn next?

The discussion on the back of the Land Rover in 1984 was about addressing that very question. What, asked Peter, if the threat was to prove true and there was no organisation devoted to the species? Why not form an organisation to specifically protect rhinos and elephants? I was less than enthusiastic, as I had spent the past 12 years very involved in the EWT and my energies were being channelled into a new game reserve and environmental education. Our role in Namibia was over and Peter was pleading for a fresh beginning. Anthony had moved to Skukuza in the Kruger National Park and he clearly supported Peter in the discussion. Since all three of us were intensely concerned about rhinos and elephants, it was inevitable that I would give in. By 1986, despite our assorted other commitments, the idea had really taken hold. I initially pushed for it to be affiliated to the EWT as a working group, because of my past connections, but Peter and Anthony felt that it should not constrain the group. Thus the Rhino & Elephant Foundation (REF) came into being, with Anthony assuming the role of first chairman.

There was widespread dismay at the prospect of yet another conservation movement encroaching on an already over-loaded ark. Competition was unavoidable as organisations wind up competing for funds and backing from both individuals and corporations, and the REF faced its most severe critics in this area. I tried to overcome these concerns by assuring myself that we had taken a firm stand in the 'rhino war'. As a specialist organisation we could devote all our energy to the emerging struggle and not be sidetracked by other conservation issues. The REF was backed by an impressive body of individuals who lent their names and support to the organisation: Dr Mangosuthu Buthelezi accepted the position of president, Ian Player and David Shepherd became patrons together with Dr David Cumming from Zimbabwe, Dr Iain Douglas Hamilton, the late Peter Jenkins from Kenya and Dr Jeremy Anderson, Dr Norman Owen-Smith (Garth's brother) and my old friend Koos Bothma, all from South Africa. These men were all highly experienced in the conservation of both species. The REF was further supported by three Homeland Boards, the Natal Parks Board (NPB) and the South African National Parks Board. The organisation was unique in that it had only a single paid staff member, Rozanne Savory, who was a living dynamo who handled everything from sticking stamps to arranging fundraising and driving us all crazy with her unbelievable energy. The REF brochure reflected the philosophy in the following words:

We live in a world where man has stretched out his hand to touch the stars, where he has left his mark upon the dark dim world of the ocean floors and where the most inhospitable parts of the earth hold no fear for him. Experience has shown that sensible application of state and private funding can reverse the decline of rhino and elephant populations.

With those words the organisation got off to a spectacular start, and staged a 'Rhino Conservation Workshop' in conjunction with the Game Rangers Association of Africa at Skukuza in 1988. This landmark event was attended by virtually everyone in the rhino world, including politicians, law enforcement, scientists, game rangers, policy makers, conservationists, fundraisers, journalists and corporate supporters. The principal financial supporter of the organisation, R. J. Reynolds, the manufacturers of Camel cigarettes, was also there. We certainly had no qualms about accepting funding, wherever it might come from. The workshop revealed the absolutely appalling loss of the black rhino throughout most of its former range in Africa. Something had to be done and done very soon, for by now the rhino war was on South Africa's very doorstep.

The horror story of the steady obliteration of Africa's black rhinos was spelled out by experts from across the continent; it was a sad tale of human avarice and greed leading to the virtual extinction of one of the earth's largest and most magnificent land mammals. The rhino war had been raging for at least ten years, starting in central Africa, and rolling down the east coast, through Uganda, Kenya and Tanzania, into Zambia and Zimbabwe, and was now about to spill over into South Africa. From a total population of 15,000 in 1980, Africa's black rhino numbered just 3,700 in 1988, and that number was dropping rapidly. On the one side of this war were the international crime syndicates that were making their fortunes supplying rhino horn to the Middle East, where they were used to manufacture dagger handles, and to the Far East, where they were used for traditional medicine. On the other side were Africa's beleaguered game rangers and conservationists. At that point in time the latter were losing. Speakers were to reveal the various measures taken to halt the slaughter. In Zimbabwe they used military strike units to seek out and destroy the poachers on the ground, and provided armed guards for individual surviving rhinos. In Namibia they relocated rhinos away from danger zones and placed them in heavily guarded intensive protection zones, with the support of the local communities.

Dr David Cummings summed up the workshop with a number of salient points:

- In the past six years there has been a 70 per cent decline in black rhino populations.
- 75 per cent of the population groups remaining consist of less than 50 animals.
- We know very little about the dynamics of the rhino-horn trade.
- There is a need for wildlife agencies to cooperate with other organisations like police and customs in all the countries involved.
- The answer may be to withdraw endangered populations to smaller areas where they can be better protected.
- Survey techniques need to be improved – many of the censuses are little better than educated guesses.
- Corrupt politicians have nullified the efforts of good conservation men and policies.
- Rhino conservation has not been put into the broader perspective of overall conservation.
- The militarist view of anti-poaching must be considered as a holding 'action'.
- There is a need to deal with the socio-economic realities of each country and bring in 'other' expertise to embed conservation in the very ethics of the country.
- The diversity of individuals is the greatest ally and force in conservation and with it must go the humility to communicate with all.

One of the recommendations of the workshop was that conservation agencies throughout southern Africa should coordinate their efforts in achieving these goals through a series of future meetings. As such, Nick Steel, then director of the KwaZulu Bureau of Natural Resources, convened a workshop at the Wildlife Society's Treasure Beach Environmental Centre in June 1989, which culminated in the following resolutions:

Management

1.1 Removal of rhino horns as a poaching deterrent is not recommended.

1.2 Legalise trade, but only on the condition that (a) funds go back into rhino conservation, and (b) there is strict control.

1.3 Artificial horn manufacture is not recommended.

1.4 Holding rhinos on private land is recommended, but only under strict control.

1.5 Boundary fences are essential.

1.6 Reducing rhino densities of vulnerable / immediate-threat rhino populations is not viable, but rather total relocation is recommended.

1.7 A captive breeding programme is recommended.

1.8 Anti-poaching mobile units and permanent camps are the best strategy – unpredictability is key.

1.9 Scout bonus scheme or incentives should be discouraged.

1.10 Scout status should be enhanced.

1.11 Scout selection should not be made on academics, but must be rigorous.

1.12 Lack of scout training is seen as one of the greatest weaknesses in the present strategy.

1.13 Deployment of local scouts should be done with caution.

1.14 Careful selection of senior field staff.

1.15 A technicon diploma doesn't make a scout.

1.16 Too much admin is keeping field staff in the office and this should change.

1.17 There are inadequate budgets for the fight against illegal hunting of rhino.

1.18 The appointment of a full-time rhino coordinator is essential.

1.19 Staff motivation is key with priorities on communication, training and remuneration.

Communications

2.1 Elevate communication – threat analysis should be done on all reserves with rhino.

2.2 Benefits from reserves should go to local communities – communities must be developed as anti-poaching support.

2.3 Details regarding a legal trade should be made public so that they can judge for themselves.

2.4 A regional Rhino Communication group should be formed.

2.5 NGOs should play an important coordinating role in combating illegal hunting – pan-African negotiations, negotiating with rhino horn traders, awareness campaigns, etc.

2.6 Conservation authorities should be involved in discussions regarding the resettlement of people alongside parks.

Law enforcement

3.1 Penalties for poaching – draft legislation must be supported and all government agencies should implement identical legislation as a matter of urgency.

3.2 Expert opinion is needed in leading evidence.

3.3 Information regarding all rhino-related 'trials' should be disseminated to all government agencies so as to keep all agencies up to date and informed.

3.4 Intelligence gathering is vital and should be disseminated between all agencies and the South African Police Service.

3.5 All privately held rhino products should either a) be surrendered to the authorities without prosecution during a limited time moratorium, or b) a sworn affidavit supplied on how the products were acquired – a possession permit may then be issued with conditions.

3.6 Honorary officers should be carefully selected and enlisted to assist with the control of illegal hunting.

What lessons did we take away from these important meetings, and have we learnt anything since? A number of important lessons were learned, which resulted in the establishment of several important bodies, including the Endangered Species Protection Unit (ESPU) of the South African Police, the African Rhino Owners Association

(AROA) and the SADC RMG and the SADC Rhino and Elephant Security Group, which was headed up by Nick Steele. The creation of the ESPU was a critical decision taken at the workshop, and turned out to be one that contributed immensely to preventing the rhino war from spilling over into South Africa. The ESPU was formed in 1989 to combat the illegal trade in wildlife products and to close the trade routes. The organisation, under the leadership of Colonel Piet Lategan, led to many interceptions and arrests and went on to achieve a high level of success, eventually operating with some 22 officers. With the change of government and politics in South Africa after 1994, the unit was unfortunately disbanded in 2003.

A few resolutions were, however, either ignored, not followed through or simply not pursued because the relevant budgets were not forthcoming. Had these not been ignored and been followed through with sufficient budget allocations, would we be in the crisis in which we find ourselves today?

Nick Steele always maintained that the best way to keep poaching levels down was to have 'feet on the ground'. This meant well-trained, well-equipped, dedicated, and properly led men, with the best backup possible. There are, admittedly, factors that make this difficult, particularly if you have little or no control over budgets, which is the problem in many state-run reserves and, we believe, in most private rhino sanctuaries. If you are reading this and you are a rhino owner or are responsible for rhino, have you taken Nick's sage advice? I often ask the question, 'Would you buy a very expensive convertible sports car and leave it out in the rain with the hood down?' The answer is a most definite no, of course, but that is exactly what has happened, especially in the private sector. Security measures to protect rhino have been minimal or non-existent, which is largely a result of the decline in poaching since 1994. Most believed or thought or hoped that the problem had gone away. Some never gave it a thought at all.

The entire Zambezi Valley, an area of some 12,000 square kilometres bordering Zambia, consists of some of the best wildlife country in Africa. An area of spectacular landscapes, it stretches from the Kariba Gorge in the west, travelling parallel to the mighty Zambezi River to the Chewore Hills in the east, and is home to an astonishing array of wildlife. The valley comprises large areas of mopane scrub and acacia woodland interspersed with ancient baobab trees (*Adansonia digitata*) and along the alluvial flood plains woodlands of ana trees (*Faidherbia albida*) and Natal mahogany (*Trichilia emetica*). At this point in time there were so few rhinos left in Zambia that it was no longer worth the poachers' efforts to find them and the stage was set for their move across the Zambezi River into the well-stocked parks of Zimbabwe. At the rhino workshop, Glen and Russell Taylor estimated that Zimbabwe still had 2,000 black rhino. The largest population of some 750 animals was located in the middle Zambezi valley between Kariba and Kenyemba. In an interview in 1988, Glen Tatham, then chief warden for Zimbabwe's national parks, said, 'It's a bush war'. The rhino war had started in earnest, although it was already seriously underway in 1984 when the last rhinos in Zambia's Luangwa Valley were killed. Poaching of rhino in Zimbabwe intensified to an alarming degree from July of that year. Zambian nationals crossed the river armed with AK-47s, G3s, SKSs, .303s and .375-calibre hunting rifles. They meant business. Zimbabwe marshalled their efforts and fought back with the support of the Zimbabwe National Conservation Trust.

In 1985 the Wildlife Society of Zimbabwe and the Zambezi Society, with massive public support and promotion, raised funds for much-needed field equipment: tents, mosquito nets, backpacks, water bottles and sleeping bags. The international NGO community also rallied. Our two American friends, Ingrid Schroeder and Babette Alfieri of SAVE US, were among them. Their support was crucial, as was that of the World Wide Fund for Nature. The REF stepped in, in due course, providing spare parts for vehicles, radios, backpacks and tents among other things. The REF also launched, at Sabi Sabi Game Reserve, a limited edition print of an original painting I had produced of a pair of black rhinos to raise funds in support of Zimbabwe's efforts. Every bit of support made a difference and Zimbabwe's rhino survival campaign became a familiar voice on T-shirts and in the media.

Glen became the commander of 'Operation Stronghold', which was part of Zimbabwe's efforts to stop the rhino poaching. He and his men, made up of highly trained individuals in specialised groups that became known as anti-poaching units, knew they were up against a very determined foe. The poachers were not afraid to fire first, and killed many parks staff and were killed themselves in turn. Julienne du Toit, a well-known and much respected South African environmental writer, interviewed Glen in 1993 and penned the following lines:

> The rhino has a face only a mother could love. And if it becomes extinct, can anybody say what a difference it will make in our everyday lives? But there's a bloody war being fought over these lumbering, half-blind creatures. In Zimbabwe they don't talk about patrolling parks. They talk war, they talk about counter-insurgency, they go out with machine guns.

In March of 1985 the right of park staff to use their weapons against poachers was given by the Zimbabwean Ministry of Home Affairs. This 'shoot to kill' policy was at first met with a good deal of condemnation and controversy from abroad. As is so often the case, Africa is told by the West what is best for them, most often by well-meaning, but misguided, people who sit so far away from the situation that they are blind to the forces at work on the ground.

To put things into perspective, I was told during the writing of this chapter that a rhino had been killed on a neighbour's farm. They are good friends who run an outstanding upmarket international safari and lodge business. In broad daylight one Sunday afternoon they heard five shots in quick succession and knew immediately what they meant. An immediate call went out to police, the anti-poaching unit was alerted and roadblocks were mounted. Poachers armed with a silenced .303 rifle had fired four bullets into a pregnant white rhino female and one into her 15-month-old calf. The cow took three shots to her head and one to the right shoulder, smashing the bone. She didn't run too far before toppling over dead. The calf received a fatal lung wound. Whoever they were, they knew how to use their weapons and knew the lie of the land. The bloody deed done, they slashed off the cow's two horns and vanished, leaving a badly wounded calf who would only die the next afternoon.

I travelled across the following morning, staying out of the way of the crime scene investigation, which was underway by police and Environmental Affairs. The scene was secured and metal detectors were in use and I was met with some very serious looking officials and staff. An air of gloom and utter frustration greeted my arrival. The smell of the rhino's death lingered and the horror of the wounds from removing the horns left me in a towering rage. The dignity of such a magnificent animal should never be reduced in this way. Three days later a black rhino was butchered in a similar fashion near Musina. In another incident a further white rhino was slaughtered. South Africa had just passed the 400 mark for 2011. The detractors of the 'shoot to kill' policy need to be present before they pass judgement and need to realise the widespread effect it has.

What is really frustrating is that the real enemy is invisible. Who are these faceless men who move between the world's capitals? They take little risk compared with the poachers who, in those days, received a pittance. The blood of about 2,500 rhinos was to soak into the soil of Zimbabwe, and alongside them the blood of at least 180 poachers and four park rangers. The killing of poachers was not a deterrent in itself, but you cannot expect men or women to defend a valuable animal, such as the rhino and the elephant, armed with radios and antiquated .303s. The mere presence of well-armed rangers sends a clear signal, but is not in itself the means to an end. One still requires all the necessary backup and support. The 1988 REF rhino workshop brought that to the fore and made plain what actions were necessary.

Everyone at the workshop was shocked at the general news concerning the black rhino in Africa. As with so many of these meetings, paper and talk was churned out trying to find ways to halt the killing, while the blood of rhinos continued to stain the African veld. Zimbabwe, the last stronghold of the rhino, was under siege.

Rhinos were now being poached by Zimbabweans themselves, and it began to escalate. Glen urged people into action, 'Time is running out for our rhino; they don't get a chance to die of natural causes anymore'. Zimbabwe's fight to save its rhinos had entered a dark hour. A senior official lamented:

> I think you have got to accept that illegal hunting is increasing in Africa for the foreseeable future in a major way . . . The emphasis should be on early detection. The state of affairs in Africa now is incredibly poor economic conditions, a breakdown of law and order, impoverished people who have no prospect of a reasonable living . . . They are going to go for rhino wherever the opportunity crops up.

The worst was still to come. Esmond Bradley Martin and Lucy Vigne, writing in *SWARA*, (the East African Wildlife Society's journal) of September / October of 1992, stated that 'the Zimbabwe Department of National Parks and Wildlife management still believed they had 2,000 black rhino in the country in 1991. The shocking reality is that there are probably only 500 to 1,000 rhino left'. The actual reality was that there were less than 500. The conservation world was stunned when the news became public. There was no simple solution given what Martin and Vigne wrote:

> There are three general reasons that rhino poaching has increased in Zimbabwe in the last year or so. First, the economy of Zambia has gone down further, giving a greater incentive for more poaching, while the Zambian authorities have been unable to prevent poachers from crossing the river border. Second, in Zimbabwe, the anti-poaching staff has become very wary: they now had poorer terms of service and there was not enough equipment nor people in the field. Third, in local currencies the value of rhino horn has gone up sharply, and the number of trade groups for the horn has increased. The horn was smuggled into Lusaka and then mostly taken by air to Swaziland or overland to South Africa for export to Taiwan.

In an urgent bid to stop the poaching, Zimbabwe commenced an experimental programme to dehorn white rhinos in 1991 and later the policy was adopted for black rhinos. Dehorning is considered a last resort in deterring poachers. Although 1–1.5 kilograms of horn remain after dehorning, the principle behind the practice is to shift the cost benefit for the poacher. By reducing the weight of the horn, the risk to the poacher increases in relation to the decreased reward. When dehorning as a poaching deterrent, the horn is cut above the dermis-covered bony ridge, avoiding the blood-rich dermal layer or horn bed. Similar to cutting one's nails, should you cut too close to the 'quick' it can result in bleeding, reduced growth and deformation. Chain saws are often used for speed, but a bow saw or large-toothed hacksaw can also be used. It is, however, important to note that rhinos developed horns for good reasons. In the case of the black rhino it is an important component of the animal's feeding and defensive abilities. The horn is also responsible for high mortality rates within the species, due to territorial conflicts, but that is the nature of the animal. Even if the horn is removed without killing the animal, the loss of the horn has a notable impact on the animal's fight for survival. The dehorning programme did not prove successful, however, especially in Hwange National Park where all the dehorned animals were slaughtered regardless. It could have been successful had all the other components been in place: anti-poaching equipment, an increase in manpower, improved salaries and benefits, etc. Sadly the opposite happened and staff were retrenched in Zimbabwe.

I wrote in the REF journal at the time, that 'unless governments make serious attempts to protect these assets and the men guarding them, we face a bleak future'. The sad saga across Africa was depressing. We had all the hype, the fundraising, the banners, the T-shirts and the media. We also had insults thrown at us for daring to shout enough is enough. Who was listening to us? Whose rhino were they in any event? There were times when my colleagues and I wondered if it was worthwhile. Of course, it was worthwhile. State-owned rhinos belong to the country, and to the world. If we can't do anything to prevent their mindless extinction, because of a belief in the efficacy of rhino horn in traditional medicine, then what are we as a species?

Areas such as Tanzania, Zambia, Mozambique and many parts of Zimbabwe are vast and we know what happened to their rhino populations. Just finding the rhino was difficult enough, let alone protecting them. The word 'stronghold', so often used in reference to the Zimbabwe rhino programme, had a most sad end, given all the effort that went into it. In hindsight, it was probably naïve to think that one could protect that many rhino over such a vast area, in the circumstances prevailing at the time. Having said that, is the same not true for our large parks today? Zimbabwe fortunately took a leaf out of Kenya's book and relocated their rhinos to private land as quickly as possible. The value of small, enclosed sanctuaries lies in the higher concentration of rangers, improved surveillance and monitoring and a greater possibility of rhino-to-rhino contact. Today there are more black rhino in conservancies than on state land in Zimbabwe.

The workshop was also an important opportunity to meet the people who, like Glen Tatham, lead the forces in the war against poachers. These are the men and women who don't get to wildlife conferences, and don't rub shoulders with the 'big' names in wildlife, but who go out on patrol night and day in all kinds of weather. They are the front-line defence and earned dismal salaries in the 1980s and 1990s and still do in most of Africa to this day. Sadly most African governments do not commit enough funding to their wildlife estates and the field staff in particular. The evidence was in plain view. Without the outside support of national and international NGOs, the battle in countries like Kenya, Tanzania, Zimbabwe, Namibia and Botswana would have been that much more difficult.

A great deal of the illegal killing of rhino had tailed off by 1999, mostly as a result of Zimbabwe and the counter measures taken to stop rhino poaching there. The war did not spill over into South Africa as was believed would happen, but had the threat really gone away? In 1994 we were down to about 2,400 black rhino in Africa and the prediction in some quarters was that the species would be extinct by 2025. The figure today stands at about 4,800. At the turn of the 19th century there were probably less than 50 southern white rhino in Africa, today the latest figure from the IUCN African Rhino Specialist Group

(AfRSG) places the figure at nearly 21,000, so somewhere someone is getting it right.

The problem is that the rhino is worth more when it's dead than when it's alive. If the animal is to survive, we are going to have to turn that around, but how do we do that and satisfy all?

CHAPTER 8

The Rise of
the Phoenix

*The rhino was only momentarily taken aback. Before I had time
to skip out of his sight he had made up his mind to charge me.
The angry thunder of his snort, mingled with a screech like an
engine blowing off steam, lent me wings.*

Vivienne de Watteville

FROM 1961 TO 1972 THE NATAL Parks Board had donated, sold and
delivered 1,109 white rhino into Africa and zoological gardens around
the world. Interestingly enough four went to Taiwan's Taipei Zoo
and four went into a park in Rangoon, Burma, where the last-known
specimens of the Javan rhino were shot in 1920. Taiwan was to be
accused of being in the forefront of the illicit trade in animals and
animal parts. The point to note here is the fact that no outward concern
existed in South Africa. As late as 1979 permits were still issued by
the Transvaal Division of Nature Conservation to move and sell rhino
horn. By 1994 the Natal Parks Board had distributed 3,465 white
rhinos around the world, and the number continued to climb. Between
1991 and 1992 the Natal Parks Board distributed 2,169 rhinos in
South Africa alone, which included black rhinos.

When the Kruger National Park (the Kruger) was proclaimed in
1926, only four or five black rhinos remained. The last black rhino, a
cow, was seen in the Kruger in 1936 and a programme of reintroduction

was instigated by the Natal Parks Board and the National Parks Board. It was in fact a very sensible decision for the Kruger, which was a prime choice for the species' introduction by virtue of its size. One needs to acknowledge the role played by the people involved, as it has proved to be the best safeguard for the species in South Africa. Prior to 1990 black rhino conservation was strictly a national affair and there were no black rhinos on private land in South Africa.

The first translocation of 20 black rhino to the Kruger took place in 1971 from Hluhluwe Game Reserve and was followed by a further group of 12 from Rhodesia (Zimbabwe) in 1972. According to Peter Hitchins, there was a total of 439 black rhino within reserves in South Africa by 1975. By 1982 no less than 70 animals had been safely introduced into the Kruger.

The bulk of South Africa's rhino of the southern subspecies, *Diceros bicornis minor*, were in the reserves of Zululand. A small population of the subspecies from East Africa, *Diceros bicornis michaeli*, had been relocated to Addo Elephant National Park in 1962 as a safeguard for the species. The last black rhino in the Orange Free State, was shot in 1842, and the last Cape rhino was shot in the Port Elizabeth area in 1853. Both the black and white rhino had fortunately been declared 'Royal Game' in 1890 and only the governor could give permission for one to be hunted. By 1895 the species was accorded absolute protection and then, strangely, in 1897 the proclamation was repealed and the species was placed in a different schedule. A licence fee was introduced, equivalent to about R20 today, for each with no more than two animals allowed per applicant. Most fortunately, both Hluhluwe and Umfolozi were proclaimed the same year, thus providing absolute protection to the species in the nick of time.

KRUGER NATIONAL PARK 1981

Peter Hitchins was very much involved in the conservation of rhinos and was literally a lone voice in the wilderness. No one was in any hurry to go near the animal and few, if any, were in any hurry to study them. The species was to become the driving force in his life and with the launch in 1973 of the EWT, he became one of its very first members, costing him R24 per annum.

Peter, together with Ken Rochat, chief capture officer of the Natal Parks Board, was directly involved in the very-first translocations to the Kruger in 1971 and was part of the team evaluating private properties in 1989. He worked for the Natal Parks Board for close on 13 years and was to devote a great portion of his life to the conservation of the species. In 1981 I was approached by Dr Anthony Hall-Martin, the senior research officer in the Kruger, for financial assistance in moving a batch of 16 black rhino to the park. As the director of the EWT I had no difficulty in persuading our board to agree. In order to derive publicity for the move, and to demonstrate our concern for the species, it was agreed that we could bring along a number of journalists to witness the arrival of the first four animals. One of the journalists invited, Charles Norman, was very well known and wrote for *Scope*, which was a widely read magazine. He was particularly well known for his writing on sport fishing. Charles was there to obtain the scoop of his life, but 'if that hadn't been necessary', he later wrote, 'I would never have been standing behind a tree in the Kruger Park, photographing the release of a batch of rhino and would not have made a wrong decision that almost caused the National Parks Board a great deal of embarrassment – and nearly my life'.

Dawn was breaking after our 16-hour journey from the Umfolozi Game Reserve with four of the eventual 16 black rhino. We found ourselves sitting atop two Land Rover station-wagons facing the loading ramp about 100 metres away. Black rhinos may be forgiven for being somewhat grumpy after a gruelling road trip and are known to take their frustration out on the first object they see. Each animal is in its own container and the rhinos are released one at a time. The loading ramp was well off into the bush so as not to be near any tourists. The first two came out calmly and vanished fairly quickly. The third, a bull, huffed and puffed a great deal and likewise was soon lost in the undergrowth. The last rhino, which was a ten-year-old female according to Ken, came storming down the ramp, only to turn around and go back up the ramp and to glare at all the officials and a cameraman sitting atop the truck. This she did a number of times, rushing back and forth, churning up clouds of dust.

Those of us on my Land Rover were so busy taking photographs we didn't notice that Charles had climbed off the second vehicle and had advanced 10 metres or so to a nice shady tree behind which he was changing his 400-millimetre lens to a shorter one. He was standing dead still, peering around now and then to snatch a picture. Our rhino soon lost interest in the container and made her way slowly down the ramp, by now quite calm. She advanced steadily in the direction of our vehicles, or more correctly straight towards Charles's tree. Every now and then she would spin around and stare back at the truck, then turn and resume her slow pace to the tree. By this stage Dick Garstang, a Kruger official, and I were urging Charles to get the hell out of there and back to the vehicle. Charles ignored us and remained where he was. He obviously believed that she would not see him, and would peel off and he would get the perfect shot. He did get the shot that he wanted, but then everything changed. The cow was now so close that Charles didn't dare move and remained frozen to the tree trunk, which was fortunately a fairly thick tamboti (*Spirostachys africana*). There was a deathly silence as we all watched, wondering what her next move would be. By now she was only about 3 metres away from the tree. Her great head came up slowly as she stared with her piggy eyes at the tree and the 400-millimetre lens hanging from a branch, swaying ever so gently in the early morning breeze. Without any warning she charged head first into the tree trunk, sending the lens flying through the air, breaking it into a number of pieces as it hit the ground.

Charles decided that it was time to leave and as he turned to run, she saw him and was after him. It is amazing what speed an 80-kilogram human being is capable of when chased by an ill-tempered rhino. As he raced between the two vehicles, his life hanging by a thread, he slipped in the soft sand and rolled under the nearest vehicle in a cloud of dust. Her speed carried her past him to the rear of the vehicle without touching him. Charles hit his head against part of the chassis when he dived under the Land Rover, which cut his scalp badly and caused him to faint momentarily. When he regained his senses, his head was bathed in blood. Peering through his blood-filled eyes, he watched in horror as the cow charged into the Land Rover again and again, crashing into the rear of the vehicle and lifting it off its wheels.

Dick and another journalist were clinging to the rooftop of the Land Rover unaware of what had happened to Charles, but fearing the worst for it appeared that she had in fact hit him. The whole episode happened so quickly and before we knew it she lost interest, satisfied with her display maybe, and thundered off. We fell off the vehicles yelling Charles's name and assisted him, alive, from under the now-battered vehicle. He looked a bloody mess, to put it mildly, but fortunately only had the gash in his head from colliding with the chassis. Dick volunteered to rush Charles through to Skukuza and bundled him into the middle seat. With Charles clutching a handful of handkerchiefs to his bloodied head, they sped off to find the doctor. About 2 kilometres down the dirt road, who had his head poking out of the dense bush looking at the oncoming vehicle? None other than the bull who had been released ahead of the cow. Dick stopped the vehicle, allowing the bull to run off, but the rhino had other ideas and now faced the stationary vehicle. Charles was later to write in his story, 'Not for nothing do my colleagues call me "abnormal Norman – the last of the big-time losers". I can't get myself almost killed, without the event turning into a comedy'.

The bull came at them like a runaway train and there was nothing they could do except release the hand break and hang on. By this stage they both knew this was going to be serious and in the next instant the rhino crashed head first into the front of the vehicle between the headlights and the radiator, sending them violently backwards as he repeatedly smashed into the bodywork before coming around to the driver's door, ripping open the metal. By now Dick had no doubt abandoned his seat with a very dazed and horrified Charles still hanging on. Having vented his displeasure, the bull wheeled about and dashed off into the bush at full gallop.

Much has been learnt since then, but long-distance relocations can still be challenging.

WATERBERG 1981

My reason for going to the Waterberg mountains in 1972 had nothing to do with settling, hunting or rhino for that matter. Experience gained on the wilderness trails in Zululand had awakened a deep interest in environmental education, especially for young children. So, I had set out to find a place, with a number of like-minded individuals who had also been on trails in Zululand, to establish an environmental school. My entry into the world of rhinos, elephants and cheetahs had not materialised at that point in time. I was employed in a position in Johannesburg, but it was not how I wished to spend the rest of my working life.

I picked up *The Star* newspaper one morning, which ran an article on a game reserve that had been developed near the town of Ellisras in the Waterberg of the northern Transvaal. It transpired that the reserve was owned by a certain Van Schalkwyk who was developing it as a game ranch that would offer hunting. This was one of the first of what would one day become a major activity in these mountains. Van Schalkwyk was a tall, tough, agreeable, cigar-smoking Afrikaner who invited me up to his reserve, which he was stocking with game. Among the animals was the first batch of five white rhinos to be reintroduced to the Waterberg in over 100 years. The cost of the five rhinos, apart from the transport, came to R800 each. At the time that seemed like a lot of money, as did Ian Player's *The White Rhino Saga*, which had set me back a whopping R5.40. Hunting and environmental education were not ideal bed fellows and my desire to get a school going sadly came to nought, as the reserve was perfect. It was to be ten years before I would return to the Waterberg. Subsequent events over the next 20 years were to define my family's role and involvement with both species of rhino, and are the reason we are still here 31 years later.

Meeting Eric 'Mchangi' Rundgren in January of 1981, in my search for a property, set the stage for the ultimate creation of a 36,000-hectare sanctuary and the achievement of my original dream to establish an environmental school for children. Eric was a living legend in Kenya, starting first as an elephant control officer in 1939, before becoming a game warden and then a professional hunter. He was the godson of

Karen Blixen's husband, Baron Bror von Blixen Finecke, and had led an extraordinary life in Kenya. In 1978 Eric and his partner, Rogers, had purchased four white rhino, which became the second batch to be introduced into the Waterberg. One was not required to have electrified fencing in those days, for rhinos and elephants were simply not available. The authorities were not thrilled about wild elephants wandering around, as they generally pay scant regard to an ordinary fence. It must have been a big moment for someone who had killed more than his fair share of rhinos, including a black rhino with a massive 114-centimetre front horn, on Mount Kenya. The return of the rhino was of great satisfaction, but it was not long before all four broke out of their cable enclosures and wandered across the river onto his eastern neighbour's property, where they settled.

Upon meeting Eric I learned that he wanted to sell the farm and that whoever bought it should carry on the work he had started and not let it go back to what it had been for 80 years: a cattle farm. Dale Parker, a fellow trustee of the EWT, joined the board in 1980 at my invitation, by virtue of his deep interest in the Cape Floral Kingdom. Dale was a farmer and a businessman who, together with his wife Elizabeth, was passionate about nature. He had inherited a large farm from his father in the Wellington district in the Western Cape and had set about preserving some of the last remaining 'renosterveld' and its bounty of rare plants. The farm is about 100 kilometres away from where Simon van der Stel had his encounter with a black rhino in 1685.

I spoke to Dale about the farm in the Waterberg while we were on an elephant count in Knysna. Unbeknown to me, Dale and Elizabeth had long desired to have a farm of their own that was truly wild. There was no doubt that this was exactly what I had found. It was not long thereafter that Dale purchased the farm and invited me to become involved in the conservation of the reserve, and allowed me to develop environmental education, which was why I had come here in the first place. This enabled my colleagues and myself to set up a programme that would allow children from primary school and older to share in an environment they would rarely be exposed to. Conita and I lived in Johannesburg, and Dale in Cape Town, so he requested that Educational Wildlife Expeditions (EWE) manage the reserve's operations, which it did until the reserve employed its own management team in 1985. Thus began a partnership that was to last for 20 years until Dale's untimely death in 2001.

During that initial period, EWE set up the first self-catering camps operation in the Waterberg, enabling families to enjoy the complete freedom of this spectacular mountain retreat. The trails for kids became very popular, so popular that in 1985, with Dale's support, the Wilderness Trust, a newly formed NGO, opened a fully operational wilderness school with fulltime staff and a capacity for 36 children. The school still functions to this very day under the Public Benefit Organisation, the Lapalala Wilderness School, which began operations in 2006. This confirmed my belief that it was essential to have well-informed youth who understood why there was such a vital need to protect areas such as this one, and why protecting biodiversity was essential to the well-being of our world. Dale purchased three more farms in 1982 and a further six white rhinos from the Natal Parks Board. Rhinos were being bought at a very low price at the time, ranging from R800 in 1972 to R2,000 in 1982. By 1988 the asking price was upwards of R20,000 per animal; it was little wonder that the system had to change. By 1991, nine years after paying R2,000 per animal, Lapalala bid R52,000 for a seven-year-old bull. The days of bargain rhino sales were well and truly over.

In 1988, following the findings of the REF's 'White Rhino Survey on Private Land', I was quoted in a press report stating that since the first Natal Parks Board rhino sales began in 1961, 149 private rhino owners in Natal and the Transvaal had bought 1,291 rhinos. The survey concluded that there were 781 rhinos on 103 properties, indicating a decline of 510 rhinos and that 46 of the farms had no rhino left at all. Makes you wonder? Surveys such as this, coupled with more realistic prices, led directly to more serious efforts on the part of private rhino owners to breed their own animals, especially since the species was now regarded as a game-ranch animal. A real value had been put on the animal, both at the supplier and consumer ends. As much as the hunting of white rhino is anathema to a broad section of the conservation world, it has, as strange as it may seem, contributed to the survival of the species.

At the time of the survey findings, questions were asked about the private sector. Could it be trusted to really cooperate in the long-term conservation of the species? Or was it a matter of simply making money? This ultimately led to the founding of the African Rhino Owners Association (AROA) in 1989, with the principal objective of improving communication and information on the whereabouts of rhinos, their numbers, management and security. The question of horn stocks remained a thorny issue and related mostly to reasons of trust, as they still do today. Some rhino owners were against revealing their rhino numbers, let alone reporting on the length of their horns. AROA was sadly to wind down as a result of the closure of the REF, which played host to the organisation, and the departure of a number of key members of the executive. Had AROA still been around in 2007/8, perhaps the private owner would have been more informed about what was coming?

By 1985 our relationship with the Natal Parks Board was most cordial, not least in my role as director of the EWT, who by now had contributed funding for black rhino and white rhino translocations to state reserves. I thought that the time was appropriate to engage in correspondence with the director about the possibility of being considered a recipient for black rhino on a custodian basis. My request fell on deaf ears and 'who did I think I was as no black rhino had ever been made available to the private sector'. It was 1986 and I reminded them relentlessly for the next four years, but my letters fell on deaf ears.

Having been unsuccessful with black rhino, I turned my attention to the river. I contacted the chief game capture officer for the Natal Parks Board, Keith Meikeljohn, for by now we were good clients. I asked him to keep an eye out for some hippos, which had been extinct in the rivers since 1962. The original owner of the house that Conita and I lived in was not partial to the animal, as they were prone to invading his gardens at night, and he had killed the last one. He also detested baboons and for years after he and his family departed, any baboon who spied us fled in absolute terror. Imagine my surprise when Keith phoned to tell me that he had a hippo bull, cow and calf from the Lake St Lucia region and asked how soon they could be delivered. The hippo had also been returned to the Waterberg.

In early 1990 I discovered a San depiction of a black rhino on the north face of the Waterberg, in a community area, which was to be the first of an eventual four. The news made no difference to my friends in the Natal Parks Board, who apparently had ideas of a more lucrative nature. The plan revealed itself when I was advised that the decision had been taken to put five black rhino, two bulls and three cows, up for public auction at the Parks Board annual auction in June of 1990. It was to be the first-ever sale of black rhino to private buyers. The rationale was to sell the animals and not, as I had hoped, to find custodians for the species. It made financial sense: the Parks Board needed the income. It was as simple as that. There were still those sceptics who weren't so sure that the private owner was up to the task; the game farming industry is a mixed blessing in South Africa.

The full story of Lapalala is yet to be written, but suffice it to say that it grew from the original 5,000 hectares to 36,000 hectares and secured some of the most important habitat and 80 kilometres of river frontage. Effectively 31,000 hectares had been transformed from degraded farmland back to a wild state. This was to be Dale's greatest Waterberg legacy. His second was his passion for both rhino species, which gave him untold joy, and now, in part, takes centre stage of my unfolding story.

PILANESBERG 1984

In 1984 the EWT convened a workshop in the Pilanesberg Game Reserve; it was chaired by Peter Hitchins and attended by leading members of the four provinces, the police, the zoological gardens of Johannesburg and Pretoria, the South West African Conservation Authority, the South African National Parks Board, the Bophuthatswana Parks Board and the IUCN African Rhino Specialist Group (AfRSG). It was accepted that the primary aim was to increase the numbers and distribution of the black rhinos in southern Africa, but a range of other factors were discussed:

- Transvaal: House in order, and we know of no poaching.
- Natal: There has been only one serious poaching problem. Two black and two white rhinos poached in 1981.
- Kruger National Park: Good security and no rhinos poached. The only problem is how the Kruger National Park can get more rhinos.
- Pilanesberg: No problems. Effective control of the rhino populations.
- South West Africa: Of considerable concern was the situation in Kaokoveld, but poaching no longer a problem in the country.

Natal remained the principal source of both species of rhino in South Africa: the state in the case of the black rhino and the state and the private sector in the case of the white rhino. Natal had already demonstrated, over a very long period, its ability to provide and restock areas. The only other source of rhinos was in South West Africa and relocations would take place onto government land to begin with and then later onto private land.

It is important to note that the workshop took place in February of 1984 and how the situation has changed today. Bear in mind the large number of private rhino owners of both black and white rhinos that developed after 1990. There are a number of factors to take into account, not least the democratic change in South Africa since 1994, the cessation of hostilities that characterised the state of emergency, and the huge influx of illegal immigrants into the country. There are now nine provinces as opposed to four. Socio-economic-political factors have to be brought into the equation too.

To further illustrate the point one needs to look at the totals for 1984 and 2011 in South Africa:

1984: White rhino: 3,250   Black rhino: 610
2011: White rhino: 20,150   Black rhino: 4,850

One of the key issues was the long-term distribution of both species and an important event took place 18 months after the workshop when, in July of 1985, six black rhinos of the subspecies *Diceros bicornis bicornis* were returned to the Cape from South West Africa after an absence of 133 years thanks to funding from the EWT. Their destination was the Augrabies Falls National Park in the north-western Cape. This was the first of what was ultimately the re-establishment, under Anthony's direction, of the south-western subspecies from South West Africa. In September of the previous year Peter and I had accompanied Anthony to four of the National Parks Board's parks on a fact-finding mission to assess the suitability of the areas for the reintroduction of the species. The Vaalbos National Park (to the west of Kimberley), Augrabies Falls National Park, the Karoo National Park and the Mountain Zebra National Park were all judged to be most suitable. Unfortunately the Augrabies Falls National Park was later to become the subject of a land claim and the rhinos had to be relocated to the other reserves. Vaalbos also fell victim to a land claim and a new park, Mokala National Park, was established with the proceeds of the payout.

The original Cape rhino (*Diceros bicornis bicornis*) is the nominate subspecies, but was regarded as being extinct, having been shot out near Addo in 1852. Others were convinced that the black rhinos of Damaraland and Kaokoland belonged to the same taxon. The distribution of the black rhino was continuous from the Cape to Etosha. As the Namibian rhino is geographically the closest to the Cape rhino, there was considerable merit in the suggestion, according to Anthony. Today the black rhino of Namibia is widely accepted on all grounds – ecological, genetic and practical – as the logical choice for the founder stock of black rhino to be introduced to the arid zones of South Africa. Today all four national parks, including Addo, contain populations of Namibian stock.

BOTSWANA 1988

In 1879 Frederick Courteney Selous observed that there were still a few black rhinos along the upper Chobe River, north-west of the Savuti outlet. Bobby Wilmot and his hunters also reported seeing black rhinos in the Okavango and on Chief's Island. By 1974 Dr Reay Smithers, in his work *The Mammals of the Southern African Subregion*, suggested that they had disappeared in Botswana. Occasional reports suggested, however, that they may still have existed in the eastern Caprivi and northern Botswana.

In 1988 Herman Potgieter and I were gathering material for a book on the Okavango Delta. Assisting us was my son Anton, our pilot Andre Pelser and Lloyd Wilmot who knows the region better than most. The plan was for Anton, Andre and I to fly to Guma Lagoon on the western side of the delta while Lloyd and Herman went at low level in Lloyd's little four-seater Cessna 175 Skylark taking photographs. We were to rendezvous later and then fly up to Tsodilo Hills, which has the most amazing San rock-art paintings. Among the cave art were numerous depictions of black rhinos, which I was anxious to record. Tsantsara pan, to the north-west of Savute, is the only one that still carries water in the drier times in this vast wilderness. Lloyd, flying low in a wide circle towards the pan, was astonished to see a rhino cow and calf running below him in the dry mopane woodland. Banking the plane, Lloyd afforded Herman, who was stationed at the open door, the opportunity to photograph them. Sure enough, it was a magnificent black rhino cow. At last we had living proof of the species' existence.

The news of the find was most encouraging and Peter made a detailed aerial survey of northern Botswana a priority. As soon as funding was available, the REF would tackle the job in order to determine the status of the white rhino, and hopefully reveal more black rhinos. Botswana's white rhinos were already extinct by the turn of the 19th century and the Natal Parks Board had undertaken the reintroduction of 90 of the species between 1974 and 1981 with funding from the Okavango Wildlife Society and the Frankfurt Zoological Society.

The long-awaited 15,000-square-kilometre rhino survey of northern Botswana finally got underway in September 1992. The operation was led by Peter with Andre as lead pilot and Anton as the principal navigator and, to make sure we stayed airborne, we enlisted the help of Johan Kotze as flight engineer. All things being equal, Botswana's white rhino population should have naturally increased to some 240 animals, bar natural mortality, since their reintroduction. Using two aircraft flying at approximately 15–20 metres above the ground, with the second aircraft 1,000 metres astern and 500 metres to starboard of the first, the survey got underway from its base at Lloyd's Camp in Savute.

Botswana today is blessed with a president, Ian Khama, who is passionate about wildlife, which is very rare in Africa. It paved the way for an excellent relationship and the full involvement of the Department of Wildlife, the Ministry of Wildlife of Namibia and the Natal Parks Board, whose personnel acted as observers. Dr Mike Knight, who is today the chairman of the IUCN AfRSG, and a pilot with considerable experience, was also along. The survey could not have had a more complete body of experienced field men under one thatched roof.

After two weeks, with 6.30 a.m. take-offs and three and a half hours of flying each morning, with follow up flying in the late afternoon, avoiding eagles and vultures frequently, no black rhinos were found and only a total of seven white. Three were poached after the survey. To add to the horror of it all, the black rhino cow and her calf were slaughtered, in two separate instances. After discovering the remains of the black rhino cow in the Savute, the Department of Wildlife in Botswana discovered the remains of her calf and retrieved her head, without its small horns, thus signalling the extinction of Botswana's black rhinos. Fortunately the survey report enabled Dr Anthony Hall-Martin, then director of special services for the South Africa's National Parks Board, and Peter to request the assistance of the crack rhino-capture team of the Natal Parks Board. They were able to save the few remaining live white rhinos in Botswana and moved them to the established Khama Rhino Sanctuary near Serowe.

The concept of a rhino sanctuary in Botswana was originally proposed by Peter Hitchins. It was initiated by the Chobe Wildlife Trust under the chairmanship of Jonathon Gibson and supported by the REF. The idea of establishing a sanctuary for both species of rhino near the town of Serowe was that of two Serowe businessmen, Ray Watson and Tony Ballantine. Serowe was a good choice, for it had a military base nearby and was far enough from any border. Serowe is, more importantly, the traditional centre of the Bamangwato tribe.

Lieutenant General Ian Khama was the head of this tribe, but was also in charge of the military, and agreed to have his family name linked to the sanctuary.

The establishment of the sanctuary came in the nick of time thanks to the generous support of the World Wildlife Fund, Hong Kong; the Chobe Wildlife Trust; and the Kalahari Conservation Society. It is unique in Africa for it amounted to a wildlife sanctuary established *by* tribal people *for* tribal people. Working closely with the government's Department of Wildlife clearly illustrates the ability of non-governmental organisations to come together in a cooperative project of this magnitude.

Botswana thus, in a hair's breath, avoided seeing their white rhinos go extinct twice in the same century.

NDUMO GAME RESERVE 1989

It was 4 a.m. and a bright moon bathed the ground with a luminous light. A fiery-necked nightjar called repeatedly in the dense bush and an owl hooted mournfully somewhere in the gloom. There was a faint snoring from the man sleeping next to me as I lay in my stuffy sleeping bag. Bar two of us, the group was shrouded in mosquito nets. The determined assault of squadrons of mosquitoes assured me that I was not alone with the night sounds of the Ndumo bush.

As I anticipated the events ahead, I forgot about the mosquitoes, the nightjar and the owl. We were on a black rhino capture operation deep in the northern Zululand bush close to the Mozambique border, and the object was to capture ten black rhinos on the eastern side of the reserve. Darting and capturing rhinos under these conditions was not without danger as the bush is extremely dense and almost impenetrable unless you are a rhino, or prepared to travel on all fours.

A single track ran past the camp from the gate, 10 kilometres away, down to a guard post and then continued onto the floodplain. The only other access was along the border. This sensitive area was of great concern to Nick Steele, director of the KwaZulu Bureau of Natural Resources, and his field men who were stretched to the limit. This piece of northern Zululand was sandwiched between the Ndumo

Game Reserve in the west, a community corridor in the middle and the newly established Tembe Elephant Park in the east. Somewhere in this bush were ten black rhino who, unless removed, were in grave danger of being poached. The objective was to relocate the animals to a safer environment and the Kruger National Park was the obvious choice. Not that the Kruger was inviolate to determined poachers, one only has to look at the statistics of the park today to confirm this, but at the time it was a far better proposition than this remote area. The understanding was that one day, when the situation changed, the rhinos could be returned, and that is precisely what has transpired. Many black rhinos were eventually relocated to nearby Tembe, where the security is far greater today.

Nick's decision was to prove 100 per cent correct, for the intended incorporation of the area, combining Tembe and Ndumo, has never happened. In fact, the very area the rhinos were taken from has been invaded by local people who demanded more land and appear to have no intention of moving.

By 6 a.m. the camp was astir. We were well taken care of by the army who provided three large rectangular tents, one of which was a full-blown mess tent with the luxury of a 'chef' with the rank of corporal. The Kruger was not known to do things by half measures and had sent their chief pilot, Hugo van Niekerk, to operate the Bell Jet Ranger. The fuel for the helicopter was funded by the REF. Ground operations were handled by some of the most experienced field men in Africa. The Kruger was taking no chances during this capture. We were accompanied by three veterinarians, Drs Kobus Raath, Vossie de Vos, Douw Grobler, and one research technician, Johan Malan. Two of the Kruger's senior rangers, Louis Olivier and Johan Oelofse, and Danie Pienaar, who was a researcher with the REF, also joined us. Graham Wiltshire and Ian Thompson from the KwaZulu Bureau of Natural Resources and a team of guards plus ten local Tongas who knew the bush rounded out the operation. Graham was later to die tragically in a light-aircraft crash while searching for black rhinos in Ndumo.

We took off into a stiff wind coming in from the nearby coast and it took two hours to find the first rhino. When we heard the words 'dart in' the entire ground force sprang into action. The helicopter gave us running commentary, advising us that the animal was heading west to the pans. A darted rhino in water is not a good idea, as the lowered head can cause them to drown very easily. We crashed over hippo-sized potholes, ducked under low-hanging branches and clung on for dear life as our vehicle raced at top speed in the direction of the helicopter. The helicopter hovered in one spot and we knew that the animal was below it, but there was no way to get to it as the vegetation was so dense. Everyone bailed off the vehicles and carried ropes, cans of water, spray and containers, drug boxes, shovels, saws and pangas towards the rhino. Michael Landman, of the Parks Board, and I were armed with cameras and stayed in the rear so as not to get in the way.

We all converged around the large bull and, while it seemed to be a mass of confusion, each person knew exactly what was expected of them. Within 40 minutes the rhino was ready to be woken from his drug-induced sleep. With a towel over his eyes and ropes secured around his head, his ears had been notched, he had been measured and generally checked out by the vets, and we were ready for the antidote. A pathway some 200 metres long had been cleared through the undergrowth and the tractor and trailer container were in position. The antidote was given and we were ready to go, with the vets at his head and two ropes spread out in front with Tongas and rangers hanging on. Blindfolded, he lumbered to his feet with the assistance of a cattle prodder in a tender spot. This part makes me shudder for it must have been bewildering to the poor animal. With a great deal of huffing and puffing we set off at a dizzying pace considering the narrow confines of the pathway. Dust swirled once or twice when he lost his balance and went down, followed by a few assistants. At the rear end the second team was hanging onto a rope attached to a leg to check the forward rush. All of us kept our mouths shut, except for the ones at the sharp end who shouted occasional instructions. The open crate was waiting as the bull thundered in and clunked into the front-end steel plate. The nose rope had to be removed from within and required steady nerves while someone attended to the back rope and the door was hastily banged shut and bolted. The entire operation had taken 55 minutes and we were one down with nine to go.

Finally, all ten of Ndumo's black rhinos were safely captured and released into the Kruger.

HLUHLUWE / UMFOLOZI 1990

When the Zulu capture staff in charge of the rhino bomas in Umfolozi were asked what they felt about the black rhino under their care they promptly answered, 'They are a gift from God'. I found that interesting because I am convinced today that they knew a great deal more than anyone else about the nature of this particular animal. They are responsible for them in the bomas and they form part of their everyday lives. But it lies deeper than that. It became very obvious to me when I had close contact with the first black rhino to return to the Waterberg, our second home for the past nine years, after an absence of some 150 years. 1990 was a year of serious drought in these mountains, but also a year of great excitement in the conservation world; the Natal Parks Board had announced the year before that they were going to put five black rhino up for auction.

The 18th of June 1990 could be regarded as one of the most momentous events in conservation in Africa. Black rhino numbers were deemed to have recovered enough to put a few of the animals up for sale. The auction was to be held in a giant marquee capable of seating 1,500 people at the Hluhluwe Sports Club in Hluhluwe, a small town supporting the wildlife and farming fraternity in northern Zululand. The conservation world was abuzz and television crews from around the world were in attendance.

Dallas Kemp, the auctioneer, announced that history was in the making as proceedings got underway at 11.30 a.m. Not a seat was to be found in the jam-packed tent, with large bodies of people lining the sides and the rear. The tent was awash with the green blazers and ties of the smartly turned-out Natal Parks Board officials – one of the rare occasions that a game ranger may be seen wearing a jacket and tie. The atmosphere was electric and it promised to be a great event. These annual auctions were not just about rhino, but a whole range of species, and were regarded as being among the best in the country. White rhinos had been an auction item since 1987, and they were second last on a catalogue of nearly a dozen species, but the last and most anticipated animals were the two black rhino bulls and three cows.

I had long believed that Lapalala was a good choice for the introduction of black rhinos, for by now the sanctuary covered 10,000 hectares. While I had repeatedly expressed my interest in becoming a custodian to the Natal Parks Board, it had largely fallen on deaf ears. Dale Parker, the owner of Lapalala, in spite of agreeing to have the reserve evaluated, was only interested in purchasing a few more white rhinos and wanted the satisfaction of knowing that the reserve was suitable for the species. His reluctance may have stemmed from a concern that we were not up to taking care of such a rare and threatened species. There were those who believed it was a bad idea to allow the private sector to become role players at all. No one could argue, however, that the white rhino had recovered largely due to the private sector's commitment.

We had arrived the previous day and made straight down to the bomas in order to view the rhinos, which was a normal event. After first viewing the white rhinos we ended up viewing the black rhinos. All the animals had been boma trained and the white rhinos were by and large relaxed, but when viewing the black rhinos, one felt instinctively that they were different. Some would be fairly relaxed, others not. One sign demanded 'quiet' and another, up at the viewing platform, made it abundantly clear that one went up entirely at one's own risk. If, for whatever reason, one was to fall into the enclosure, the chances of coming out were zero. That's exactly where I found Dale, who continued to keep his thoughts to himself as he observed the rhino peering up at him.

Erica Platter, a well-known writer, was one of a score of journalists attending the event and later was to write a delightful piece for *Style* magazine:

There wasn't a suit to be seen, aside from Norma Rattray's cunning little topee, and a sprinkling of bush-fatigued stalkers. The only ties were regulation Natal Parks Board green, a blue blazer denoted an auctioneer, and Ian Player wore sand forest green. There were very precise directions for getting to the auction site, a scatter of army tents and a circus marquee on the rugby field of the Hluhluwe Sports Club. And just over the road dozens of private planes flew in for the day, landing on the village bush strip.

The event was reminiscent of a carnival, and by the time the exhausted gathering arrived at the last item, the tension was unbearable. Dallas Kemp kept reminding everyone that black rhinos 'must survive the greed of man', whatever he meant by that remark, building up the tempo as only an auctioneer can. He opened the bidding at the reserve price of R1 million and Fred Keeley, a businessman and conservationist, immediately bid R1.1 million. No one else bid and a deathly hush came over the entire gathering, which clearly surprised everyone considering nine properties had been approved in a stringently vetted assessment for size, security and habitat. At this point the atmosphere became unbearable as all eyes and TV cameras focused on the lone bidder. Up to this point, Dale had not said a word to me and had earlier chosen a number of white rhinos. We had duly registered as white rhino buyers, and had been given the black disc that marked us out as such, but we had not taken the green disc that indicated a potential black rhino buyer. At this point Dallas was getting desperate, pleading that the five black rhinos were worth way more than R 1.1 million. I knew that Dale shared this opinion and I could see that he was clearly troubled. In the dying moments before the hammer fell he turned to me and asked me what I thought. I felt that I had been waiting my whole life to give the answer. Dale had come to trust my judgement over our ten-year association, and I never hesitated for one moment. I whispered, 'Put your hand up'. He did so and upped the bid by R100,000. Dallas recognised Dale and shouted out, 'Oh, it's Dale and Clive'. An official ran down the aisle behind us and thrust a green disc into my hands, which I promptly held up. The bidding then rose rapidly to R2.2 million, which was Dale's final bid, and the hammer fell. For the first time ever the black rhino had real value and the private owner had been entrusted with their care. I kept both the green and the black disc. After working for the conservation of black rhinos for the past 19 years, the time had arrived when we were able to work directly with the living animal, and I felt I deserved them. The press reception afterwards was phenomenal. Dale quickly disappeared, insisting that I face the cameras and reporters. As the face of Lapalala, some of the press linked me to the purchase, assuming that I had bought the rhino in partnership with Dale. While I did my best to orchestrate the outcome, I certainly did not write the cheque.

Lapalala originally had four scouts trained in white rhino tracking, who also did fence and general reserve patrol. With the arrival of the five black rhinos we upped the number of scouts to six and they received proper field-ranger training. I appointed Andries Mokwena, a Pedi cattle herder from the nearby community of Bakenberg, who we had previously employed in 1982, as the leader of the scouts. The rhinos remained in bomas for three months after their arrival. One of the scouts' tasks was to collect daily browse for the rhinos, and they got to know each of the animals, learning their personalities, traits and actions. They soon knew which rhinos they had to be careful of and which had a sense of humour. Each rhino had been named by the Zulus back in Umfolozi, just as they do with their Nguni cattle, and we retained the names. The one male was Mehlobomvu, Red Eyes, whose eyes seemed permanently bloodshot, and the other was Makula or Big Balls. The three females were Punyane, or Tiny, Nkane, or Cat's Eyes, although she became Garfield to us as she had that distinct look of Garfield the cat, and finally Masasaneni, the Zulu word for prostitute. Black rhinos had not occurred in these parts for 130 years and the Pedi had never previously seen or worked with them. The animal represented nothing to them, other than respect.

One thing we all learnt was that rhino reverted to type once released, and there was no way you could take liberties with any of them, with the exception of the female Punyane. White rhinos are very different from black rhinos, and can become very used to the presence of humans and vehicles. They are far more relaxed than black rhinos and can be approached with relative ease. I choose my words carefully, and don't want anyone to underestimate the capability of a white rhino under any circumstance. I believe more incidences have occurred when liberties have been taken with the animal.

For the next 14 years black rhinos were our neighbours. Two male black rhino calves and a female white rhino grew up in our garden. The first black rhino, named Bwana, was a day old when found and was rushed to the Onderstepoort Veterinary Institute. He was then placed in the hands of a most remarkable woman, Karen Trendler, who miraculously nursed him back to health at her animal care centre near Pretoria. After six months he came back to Lapalala and Doornleegte became his new home where, under Conita's watchful eye and the assistance of her Pedi staff, he was raised to adulthood. Conita went on to raise a female hippo before returning her to the wild where she joined up with the wild hippos we introduced into the Palala River system. She was followed by another orphaned black rhino male, who was successfully integrated into the wild, and a white rhino female who also went back to the wild and produced calves. The final orphan, Moeng, was a badly injured, prematurely born, black rhino female. She was placed in Karen's care and eventually returned to Conita for ongoing recovery.[4] One Sunday evening, in August 2008, she was slain in her holding pen by poachers armed with a handgun. Her horn was not even 10 centimetres long. The rhino war had recommenced. Moeng's death was a shattering forerunner to the blood bath that has followed. What the perpetrators don't care about is the valuable role she played as a role model for thousands of adults, children and teachers. We don't know who committed this appalling act, and the police have never been able to find out. We do know that it had to be someone who knew us and our movements, and was possibly to be found within our own ranks.

Anton married his fiancée, René, at Lapalala in 1994 and they managed a neighbouring reserve. They were approached by Dale in late 1996 to join the fulltime staff of Lapalala as the management

---

4 Conita's biography about her journey as a foster mother is currently being written by a close friend, Sarah Smith, and reveals just how extraordinary these animals really are, and will dispel much of the ignorance surrounding them.

team of the eastern sector, following the purchase of an adjoining 12,000-hectare property, which had seen the reserve grow to 36,000 hectares. The integration of this property allowed the reserve to function as a single rhino sanctuary. This realised two of Dale's greatest wishes: the protection of 80 kilometres of river frontage and the expansion of the sanctuary for both species of rhino. To his credit he agreed to my request in 1990 that we undertake daily monitoring of the black rhinos. The northern Waterberg bush can be extremely dense and is often very rugged. I appointed Glynis Brown, who was in tourism, to capture the daily observations and locations of each known animal from the field rangers. I learnt this from my Namibian friends, but the two situations cannot really be compared.

Itala Game Reserve in northern KwaZulu-Natal was the setting for an IUCN AfRSG meeting in July of 1998 and, as usual, I shared a room with Tony Conway of the Natal Parks Board. The group, which I had been invited to join in 1994, came about as a result of the introduction of the black rhino in 1990, and the founding of the AROA, and had little to do with my position within the ranks of NGOs. The organisation played an important role in the conservation of both species of rhino in Africa, and membership is largely made up of scientific and management authorities at state level. Prior to 1990 no privately owned rhino members were present. I was privileged to serve on the group for 14 years.

During an afternoon session on range expansion, the question of the preparedness of one of the state reserves to receive a large batch of black rhinos was discussed. The outcome was that the reserve in question was not considered ready. The planned relocation was large, amounting to nine females and five males. Later, as was customary, Tony and I enjoyed a beer after the meeting closed for the day. I asked him whether they wouldn't consider selling the entire group, rather than having a state reserve lose out to another jumping the queue. I emphasised the fact that jealousy occurs at all levels, knowing full well that the Kruger National Park would take all the animals providing they came with no price tag. Why not sell them and generate much needed funding? It's very easy to talk like that when it's someone else's money, and I had not discussed the matter with Dale Parker at all, but I nevertheless felt that this was an opportunity not to be missed. The Parks Board had already made the decision to remove the rhinos and I thought that it was worth him trying. The new section of Lapalala Wilderness was perfect. All I had to do was convince Dale.

The fact that Anton and René were resident in the area made all the difference in Dale's decision. He agreed after getting the okay from Dr George Hughes, the director of Ezemvelo KwaZulu-Natal Wildlife, and his discussions with Tony. I was overwhelmed at the prospect; all the lessons Peter Hitchins and I had learned from visiting five of Kenya's private reserves and three national parks in 1993, arranged by Kuki Gallmann, had been worthwhile. The Kenyans were the leaders in black rhino conservation on private land in those early days, and there was much we were to learn.

Dale agreed to the purchase of all 14 animals, which necessitated the rapid construction of suitable holding pens. Anton and his team, with the help of Clive Ravenhill, reserve manager of the western sector, soon completed them, and we were shortly thereafter able to receive the first five. A young game ranger, David Bradfield, had pestered me for some time for a job working with rhinos, but my answer had always been no. He had been offered a position with a large state reserve, Songimvelo, in the Lowveld, and I advised him to take the position to gain experience. When the time came to expand Lapalala's rhino programme, David was the perfect choice. He took over the rhino monitoring field staff and they taught him the ropes very quickly, as he was expected to accompany them rather than sit back in the office recording data. David and the team developed into a field ranger monitoring and capture team regarded by some of the most prominent veterinarians in the country as without equal, an opinion that I share to this day.

At the outset of black rhinos being introduced onto private land, a workshop was held in Lapalala to set down norms and standards, as the authorities were determined to ensure that the private sector toed the line and played their part. I was equally determined to follow these to the letter, and to prove that the private owner was up to the responsibility, which I had publicly stated at the press conference after the 1990 auction. Our field rangers had worked with the black rhinos since their release in late 1990 and knew the precise location of each animal and could identify them by their individual tracks. Daily records were kept of every individual and were later computerised. If you want to know anything about this animal, then no one knows them better than the men who spend their daily lives in the field with them. Peter Hitchins taught us that, and was a frequent visitor. At one point he stayed with us for a year writing up his research work and often advised the field staff.

While we are on the subject, let us put one misconception about the black rhino to bed once and for all. The black rhino, far from being stupid, is an intelligent animal. One makes a great error of judgement in assuming that they are stupid, brutish or prehistoric.

Black rhinos are most certainly dangerous. The only reason that more people are killed by elephants in Africa every year is because elephants number in their tens of thousands and black rhino do not. They are usually solitary and prefer to stay as far away from human scent and sight as possible. If you disturb a sleeping rhino, and it can smell you upon waking, it will run away in most instances. If you surprise the animal, and it cannot smell you, but can hear you or see you, it may very well charge. Although its aggression may have to do with poor eyesight, I am inclined to believe the rhino's natural reaction is one of defence. The rhino has evolved with a horn on its nose to allow it to feed, and to allow it to defend itself. If a rhino senses a threat, but cannot smell anything, it will stand with its head fully erect facing the direction of the threat, sniffing and listening. A loud snort may then herald a charge, which is performed with the head held down, accelerating with constant huffing. To turn and run is the worst possible decision. You must get up a stout tree as fast as possible. If it is sufficiently riled it will pound the tree with horn or chest and will even leap up to hook you down. Remember that you are invading their space and, as each animal has its own unique character, they do react unpredictably.

Being armed with a double-barrelled rifle, or sitting behind a desk, does not qualify a person to pass judgement on the rhino. Unfortunately, most of what has been written about the animal through the ages comes from these very people. Sadly, most 19th-century Africana literature dismisses the animal as worthy of nothing more than providing a mountain of meat for their followers, the delicacy of its tongue for dinner, and labels it casually as stupid. They are generally secretive, shy creatures and largely nocturnal and are consequently not easily studied, which has largely contributed to the unfounded reputation they have earned. 'Stupid' takes on a different meaning if you enter their domain, and the following may well act as a guide for anyone who desires to become better acquainted.

The new arrivals were held in pens for less than a week and released one at a time on consecutive days. This is always a difficult time as they have to establish their new home ranges. The sooner this process is accomplished the better, as it enables each one a reasonable period of time to settle in. The releases were done at dawn by David and one other staff member, who would very quietly slide the heavy exit gate open and move away immediately. No monitoring was to take place during the introduction phase in the east. One animal, a large bull, ambled out and soon disappeared, much to David's relief, and he reported that all was fine to Anton. During the night the bull ended up on an internal road some 6 kilometres from the bomas and had gone to sleep next to some dense bush a few metres from the road. Sometime after 7 a.m. Clive Ravenhill came along the road on his way up to see Anton and noticed fresh rhino tracks in the soft sand. He turned the engine off and proceeded to follow the tracks on foot in order to confirm the rhino presence near the river boundary. Clive was some 100 metres from his vehicle, scanning the ground. He was unaware of the rhino, which had been awoken by the sound of the vehicle and was now on its feet. The bull could hear, smell and was shortly to see a rugged, bearded, floppy-hatted human figure in the middle of the road. Disturbed, nervous, unsure of its surroundings, with its worst enemy making straight towards it – ask yourself what you would do.

The first indication Clive had of the charge was the tell-tale blast of air, which all of us know only too well, and the rhino was heading straight at him. With no tree in sight, and his heart pounding, Clive knew that if he turned to run back to the vehicle he was doomed. The rhino was just too close. His only choice, which he made in a split second, was to run forward and to his left and to dive over a nearby fence, which was fortunately a buffalo enclosure. He got over the fence just as the rhino collided with the upright and bounced off. Clive was getting onto his feet when the bull spun around and went after him again. This time the rhino charged straight through the fence as though it was not there. Clive scrambled across some jagged sandstone outcrop and the bull lunged over him and struck him a blow below the right knee. Clive was lying on his back by now, pummelling the rhino with his feet, when for no reason the animal lost its interest, looked up, turned around and went out through another mangled section of the fence.

Terry Matthews, a former big game hunter turned sculptor from Kenya, had a far worse encounter with a black rhino cow in Kenya's Nairobi National Park. This all happened in 1988 and I was fortunate enough to visit the park in 1993 and see these spectacular animals (*Diceros bicornis michaeli*), which are physically larger than their southern counterparts with very distinctive rib markings. The beauty of this park is that the rhino are easily visible due to the open grasslands. Terry was trying to get subject material on foot for a sculpture of both the cow and her young calf. With little or no warning the cow charged, tossing Terry right over her head in spite of the fact that he is a large man. Her horn sliced into his abdomen, passed through his stomach and stopped 6 millimetres short of his heart. His liver, spleen and lungs were severely damaged by the time he landed heavily on the ground behind her, which further damaged his ribs and vertebrae. Still conscious, Terry must have been amazed at her immediate loss of interest in him. She stood within a metre of him for a few moments and then trotted back to her calf. Terry spent five hours on the operating table and miraculously recovered. In a later fax to his wife we expressed our shock at the news, for the photographs depicting the lightning-speed attack were horrific, and prayed for his recovery, which took place over time.

BLACK RHINO RETURNS TO THE CAPE 1991

One of the most commendable commitments to rhino conservation is that of two private individuals, Lucky Mavrandonis and his partner Sue Downie. They were the driving force behind a black rhino monitoring project with David Shepherd in Namibia's Kaokoveld and, through their company's support of the EWT over many years, raised much-needed funds for endangered species. They were certainly not newcomers to conservation, but were not exactly experienced rhino experts when they took on the conservation of the animals after retiring from the corporate world.

Dr Anthony Hall-Martin, senior research director of the National Parks Board at the time, proposed that they monitor a black rhino, Shibula, of the subspecies *Diceros bicornis bicornis*. Shibula had been brought back from the Lisbon Zoo in Portugal in August 1991 with funding from the David Shepherd Foundation and had been released into the Addo Elephant National Park. In 1994 she successfully gave birth to her first calf, Dundagos, or Dundi for short, and was later tranlocated to an expanded Mountain Zebra National Park. The upshot was that Lucky and Sue registered a project to monitor breeding rhino populations in both parks.

Much of their monitoring is fairly long range, using a spotter scope, and if conditions are favourable, they work out a safe way to get closer to photograph and positively identify each individual and to monitor their condition. On average they remain undetected 80 per cent of the time, which enables them to observe the rhinos' natural behaviour. The habitat plays a role in the behaviour of rhinos and observations in arid regions are likely to be somewhat different from those in dense bush and closed-canopy woodland. This work is not for the faint hearted and conditions can vary from freezing cold to blazing heat with temperatures in the 40s.

After nearly ten years of monitoring, they have built up over 1,200 hours of observations and some 900 days in the field. They found that rhinos are not solitary and aggressive, but that they have a well-organised social structure and interaction. They found the bulls to be gentle and cautious with young calves, which has not always been the case in my experience. I have witnessed serious injuries to calves and even females. They did confirm the frequent use of the horn in feeding.

A remarkable couple who unselfishly chose to make rhinos their passion, Lucky and Sue have really put their heart and soul into their project. It has provided very valuable information and has enjoyed the patronage of the David Shepherd Wildlife Foundation. They took the project a step further by setting up a Rhino Security and Protection plan in the Vaalbos National Park, Augrabies Falls National Park, the Karoo National Park and the Mountain Zebra National Park, in conjunction with SANParks, with financial support to the tune of over R780,000. Herein lies the secret to rhino protection: dedication by two individuals, vital funding enabling the upgrading of security, surveillance and response, as well as, and this is vital, increasing the motivation and morale of the field rangers. NGOs and individuals can make a difference and if the rhino is going to survive in the long term, this is one very valuable formula.

These are but a few of the notable achievements in rhino conservation in southern Africa by the official conservation authorities, the private rhino owner and the NGO movement since the end of the last rhino war.

The phoenix was slowly rising from the ashes of the past mindless slaughter.

CHAPTER 9

Silence Will Speak

Good intentions, like some African rivers, are apt to run into sands of
reports, committees, conferences and global strategies, which keep a lot
of people busy, but do not halt the poacher with his gun or poisoned
arrow, the smuggler in his dhow, the importer with his fake documents
. . . While people pass resolutions, rhinos die.

Elspeth Huxley, Introduction to *Rhino Exploitation*

I HAVE BEEN STRUCK BY THE volume of literature that has been produced
on the rhino while researching this book. It is almost overwhelming
– there are books, papers, reports, files, press releases, cuttings and
correspondence. Having been involved with rhinos for close on 40
years now, I also have boxes and boxes of the stuff. I am no longer a
member or employee of any organisation involved with the rhino, but
I have hung onto the mountains of paper that I accumulated over all
those years, including the endless proposals on how to 'save the rhino'.
My self-imposed task was to go through it all to try to get an objective
overview of the rhino situation today. The objective of this chapter and
the following is to assess the past and examine the present. They will
also hopefully remind us that all the paper that has been churned out
over the years has been for an animal whose survival should be the
object of all of our concerns.

We have come to the brutal realisation, in these first two decades of the 21st century, that the rhino once again lives in very uncertain times. The decades prior to 1994 were characterised by the rhino wars, which saw thousands of rhinos poached to feed the insatiable demand from the East. The battle to save the species began to tail off from the mid-1990s, the continental population of black rhino having declined to an estimated 2,400 animals. Mozambique saw the white rhino become extinct twice, and the same very nearly happened to Botswana. South Africa was the least affected, in truth, although low-level rhino poaching in the Kruger National Park and the KwaZulu-Natal reserves remained a concern.

South Africa, as I have shown, had an appalling decline in wildlife in the 18th and 19th centuries. We witnessed the extinction of three species, and came far too close to exterminating both black and white rhinos. The efforts that have been made since then to redress the evils of the past have been phenomenal. We should marvel at a country that, having almost lost all its mega species, now ranks as the most advanced in the world in terms of wildlife recovery. The combined efforts of the state and the private sector, especially in the area of wildlife ranching, managed to turn the situation around.

If one considers the decline of Africa's rhinos since the 1970s, it is clear that the conservation world reacted to the threat timeously and effectively. The pages of this book testify to that: the setting aside of specially protected areas; translocations to safer reserves; the involvement of the private landowner; the training and equipping of rangers; the establishment of the Endangered Species Protection Unit; the formation of the Rhino & Elephant Foundation, the African Rhino Owners Association and the SADC Rhino Management Group; massive NGO support; considerable media awareness; and workshops to come up with ways to stop the killing. During the latter part of the 20th century, the rhino was pulled back from the brink of extinction. But in 2011 poachers killed 448 rhinos in state and private reserves, and maybe more that have yet to be accounted for. Did we win the battle but lose the war?

Traditional medicine is an age-old practice in African cultures, and remains widespread in both rural and urban South Africa despite easy, and often free, access to modern medical care. There are initiatives in place – of varying efficacy – to educate the purveyors of traditional medicines about the consequences of plundering natural resources for short-term benefits. The indiscriminate harvesting of increasingly scarce plants and the killing of specific animals, such as the pangolin and the hedgehog, are issues of great concern to all associated with conservation.

The rhino is no different, except that its horn is used in the traditional medicine of distant societies – societies that are uninterested in the unsustainability of its procurement, indifferent to the cruelty that characterises rhino poaching and ignorant of the consequences for our environment. The practitioners of traditional medicine in the East who continue to promote the use of rhino horn in various medicaments do so without any concern for the disastrous effects their demand is having on the rhino population of Africa. We are well aware of these issues. Our problem is that, as a result of our success in restoring rhino populations to reasonable levels, South Africa has become the principal repository of rhino horn in the world. As a consequence, we have turned the poachers' attentions on ourselves. PRICE OF HORN

This is, in many ways, due to the unbelievable escalation in the price of rhino horn. In 1979 the average price for African rhino horn in South East Asia was US$550 per kilogram, by 1993 it was between US$750 and US$1,000 per kilogram, and today it is somewhere in the region of US$60,000 per kilogram. The stakes are so high that poachers are more than willing to take enormous risks. They make a good living from their bloody work and are certainly not all the starving peasants that some people would make them out to be. A new breed of poacher has emerged – one who often has military training and is experienced in handling weapons; one who is far more difficult to track down, and dangerous, in the bush; and one who is, it is suspected, supported by sectors of the very industry that seeks to protect the rhino. They are the physical embodiment of the international crime syndicates from Eastern countries that drive the international trade in rhino horn. Despite the actions of the conservation authorities and private rhino owners in South Africa, the threat persists. Kill one poacher (26 were killed in 2011 alone) and there are others waiting to take his place.

In 2012 we sit with a very dark cloud over our country as a new menace faces our rhino populations. Although only 120 rhinos were poached in South Africa from 2000 to 2007, a new round of killing began in 2008 with 83 deaths. Our five-year-old orphaned female black rhino, Moeng, was the third to die that year. The top of her head was slashed open and her small horn was removed – the second rhino war had begun for me and my family. It was to be the beginning of a very bloody and horrific attack on rhino in South Africa on private and state reserves. The killing escalated to 122 deaths in 2009 and 333 deaths in 2010. The figure for 2011 soared to 448. At the time of writing, in May 2012, the total for the year is already over 217.

Not even the rhinos displayed in the world's museums have escaped the onslaught. Clever thieves, rather than traditional poachers, have found ways to penetrate these institutions and remove the horns from mounted exhibits. The statistics are shocking and involve our own museums. Since 2007, fourteen horns have been stolen from six South African museums, two of which were taken from a 100-year-old white rhino exhibit at the Iziko South African Museum in Cape Town. Even a fibreglass replica horn was stolen from the Albany Museum in Grahamstown. Another example is the world-record horn of the white rhino shot by Roualeyn Gordon Cumming in 1847, which was brazenly stolen from the family estate in Scotland. If we do not halt this onslaught, we will witness the unravelling of the successes of the past decades of excellent conservation work.

The first rhino war had begun to tail off by 1995, the poachers were slowly returning to their former lives, rhino numbers had stabilised and started to grow. Within the next few years the Rhino & Elephant Foundation had fulfilled its mandate and closed its doors; the African Rhino Owners Association slowly faded without the support of the REF; the Endangered Species Protection Unit was disbanded in 2003; NGOs moved on to the next crisis; the media reportage about the rhino carnage no longer graced the front pages; and the workshops stopped. The general public and the corporate sectors, who played such an active role during the rhino war, turned their attention to other things, and an ominous silence fell across the rhino world. The number of private rhino owners was increasing along with the value of live rhino – an industry was being created and the rhino world became bullish.

The impending threat to South Africa's rhino populations due to increased poaching was made clear at the 14th meeting of the IUCN's Conference of the Parties (CoP)[5] in June 2007. The Department of Water and Environmental Affairs (DEA) was there, with 14 delegates, as were the AfRSG, the World Wide Fund for Nature (WWF), TRAFFIC (the Trade Records Analysis on Flora and Fauna in Commerce – the wildlife monitoring network of the WWF and IUCN) and others. Red lights were clearly flashing, but was action taken to alert all stake holders, particularly the private rhino owner? Was the government really taking the matter of rhino conservation and the crime of poaching seriously enough?

In his preface to Esmond Bradley Martin's book, *Rhino Exploitation*, Lee Talbot, director general of the IUCN from 1980 to 1982, wrote the following: 'A threat to a species or an area was perceived and conservationists reacted to the threat. Consequently, reactive conservation focuses on the effects, not the cause – therefore it usually treats the symptoms, not the basic illness; it emphasises cure, not prevention'. These words have a greater significance today than they did 30 years ago.

Esmond's study, which was mostly funded by the WWF and the IUCN, commenced in 1979. It focused on the international trade in rhino products – a practice that has gone on for thousands of years in

---

5 During the 1960s many countries became aware that over-exploitation of wildlife through international trade was contributing to the rapid decline of many species. They realised that something needed to be done to protect these species for future generations. CITES came about due to a resolution adopted in 1963 at a meeting of members of the IUCN. The resolution was further developed at the UN Conference on Human Environment, which took place in Stockholm, Sweden, in 1972. The text of the convention was finally agreed on at a meeting of about 80 countries in Washington, DC in 1973. CITES then came into being in July 1975. The primary forum at which CITES issues are decided is the Conference of the Parties (CoP).

China and South East Asia – and the beliefs and misconceptions in the age-old practice of using rhino horn in traditional medicine. The study debunked the myth that rhino horn was used as an aphrodisiac. It was not, and is not, used for this purpose. It is used as a remedy to relieve a whole string of ailments from headaches to arthritis. A study in South Korea in 1993 revealed that 79 per cent of their doctors (there are over 16,000 practitioners of traditional medicine in South Korea) believed that rhino horn was an essential medicine.

The WWF wanted to deal directly with the cause of the problem to stop the rhino horn trade. So, from October 1982 to February 1983, Esmond visited ten Asian countries to:

> discourage pharmaceutical wholesalers from further dealing in rhino products, and to explain to practitioners of traditional Chinese medicine why they should no longer prescribe rhino drugs, and to publicise in the mass media the plight of the rhino in Africa as well as in Asia, so that consumers would be more willing to use substitutes.

Esmond has since travelled widely, from the Arabian states to virtually every country in South East Asia, in order to uncover the facts surrounding the use of rhino horn. He is considered the world's leading authority on the international trade in rhino products and has served on the IUCN African Rhino Specialist Group since the 1980s. The AfRSG is one member of several groups that make up the Species Survival Commission (SSC) of the IUCN. The AfRSG comprises official representatives of the rhino range states and rhino specialists in the scientific, veterinary, field management and trade fields. The mission of the AfRSG is 'to promote the long-term conservation of Africa's rhinos and, where necessary, the recovery of their populations to viable levels. It is charged with providing and improving technical information and advice to both government and non-governmental organisations, and with promoting conservation activities to be carried out by these agencies'. One of the most vital functions has been to compile and maintain a database on the numbers of African rhinos. The international trade in rhino horn has, therefore, been a long-standing issue from the inception of the group and one that arrests everyone's attention, given the current crisis.

As members of the AfRSG, Esmond and I have travelled to many rhino meetings over the years and his tenacious ability to obtain data has never ceased to amaze me. In March 2012 I asked him what his impressions of the rhino situation were after investigating the trade for the past 30 years. I asked him why there has been such an upsurge in the demand for rhino horn since 2008, especially in view of the considerable efforts to encourage the use of alternatives, as set out in his book.

Esmond said he was very discouraged about the recent sharp increase in rhino poaching in Zimbabwe and South Africa. He argued that the renewed onslaught is due to the increase in demand for rhino horns in Vietnam and China, because of their increasing personal wealth, and the lack of adequate law enforcement in Africa and Asia. He felt that the efforts to curtail the illegal rhino horn trade, and to promote the use of substitutes for rhino horn in traditional medicine, have been inadequately funded over the years because most conservation money is ploughed into the necessary protection of rhinos in situ. Esmond, and his colleague Lucy Vigne, struggled to encourage law enforcement to fight against the illicit rhino horn trade. They have often lamented the fact that the considerable efforts in recent years to understand the demand for rhino horn, and to support the use of alternatives in Asia, have simply not been enough. EFFECT/CAUSE .

As Lee Talbot pointed out, we tend to deal with the *effect* of the problem, which is the illegal act of killing rhinos, rather than the *cause*, which is the demand created by the medicinal use of rhino horn. Those on the ground, who are responsible for the conservation of rhinos in South Africa at the moment, have little choice to do otherwise. We are fighting fire with fire and we appear to be losing, so far. The escalation of the rhino killings is an appalling testament to what has overtaken us. How has this come about and why did we not learn any lessons from the past? Why did we not do more to address the cause?

Putting to one side the debate on the question of legal trade in rhino horn, which will be discussed in depth in the following chapter, we need to take a look at the actual practice of conservation of rhino on the ground; and both the state and private landowners need to answer a number of questions honestly about the actions they have taken since the end of the last major decline of rhino in southern Africa 15 years ago.

In a paper published in *Nature* in 1988, Prof. Nigel Leader-Williams and S. D. Albon stated, with specific reference to the 16,000-square-kilometre range of Zambia's Luangwa Valley, that in order to achieve a zero decline in the rhino population, spending should have been US$230 per square kilometre per year. The government was only spending US$11 per square kilometre per year, augmented by external donations that amounted to a further US$10 per square kilometre per year, which was a total of less than ten per cent of the suggested figure. If one multiplies the suggested 1988 figure of US$230 per square kilometre per year by the 20,000 square kilometres of the Kruger National Park, for example, one gets a figure of about US$4.6 million (about R35 million) required per year to effectively protect their rhinos. Based on these figures, I shudder to think what the figure would be today, and some even advocate a higher figure per square kilometre! We have to ask ourselves if this is realistic and, if it is, where the funding will come from.

On the 26th of January 2012 the Parliamentary Portfolio Committee on Water and Environmental Affairs convened a meeting in Cape Town to study submissions from members of the public. The committee's notice read: 'Rhino poaching: a threat to the hard-won population increases achieved by conservation authorities'. In his presentation to the Committee, Michael Eustace, an asset manager in Johannesburg, brought the point home with startling clarity:

> Kruger has increased the amount of anti-poaching efforts in 2011 by about 50 per cent over the 2010 level. Also the army have been co-opted and now patrol the border with Mozambique. Nevertheless, rhinos poached have increased from 146 in 2010 to 252 in 2011, or

by 73 per cent. Twenty one poachers were shot dead in skirmishes in 2011 and 82 arrests made. (Nationally the rate of rhino-poaching convictions relative to arrests is less than 5 per cent). While there have been some notable successes, Kruger is clearly not winning the war. They have some 10,000 rhinos, or 48 per cent of the national herd, and with rhinos having been wiped out in countries to the north of South Africa, Kruger has become the focus for poachers.

Kruger is 20,000 square kilometres in extent and has a 400-kilometre border with Mozambique. It would be prohibitively costly to patrol effectively. Kruger currently has 400 rangers who patrol the park, i.e. 50 square kilometres per ranger. I doubt that one ranger could effectively protect more than 10 square kilometres per day. This implies a required force of 2,000 rangers or five times the current force. Assuming only half the park needs to be patrolled intensively, because rhino are concentrated in one half, then 1,000 rangers would be needed. The cost, including overheads, of an additional 600 rangers would be approximately US$10 million (R80 million) per annum or more than the annual surplus of the South African National Parks, which was R52.6 million for the year to March 2011. It is not possible for SANParks to finance 1,000 rangers, and even if it were, there would still be a weakness that undermines law enforcement efforts in most parks in Africa: corruption among the law enforcers.

I made 13 suggestions at the same meeting, directing my concerns mainly towards security and commitment to a number of issues:

The most critical [issue] being the serious constraints in the lack of adequate budgets to deal effectively with the threat on the ground: poaching. If the state wishes to seriously address the issue, this has to be a priority otherwise it [the state] is in danger of abdicating its responsibility as the custodians of the country's natural heritage. You can pour as many men as you like into a park but unless they are motivated, well equipped, trained and properly led, and certainly not subject to strikes,[6] you are wasting your time.

So, we also have to ask how well our national wildlife estates are being managed today. In a hard-hitting *Sunday Times* article published in November 2010, Dr Crispian Olver, a former director general in the Department of Environmental Affairs, reported on a review he had completed for the government on the effectiveness of the conservation system in South Africa. The report pointed out that there are 15 official conservation management agencies in the country, of which only five were performing 'adequately to well' and that even these were showing signs of distress. It is particularly disturbing to note the inability of official conservation agencies to function effectively, which was clearly revealed during the recent upsurge in rhino poaching. In order for an agency to function effectively, it must have an adequate budget – an adequate *operating* budget, not one that is expended on office-bound administrative personnel. Unfortunately, this is not the case. A further issue, suggested by Martin Brooks and Richard Emslie in 1997, which has largely been overlooked, is the consequence of the 'transformation of the civil service coupled with declining budgets leading to many skilled and senior conservationists taking retrenchment packages, causing a skills shortage and reduced effectiveness of some provincial nature conservation departments'. Against this background, the policy of the present government to further reduce the budgets of these agencies is surely a prescription for disaster. I accept that one cannot eliminate poaching completely, but is enough being done to limit this crime? Has the state abdicated its responsibility, or is the situation more complex than that? The amount expended by private owners, in terms of security or monitoring, was, until very recently, close to zero in many instances. Is the proportion of rhinos being lost not directly related to the shortfall in what should, I repeat should, have been spent to protect them? Is funding the main issue?

---

6 This fact was sadly demonstrated in February 2012 when the field rangers of the Kruger National Park threatened strike action at a most critical period in the ongoing rhino crisis. Is this an indication of the level to which the field ranger of Africa has sunk, destroying the long and proud history of this noble profession?

Apart from delegation visits to and from Vietnam in 2010 and 2011, there is little evidence that government engagement at the highest political level is effective, committed or ongoing, especially in respect of South Africa's relations with China and other countries known to be end users of rhino horn. Although there seems to be more effort being made in 2012, what is the South African government doing to persuade their Chinese counterparts to forcefully attend to rhino horn dealers? Are they even aware of the problem? Are they concerned about it? I doubt that South Africa is going to demand that South East Asia actively enforces the prohibition of the illegal trade in rhino horn, which China has already done on paper, yet the Chinese have no problem executing South Africans for drug-running and would probably do the same if a South African poached a panda bear. Would South Africa call for such action as the Pelly Amendment?[7] This is not very likely, given our new-found political relationship.

In August 2011 Dr Ian Player, in an article in *Business Day*, attributed much of the original recovery in rhino populations to the opportunities provided by the legal hunting of white rhinos since 1970. The financial rewards for the wildlife rancher from legal hunting, and the consequent increase in the value of white rhinos, is generally accepted as a major factor in the recovery of the species, but it has introduced its own suite of problems, which are not always evident. The wildlife ranching of rhinos has been hugely successful, but parts of the industry may, unwittingly, have begun to cannibalise themselves. South Africans in the hunting and wildlife ranching industries have often been blamed for fuelling the demand for rhino horn by playing a role in the illegal supply chain. This is particularly focused on the practice of pseudo-hunts, where South African ranchers abuse legal hunting permits to allow 'hunters' from the Far East to kill rhinos, whose horns are then sold into the black market.[8] It is, in fact, more

---

7 An amendment to the Fisherman's Protective Act of 1967 that allowed the prohibition of the importation of fish or fish products from a country that threatened the effectiveness of an international fishery conservation programme. The amendment also applies when foreign nationals are engaging in trade or taking in a manner that diminishes the effectiveness of any international programme for endangered or threatened species.

8 According to Dr Kobus du Toit there were about 1,150 legal hunts between 1971 and 2004, or 34 per year. The figure increased dramatically between 2005 and 2008 when

likely that the industries delayed the inevitable resurgence of poaching, which has been driven by Asian consumer demand. It is quite possible that the tight regulation of the South African rhino market, including the domestic moratorium on horn sales, and restrictions on pseudo-hunts, caused a supply constriction during 2008. This most likely resulted in a price increase, which then created a stronger incentive for poaching. It may be more sensible to allow ranchers to continue with controlled hunting as a means of maintaining real value and to ensure that only accredited buyers will ever be considered. Official conservation agencies that sell surplus rhinos have similarly become very dependent on sales to fund their operations. The real question then is: How well have rhino buyers been scrutinised? Have the provincial authorities monitored the properties of prospective buyers in the past? What security and ongoing monitoring measures have been put in place, if any? Who, for example, signed off on the 200-odd rhinos that were sold to China between 2006 and 2009? Ironically, these animals are probably much safer than the rhinos in Africa.

One of my objectives during my time with the AfRSG was to ensure that the private sector played a meaningful role in the conservation of rhinos. This view was not shared by everyone in the state conservation fraternity in South Africa. Their scepticism was understandable, for the private sector, as I had learnt during my time with the EWT and the REF, had not always demonstrated the highest standards and ethics. But in many respects the private sector has led the way in rhino conservation. The resurgence in poaching that began in 2008 has galvanised the private rhino owner in a manner not seen since the late 1990s, resulting in widespread action. It has taken action when necessary and is generally way ahead in terms of preparedness and mental outlook compared with its state counterparts. Rhino

---

338 rhino were legally hunted, or 85 per year. An estimated 80 per cent of these animals were hunted by Vietnamese, which strongly suggests that the majority of these rhinos were hunted solely for their horns and sale into the black market. In early 2008 the DEA published relevant legislation putting new controls in place and limited the hunting of white rhino to one animal per person per year. However, there were reports of each member of so called 'families' from the Far East hunting a 'trophy'. The restriction did, nevertheless, reduce the number of rhinos hunted by Vietnamese. What followed, however, was an increase in the number of rhinos poached on private land. Whether there is a connection remains to be proven.

conservation requires a focused operational mentality and a high level of commitment and I would recommend that the state parks consult the private sector security specialists and work more closely with them in the future.

To the best of my knowledge there was only one South African NGO, the WWF, involved with rhino conservation in South Africa in 2008. Their Black Rhino Range Expansion Project began in 2003, with the aim of increasing numbers and growth rates of the subspecies *Diceros bicornis minor*. Today the number of NGOs 'saving the rhino' is around 250, although most of these organisations are focused on fundraising and awareness. The concern, however, is that very little genuine co-operation exists between them. The naiveté of many of these individuals and groups is obvious, especially since a lot of their opinions are so often based on emotional perspectives. Dr Richard Emslie, speaking in his private capacity, noted the following: 'As you know, a plethora of new NGOs claiming to be "saving rhino" have sprung up and I suspect a good few of these are opportunistic and looking to jump on the rhino bandwagon to make money for their principles'.

The renewed response from the public and corporate sector, which was so evident in the last rhino war, however, has been most encouraging. Three months after Moeng's death in 2008, I received a call from Peter Hitchins who was very alarmed at the upsurge in poaching. I introduced him to Yolan Friedman, the CEO of the EWT. Although the EWT had been inactive in the rhino field for some years, the organisation had a long track record in rhino conservation. Subsequently Yolan, with the EWT, the Game Rangers Association of Africa (GRAA) and the Wildlife and Environment Society of South Africa (WESSA), organised a workshop in June 2009 to address the threat of poaching. The event was hosted by SANParks at Skukuza in the Kruger National Park. The workshop, 'Strengthening the security of rhino in South Africa', resolved to focus on three areas: law enforcement through the recently initiated Poaching Investigators

Crime Forum; tracking the trade in rhino horn through an existing project coordinated by TRAFFIC; and working to ensure the in situ security of rhino, especially on private land.

Following the workshop, the EWT established the Rhino Security Project. The project would focus on rhino security concerns on privately owned game farms as well as in formally protected areas; improve communication between rhino owners and the relevant government officials; support improved investigations into rhino poaching incidences; work with relevant bodies to identify causes and drivers of the trade in rhino horn; and enhance current knowledge on the demographics of rhinos in situ in collaboration with other existing initiatives.

In the meantime rhinos were being killed at an alarming rate. The consensus within the wildlife industry was that a follow-up workshop was necessary, so Peter Hitchins, Pelham Jones and Paul Phelan facilitated a workshop, which was held in Midrand in November 2009. This workshop effectively established the Private Rhino Owners Association (PROA), under Pelham's leadership.

The Midrand workshop was followed by the Lead SA Rhino Summit in August 2010, which was attended by the Department of Water and Environmental Affairs, SANParks, the Hawks, the South African Police Service, the South African Veterinary Association, WESSA, GRAA, PROA, EWT and others. The workshop agreed to: the creation of a national anti-rhino-poaching hotline; the coordination of intelligence from all groups to a National Wildlife Crime Reaction Unit; the establishment of a national fund-raising campaign for specific anti-poaching initiatives; and the running of an information campaign about rhino poaching and the use of rhino horn.

Having been a participant at the Midrand and NGO workshops, it was only in October 2010 that the Minister of Water and Environmental Affairs organised a two-day National Rhino Summit to discuss the increase in the poaching of rhinos in South Africa. At the summit a National Strategy for the Safety and Security of Rhinoceros Populations and Horn Stocks in South Africa was approved and implemented. The establishment of an interim National Wildlife Crime Reaction Unit

(NWCRU) within the DEA, which was proposed at the Lead SA Rhino Summit, was also announced. A feasibility study to determine the viability of legalising the rhino horn trade in South Africa, a dehorning impact study, and a global competitive market research study relating to rhino horn were commissioned.

The EWT, that remains one of the leading NGOs in the current crisis, was commissioned by the DEA to undertake two of the above-mentioned studies and consequently held a workshop in March 2011, 'Perspectives on dehorning and legalising trade in rhino horn as tools to combat rhino poaching', as part of the research.

The PROA, which was established at the Midrand workshop, was formalised as a 'Chapter' of Wildlife Ranching South Africa (WRSA), and is now at the forefront of the action and has been setting the example for how things need to be done in the future. This group, headed by Pelham Jones and his colleagues, works tirelessly and has:

> established an excellent working relationship with a number of authorities directly involved in the rhino-poaching saga, including the Hawks, National Prosecuting Authority (NPA), The Department of Environmental Affairs (DEA) at national and provincial level, the South African National Parks (SANParks) and in particular the National Wildlife Crime Reaction Unit (NWCRU) of the South African Police Service. This interaction covers a wide spectrum of activities from investigations to providing information, and calling for assistance on behalf of rhino owners.

The PROA works closely with a wide range of organisations, including NGOs, private security companies and rhino owners, and helps to coordinate and implement rhino preservation projects, while at the same time serving on a number of NGO committees. These include the EWT, WWF, SADC RMG, TRAFFIC South Africa, and professional and amateur hunting associations.

Many high-profile South African NGOs and corporations have responded generously and vocally to the growing crisis. The Game Rangers Association of Africa (GRAA), whose members comprise an indispensable element in the battle against rhino poaching, needs our support more than ever. Without the truly dedicated game ranger on the ground we will lose both the battle and the war.

It is hugely encouraging to note the financial support streaming in from many of the world's leading NGOs, who realise that severe governmental budget constraints are increasingly hampering the official conservation agencies' field forces. These include the EWT, Save the Rhino International, the David Shepherd Wildlife Foundation, the International Rhino Foundation, stoprhinopoaching.com and the South African Hunters and Game Conservation Association (SAHGCA). Projects include the determination of DNA profiles of all rhinos in South Africa, but much of their effort has been centred on the training of field staff and the provision of vehicles and specialised equipment to combat the poaching threat.

All of this effort is, of course, focused on the consequences of poaching, the effect. Only 163 rhino were killed between 1995 and 2007, a relatively low number. Why was attention not focused on the cause during this relatively quiet period? We had 13 years to work on the cause – and didn't! Since the start of the second rhino war in 2008 at least 986 rhinos have been poached in South Africa, and there is now a huge scramble to save the rhino. We no longer have the luxury of time to deal solely with the cause at this stage, but at some point in time the issue must be addressed.

The government and the private sector need to demonstrate urgently to the country, and the world, that they can work constructively together and that they are committed to overcoming this scourge. In order to survive, the rhino needs the positive intervention of humankind more than ever before.

CHAPTER 10

Which Way
the Rhino?

*A fair result can be obtained only by fully stating and balancing
the facts and arguments on both sides of each question.*

Charles Darwin, *On the Origin of Species*

African Rhino: Status Survey and Conservation Action Plan, by Drs
Martin Brooks and Richard Emslie, should be prescribed reading for
anyone involved in, and concerned with, rhino conservation. They
succinctly capture the crux of the matter, in terms of cause and effect,
when they state:

> It is a simple but undeniable fact that if there was no demand for rhino
> horn, there would be little or no rhino poaching. Controlling the illegal
> supply of horn through anti-poaching measures is a very expensive
> strategy, and its long-term effectiveness is threatened by declining
> budgets. It is important to discover what drives the rhino-horn trade,
> and examine the potential for reducing illegal demand.

Although it has been 12 years since this important document was
produced, conservationists find themselves once again examining 'the
potential for reducing illegal demand' for rhino horn. Despite the
apparent success of the rhino wars, the widespread killing of rhinos
for their horn began again – because the *cause* had not been dealt with,

164

the *effect* was back. The *effect* requires immediate action, of course, as it did during the first rhino war, but the *cause* requires a long-term solution.

There are many proposed options to reduce the poaching of rhinos: poisoning and/or dyeing the horns of living animals; flooding the market with horn from government and private stockpiles; increasing the numbers of armed men on the ground; employing private anti-poaching units; using radar and fibre-optics; dehorning rhinos to minimise the incentive for poachers; harsher legal punishment; more intelligence agents; and the list goes on. All of these are, however, dealing with the effect and not the cause, i.e. with the killing and not the demand. In reality there are two major schools of thought that address the cause: the first is to focus on education and continue with the ban on the illegal rhino horn trade; the second is to legalise the international trade in rhino horn.

Michael 't Sas-Rolfes, an environmental economist, argues that, although education is important, it will not successfully deal with the cause:

1. Re-educate the East?

> Firstly, it is predicated on the conviction that rhino horn has no medicinal value. However, this is not a universally accepted fact – far from it. Just because Western reductionist science has not (yet) established a healing effect for rhino horn does not negate the deeply held beliefs and rich ancestral experience of an Eastern culture that adopts a more 'systems-based' approach to medicine. Even in Western society, naturopathic and alternative approaches to medicine and healing enjoy substantial (and probably increasing) public support. The 'rhino horn is not medicine' dictum will not be universally accepted.

Secondly, it is disingenuous to argue that the use of rhino horn medicine necessarily causes poaching when horn can be obtained by non-lethal means. The core group of [traditional Chinese medicine] adherents already know this, which is why they are exploring the option of captive breeding and shaving horn off live animals. Furthermore, ethical arguments that live rhinos have the 'right' to retain their full horns do not carry much weight in a world where animals, such as sheep or wild vicuñas, are habitually sheared for their wool. Many, if not most, Asian consumers will most likely place their own 'rights' to acquire medicines ahead of those of rhinos.

Thirdly, a general publicity campaign may have an impact on marginal (fringe) consumers, but is unlikely to reach those actually responsible for paying the extraordinary high prices that are driving the poaching problem. Those people are determined to acquire horn for reasons based on deeply held convictions about medicinal value or niche cultural status and may well be dismissive if not defiant of mainstream Western-influenced opinion.

In a column that appeared in the *Daily Maverick*, Ivo Vegter argues in the same vein that:

Many environmentalists and armchair liberals are of the view that 'we' merely need to educate the backward Orientals about the lack of medicinal qualities of rhino horn. This is rich coming from a group that routinely advocates the use of unproven herbal remedies. It is also supremely condescending. Imagine the Chinese coming to Africa and telling us to stop using muti, or better yet, instructing wealthy elites about the superstition that homeopathy works. We'd tell them to mind their own business and sod off back to China, and rightly so. Even if the Vietnamese and Chinese are wrong about rhino horn, re-educating half a billion people is as tyrannical as it sounds. And even the communists failed at that.

While education must continue, it seems that the problems facing it are overwhelming. Not only do we have to address, and try to change, entrenched ideas in a population halfway around the world, but we have to do so with extremely limited funding. Who will foot the bill for an extensive international education campaign? As a country trying to resolve our own social complexities, dealing with unemployment and the alleviation of poverty have to be our priorities. We can barely find the funding to adequately protect our rhino, let alone educate the East Asians.

2 . Legalise poaching

The second part of the solution, the continued bans on the trade in rhino horn, is the most controversial and has been for a considerable period of time. In 1996 Eugène Joubert wrote in his book, *On the Clover Trail*, that 'the ban on the trade in rhino products was born from the notion by developed countries that the demand will diminish if they can stop the supply'. Let us, therefore, briefly reflect on the rhino's history at the Convention on International Trade in Endangered Species of Wild Fauna and Flora (CITES).

In 1976, at the first CITES Conference of the Parties, or CoP1, the *Rhinocerotidae* spp. were listed on Appendix I, which prohibits international trade in species that are considered to be under threat of extinction. At the time there were approximately 35,000 black rhinos in Africa. The market price of rhino horn increased considerably over the next few years, from between 400 and 700 per cent depending on the consuming country. Taiwan's price grew a whopping 2,800 per cent! The illegal trade continued and Asian stockpiling further drove demand. By 1980 Africa's black rhino population was under 15,000.

In recognising that the Appendix I listings had failed to halt rhino poaching, CoP3, in 1981, passed Resolution Conf. 3.11 on the rhino-horn trade. This called on nations that were not part of CITES to take measures to prevent the international trade in rhino products and it called for a moratorium on the sale of all governmental and parastatal stocks of rhino products. Rhino poaching and illegal trade continued, however, and between 1981 and 1987 black rhino numbers in Africa dropped to 3,800.

As a result, a stricter resolution was adopted at CoP6 in 1987. The resolution called for the complete ban on trade in all rhino products, both internationally and domestically, as well as the destruction of government rhino-horn stocks. Resolution Conf. 6.10 was subsequently ignored by several consumer countries and range states. The illegal rhino-horn trade and poaching continued. From 1987 to 1992, Zimbabwe's rhino population dropped by 75 per cent, despite their 'shoot to kill' policy.

Dissatisfied with the performance of CITES' ban, the governments of South Africa and Zimbabwe felt that a controlled legal trade in rhino horn would be sensible. At CoP8, in 1992, South Africa proposed to down-list its white rhino population to Appendix II, which allowed trophy hunting, and Zimbabwe proposed to down-list both its white and black rhino populations to Appendix II. The proposals were turned down. By 1993 Africa's black rhino population was down to about 2,500 animals.

Then at CoP9, in 1994, in Fort Lauderdale, USA, South Africa again proposed that the white rhino be down-listed to Appendix II. This time the member states approved the proposal and the white rhino was down-listed. Remember that the white rhino population in Africa had grown substantially, from about 2,400 in 1976 to around 7,000 in 1994, of which nearly 6,400 were in South Africa.

At CoP10, in 1997, in Harare, South Africa proposed a trade in 'parts and derivatives' and recommended 'a zero quota for the international trade in such products'. They requested support 'to investigate the possibility of establishing bilateral trade in these products with appropriate controls that will prevent the laundering of illegal products'. This meant that there would be no legal trade until the next conference. This was proposed so that a set of controls could be put in place before actual trading would begin, which would allow South Africa to deal openly with the authorities of consumer countries without any potential negative political ramification. George Hughes, representing South Africa, argued that:

> The reasons behind the proposal were simple – after 15 years of total CITES protection the world status of rhino populations, with the exception of the southern race of the white rhinoceros, had steadily worsened. The CITES ban (and within the country bans on trade) had apparently merely exacerbated a deteriorating situation with no indication of any change in trend. Both South Africa and Zimbabwe feel that a new approach to the conservation of rhinoceros is necessary.

He further insisted that:

> It is well established that legislation of trade results in improved intelligence, as the legal entrepreneur informs on black market

activities, and that a dependable supply of products depresses black market prices.

The CITES secretariat wanted to rule on the proposal the same day, as it was late, and South Africa accommodated them by agreeing to a public vote. On the 18th of June South Africa's proposal to legalise the trade in rhino products was rejected, with 60 in favour and only 32 against (a 61 to 31 vote would have seen the proposal passed!). I believe the South African delegation made a strategic error when they did not insist on a secret ballot the first time round. It thus came as a shock when, in the second vote, by secret ballot, on the 19th of June, the proposal was rejected with 48 against – the vote was now far from the two thirds majority required for a change. There was clearly much lobbying on the evening of the 18th, considering everyone knew how the various countries had initially voted.

There is a growing belief in South Africa that the ban on the illegal rhino-horn trade has not prevented the slaughter of a single African rhino. Many of South Africa's most experienced conservation voices, who have no vested interest in the legal trade in rhino horn, are seriously concerned about the fate that has overtaken rhino conservation in southern Africa. Leading the call is Dr Ian Player who needs little introduction; Dr John Ledger, former Director of the EWT; Dr George Hughes, former CEO of the Natal Parks Board / KZN Wildlife; Dr John Hanks, Consultant; Michael Eustace, Asset Manager; Michael 't Sas-Rolfes, Environmental Economist; and Dr Herman Els (SAHGCA), to name but a few. They are, along with every other South African, shareholders in the country's national herds and have every right to voice an opinion.

South Africa has not submitted any proposals relating to the rhino since CoP11 in 2000, and now CoP16 is on our doorstep. The rhino faces a bleak future if the current poaching trend continues unabated. If we succeed in dealing with the present upsurge in poaching, will it just be a matter of time before the poachers return again? CoP16 takes place in March 2013 in Bangkok. Will South Africa try again? Will we have our house in order in time? How many more rhinos will we have lost by then?

In July 2011 I received a paper from Michael Eustace entitled 'Rhino Options'. He predicted that as many as 438 rhino were likely to be killed in southern Africa that year. He was very close, as 448 were in fact poached. He argued that:

> Poachers are likely to kill 438 rhino in southern Africa this year. Add another 150 to be killed in pseudo-trophy hunts and the total becomes 588. This produces 588 of what I call horn sets.
>
> In order to calculate the total supply of horn, illegal sales by farmers of 100 horn sets, and 200 horn sets from natural deaths that are collected and sold illegally into the market, need to be included. This adds up to a total market size in 2011 of 888 horn sets.
>
> These figures are, of course, an approximation.
>
> The wholesale value of the horn sets at R140,000 (US$20,000) per kilogram, at an average weight of 4 kilograms per horn set, amounts to R497 million. Most of this money goes to criminals as there is a long-standing ban on trade by CITES, of which South Africa is a party.

The point he emphasised is that if there existed:

> a regulated legal trade, through a single channel to Chinese state pharmaceutical companies, southern Africa could make R497 million per annum for parks and conservation and, importantly, there would be no need for the killing of even one rhino.[9]

In conclusion he states:

> It is hard to believe that the world, as represented by CITES, can choose to continue with a failed strategy (the ban on trade), sacrifice

---

9 Eustace's figures are based on the average of 4 kilograms per horn set taken from poached rhinos. If the trade was legalised the animals would not be killed, of course. Approximately 1 kilogram of horn can be harvested from a rhino each year, but there would be far more animals involved in the process than the estimated 888 horn sets that were supplied to the black market in Eustace's figures.

588 rhino per annum and fund criminals, when there is potential from a regulated trade to produce annual profits of billions for African conservation and secure 168 parks, all without the need to kill one rhino.

It seems then that the conservation agencies in South Africa, particularly CITES and the DEA, who will have to make the final judgement call, would be foolish not to legalise the rhino horn trade and should start planning for the allocation of funds forthwith. But things, as always, are not quite as simple as this.

Dr Richard Emslie, for example, argues that one of the major issues we have in tackling the issue surrounding the legal rhino-horn trade is that 'we don't know enough about end-user dynamics at this moment. We are not sure where all the horn is going to and for what purpose'. He goes on to insist that 'consistent funding must go into rhino-horn trade studies to ascertain who is buying and selling the horn, and for what purpose rhino horn is nowadays being consumed. We knew more about this in the 1980s and 1990s, but not enough in the 2000s'. TRAFFIC noted this same thing in 2007, agreeing that 'the precise nature of markets in East and South East Asia is not fully understood. For example, the degree of speculative buying of rhino horn, as compared to purchases to meet current market demand, has not been ascertained'. Is it possible that this new threat to our rhinos has nothing to do with consumer consumption, which is taken for granted, but is rather linked to the investment potential of rhino horn?

Susie Watts, a consultant to the Humane Society, suggested this very possibility in a recent communication:

The biggest problem in South Africa, until now, has been a complete inability (or unwillingness!) to spend any time focusing on the markets. To some, it was a question of 'out of sight, out of mind'. Back then, I couldn't believe that they thought the crisis could be solved simply by improving security at home, with no reference to developments in the markets.

Now we have new markets, and they're a whole different thing.

We are back to the drawing board when it comes to figuring out how to deal with them. We also have a scenario where the horn is not easily available in the pharmacies [in the East] and where immediate consumption is not the driver of poaching. Just as in the West, where the advice since the global financial crisis began has been 'buy gold', it's very possible that, in the Far East, it has been 'buy rhino horn'. I suspect that a lot of it has been stockpiled as a hedge against future investment crises. I have no solid evidence, but it makes sense.

Either way, legalising the trade is not going to help. There are so many millionaires and billionaires in China now (and increasingly in Vietnam) that they can continue hoovering up the rhino horn ad infinitum. They can release it into the markets as slowly as they wish in order to keep the price high. Legalising trade will only make those people even richer, because they will pay the highest prices and continue to operate as a monopoly.

Michael 't Sas-Rolfes suggests that conservationists and the general public, who are typically unfamiliar with economic principles, habitually express concern about the market for rhino horn being too big for the supply. What they often fail to grasp is that markets have two dimensions and that both are variable. The one dimension represents the number of people who would be interested in acquiring a product and the amount of product they desire: this determines the quantity demanded. The other dimension is the price they would be willing to pay to obtain a product. These two dimensions are interdependent: at prices closest to zero, the quantity demanded will be greatest; as prices increase, the quantity demanded will decline.

Demand is, therefore, a relationship between price and quantity and not a fixed number. To state, for example, that 'the demand for rhino horn is 10 tons per year' is meaningless without specifying an associated price. The current amount of horn traded at the current price may indeed be 10 tons a year, but if the price were to change, the amount of horn traded would most likely also change. The amount traded does not reflect demand as such, but merely the quantity demanded at a specific price at a specific time.

Flood the market.

When thinking about the demand for rhino horn, it is more helpful to think about market size as measured by its value (the average price multiplied by quantity traded). It is important to realise that a (hypothetical) market that trades only 10 tons of rhino horn at an average price of US$1,000 per ton per year is effectively the same size as a market that trades 100 tons at only US$100 per ton per year. The value of both markets is US$10,000. Now if the average price in the first market had to rise to US$1,200 per ton per year, the first market would actually be larger in value (US$12,000) than the second, despite the fact that it trades only one tenth as much product. Since it is market profitability that drives poaching and illegal trade, this leaves us with the interesting paradox that a high-value market moving smaller quantities could potentially pose more of a threat to an endangered species than a lower value market involving larger quantities.

'There are two aspects of the rhino-horn market that should be of concern and are poorly understood' according to 't Sas-Rolfes: 'market size (as measured by total market value) and persistence of demand in the face of rising prices (as measured by so-called price elasticity)'. But, as George Hughes put it at CoP10 in 1997: 'Existing trade data worldwide give an inaccurate measure of the past and present demand in the consumer markets, because as controls are tightened, the trade becomes increasingly covert'. The problem then is: how does one accurately study these two elements, or even clearly understand them, when they both operate in the illegal underground economy? So we find ourselves in a position where we know what needs to be done, in terms of research into the market for rhino horn in the East, with seemingly no way to do it. We can speculate about the Asian markets, particularly the rhino-horn investment markets, until the cows come home, but without hard evidence to support the theories we find ourselves back at square one. Perhaps more than ever we need a 'trade with a zero quota' proposal?

The other question arising from Susie Watts's comments, apart from our lack of knowledge of the markets, is how much do we know about the end user? At dinner one evening, while visiting Hong Kong, my Chinese host said to me: 'the Cantonese will eat anything with four legs except the kitchen table'. I was enquiring as to what we were eating and he thought it was better that I did not know. The problem for us in South Africa is that we know so little about Chinese culture and customs that we may never fully understand their mindset.

A friend living in California, Dr David Cumes, who is also a qualified sangoma, believes that in the case of the Chinese, the placebo effect of rhino-horn medicaments is exacerbated by their magical beliefs in the horn's properties. One of David's contacts, who must remain anonymous, is well known locally and frequently visits China. He suggests that 'You are probably up against the "new rich" who were just peasants and have no scruples. They are easily persuaded by traders that this stuff works for sure and the business is good. A "spiritual" value does play a role, but its more about magical superstitious thinking, which is rife in China'.

If we are to deal effectively with the demand for rhino horn, then the South East Asians must be part of the debate around these critical issues.

The debate on legalising the trade in rhino horn has opened a can of worms among the various NGOs operating in and around South Africa, which was to be expected, of course. I have endeavoured to canvas as broad a body of opinion as possible among the state agencies and the NGOs, but unfortunately a few key institutions were unable to respond to our requests for input in time. While we have been unable to consult with all related parties, the response from those that we have contacted has been gratifying.

Cathy Dean, of Save the Rhino International (SRI), one of the long-standing organisations working for the conservation of rhinos, argues that:

> Save the Rhino International is generally in favour of sustainable use, believing that conservation efforts must, as far as possible, be income-generating in order to avoid over-reliance on international donor support . . . However, we have not yet reached a position on the

debate over legalising the trade in rhino horn. We are concerned that occasional, one-off sales of elephant ivory have not reduced poaching for ivory. We would like to see more detail on how a trade in rhino horn will be regulated, how the proponents would ensure that income generated goes back into rhino conservation efforts, and on the likely impact on demand of legalising the trade.

Melanie Shepherd, spokesperson of the David Shepherd Wildlife Foundation (DSWF), has the following viewpoint:

The David Shepherd Wildlife Foundation is against the opening of trade in rhino horn. The sheer size of the potential market for a legalised rhino-horn trade means that we have to get it right first time. You cannot conduct an economic experiment with the consumption patterns of hundreds of millions of people and then expect to be able to reverse it overnight. Once rhino horn is legally available, demand will soar, as it has with ivory. CITES may well be starting to regret opening up legal ivory trade with China – those responsible for elephants in range states certainly are – and they simply don't have the resources to combat increasing wildlife crime. Ivory prices, elephant poaching and ivory smuggling were all supposed to fall as a result of this experiment. The opposite has happened. It's not a case of people switching from illegal to legal ivory. They're now buying both.

The International Rhino Foundation (IRF) stated that they had not yet taken a position on legalising trade in rhino horn because wildlife trade economics were complicated. They went on to say that:

There are still a lot of information gaps which need to be filled before we do so: What are the current rhino-horn trade dynamics? What are the legal incentives for rhino-horn production? What happens if the demand in Asia rises if legal trade is allowed? Will farmed rhino horn be able to meet demand or will the rampant killing of rhino continue?

Consumer countries have signed on to CITES and have banned trade, but what are the ramifications if a legal trade market is opened up? How would private owners of rhinos, especially in South Africa, be regulated with respect to horn harvest? How would the risk of the corrupt elite (e.g. in African countries) taking control of rhino resources be managed if legal trade is allowed? And if trade is legalised, what can we do to protect rhino populations (short term) until, and during the time, controlled trade (long term) is implemented?

Dr Michael Knight, chairman of the IUCN African Rhino Specialist Group and the group's scientific officer, Dr Richard Emslie, are of the opinion that what is needed is 'an objective and rational look at the pros and cons of ALL alternative options to see which one, or a combination of them, will most likely':

1. Reduce illegal killing of rhinos
2. Reduce black-market prices for horn in South East Asia
3. Reduce market demand for illegal horn in South East Asia (achieving 2 should contribute to this)
4. Generate sufficient incentives to encourage the spread and continuation of rhinos onto private and community land (critical to expanding range and keeping numbers growing rapidly and to prevent overstocking and declines in performance in established populations)
5. Generate more, and sustainable, funding to increase law enforcement and intelligence to try to ensure we get to more poachers before they kill rhino

The need for research into all the issues is clearly the driving force behind the arguments over the legalisation of the rhino-horn trade. The EWT is, however, already involved in the research necessary to make an informed decision. Yolan Friedmann, CEO of the EWT, said that:

The EWT has been commissioned [by the DEA] to do the research into the feasibility of legalising the rhino-horn trade, and this report will be completed in a few months' time only, as it requires a lot of surveys, research, etc.

Until then the EWT cannot formulate an opinion and besides, we too want the results of this information to find the facts among the massive amounts of public disinformation, emotional hysteria and personal perspectives with clear subjective viewpoints.

The rhino crisis will not be solved in the public or media domain and those who insist on arguing their points in this space seem to be missing the importance of a balanced approach towards improving law enforcement, increasing anti-poaching unit support, weeding out corruption, improving permitting processes, etc. as if legalising the trade is alone the one magic bullet we have all missed! They select their information and then pad it with massively emotional arguments that simply polarise communities and we are therefore sticking to the fact-finding process we have started, which will inform not only an opinion, but also a process that has to be followed. Like it or not, the DEA and CITES are the only two entities that can legalise trade, and unless we work within these systems, we will get nowhere.

It is clear then from the queries, concerns and worries from various quarters that the NGOs are, for the most part, doing everything they can to ensure that, should the legal trade be approved, all issues will have been ironed out prior to the first transactions with the East.

In 1994, when I was Chairman of the REF, I made a statement at a symposium on utilisation, that the trade in rhino horn should be unbanned. I was quoted as saying that 'in our opinion, it [the ban] has not saved a single rhino'. I went on to caution that 'the Foundation does, however, issue a warning of the complexities in resuming trade in rhino horn, and makes a consequent plea to those responsible in deciding the issue to be circumspect in their approach'. That was 18 years ago! Has South Africa addressed these 'complexities'? The concerns raised by all the NGOs clearly indicate that we haven't, but they do reiterate the caution and due diligence required. Do we know enough, do we have enough detail, could we regulate? What about stock-piling?

Legal trade will not halt poaching altogether, of course, and will never be a silver-bullet solution in and of itself. Trade in diamonds and gold in South Africa is legal, but in spite of legislation the smuggling of both continues. As Gerhard Swanepoel argues, 'Legalisation without any proper counter measures, such as legislation and strict controls, will only create a parallel opportunity for the illegal trade to exist with the legal'. But even if the legalisation of the rhino-horn trade does not stop poaching, it will certainly reduce it.

If the results of legalising the ivory trade are correct, then it must be assumed that the demand for rhino horn will increase when the rhino-horn trade is legalised. The increased demand will be good for those supplying horn from harvesting or legal hunts, of course, because their profits will increase with the demand.

A legal trade would provide the government a substantial income if Michael Eustace and Michael 't Sas-Rolfes are to be believed, and I would argue that their figures are largely correct. The increased profits would surely allow for sufficient funds to be channelled into the regulation and monitoring of the entire industry and would certainly address the biggest issue in the state conservation agencies – reduced budgets.

It would therefore be in the state's interest to channel funds into protecting the increasingly valuable commodity of their rhinos, as it would be for the private rhino owner. So, one would assume that the money earned from the legalisation of the trade in rhino horn would serve to improve conservation of both state and private rhinos.

All of this, of course, is speculative and rests on the outcome of the various studies on the rhino-horn trade that are taking place at present, and those that still need to take place, to determine whether a legal trade is feasible and if South Africa has the ability to handle the international trade with the East.

Even if legal trade worked for South Africa, and its private rhino owners, what guarantee is there that it would work in the rest of Africa, let alone the Asian countries? Could the rest of the world's rhino population survive a legalised trade? It is critical that we do not view the two species of African rhino in isolation from the three Asian species, which have entirely different circumstances affecting their long-term survival. As SANParks spokesman, Wanda Mkutshulwa, put it: 'What happens to the country that has fewer than 50 rhinos? What happens to the country that has 10 rhinos left? What happens to the Sumatran rhino that is almost extinct? We need to ensure we aren't going to open the floodgates for those animals to truly go extinct'.

The ancient Mesoamericans undertook a form of ranching with a wild native bird of the Americas. They domesticated *Meleagris gallopavo gallopavo*, better known as the turkey, nearly 3,000 years ago. We can be grateful to them, for if they had not done so it is possible that the species may otherwise have become extinct. We also have the 16th-century Spanish conquerors of Central America to thank. They took the domesticated birds back to Spain by way of Turkey, where the bird acquired its name, and introduced it into the rest of Europe. My interest stems from the absolutely astonishing number of turkeys that American citizens consume on Thanksgiving Day each year, not to mention the millions of turkeys consumed annually for Christmas dinners!

Wild turkeys still exist in America, and the point is not to trivialise the situation of the rhino by drawing comparisons, but to note what ranching has done. Ranching is about making money whether it is through hunting, the sale of live animals or the trade in animal products. It seems to me that we are quite possibly facing a future where we could have farmed rhinos without horns (due to regular harvesting); ranched rhinos with and without horns (depending on their use); and 'wild' rhinos with horns, but at least we will have rhinos.[10]

Not all rhino owners should be viewed as having the same objectives in terms of their involvement in a possible legal trade. In South Africa

---

10 At the time of the Inca civilisation it is estimated that there were 1.5 million vicuñas (a relative of the llama), which were prized for their extremely fine wool. Efforts to protect the animals as far back as 1777 proved ineffective as poachers were all too willing to disregard restrictive laws in order to cash in on the valuable pelt. This led to the wholesale slaughter of the species. The vicuña population was down to approximately 6,000 by the time it was declared endangered in 1964. Today herding, capturing and shearing, in essence ranching, takes place annually and the population has grown to about 350,000.

we have three types of rhino owners, generally speaking. Firstly, we have the state with its national parks and provincial reserves that are concerned with biodiversity conservation, which includes tourism and education. Their prime objective is not breeding and selling wildlife per se, and I don't anticipate that they will ever 'farm' rhinos. They will, however, continue to sell live rhinos, as all ring-fenced reserves have a limited carrying capacity. They will also, no doubt, harvest rhino horn, if only from naturally deceased animals, and sell the horns to pay for their ongoing conservation.

Secondly, we have the wildlife rancher. This is the private owner who manages the extensive production of wildlife on large tracts of land and is generally involved in the wildlife industry as a business. They are very likely to be involved in some form of tourism or hunting, or both. These owners may harvest rhino horn from naturally deceased animals and may occasionally harvest horn from living rhino by dehorning, where the horn is cut above the dermis-covered bony ridge, allowing for the horn to regrow.

Thirdly, we have the wildlife farmer who manages the intensive production of animals in small fenced camps. These rhinos are intended both for live sale and for the harvesting of horn (which is supposedly stockpiled for when the trade is legalised). Although trading in rhino horn is illegal in South Africa, farming rhinos is not, and does take place. They are in the business to make money from stock and the rhino represents nothing more to them than a Bonsmara cow does to a cattle farmer. The wildlife farmer is able to harvest the horns from his rhinos every 12 to 18 months and hopefully a calf from the females every 24 to 30 months.

All three types of rhino owners make a valuable contribution to the species, but at the end of the day each do it for different reasons. I think that over the last 15 years a dramatic shift has taken place, from the *conservation* of rhinos to the *ranching* of the species. This is evidenced by the huge number of private sales that take place each year and a market, largely driven by the sale of surplus animals at auction, where the price is often determined by trophy hunters and where rhinos are sold by the inch! SANParks and Ezemvelo KZN Wildlife have, in essence, been ranching for years. KZN has been doing so since the 1960s. Between 2005 and 2008 SANParks, Ezemvelo KZN Wildlife and the North West Province sold 581 rhinos, which resulted in earnings of R98 million. During the process of sale and relocation, the rhinos have to be darted. If the rhinos were dehorned during this exercise, and if we assume that 4 kilograms of horn were removed from each animal, its value, based on Michael Eustace's figures, would have been around R 325 million!

By the end of 2005 about 3,300 of the world population of 14,540 white rhinos were held by the private sector. By the end of 2011 private owners held an estimated 5,000 white rhinos with the balance of approximately 15,000 animals in the care of various state agencies.[11] Many of the private owners would happily make use of a legal rhino trade, and even occasionally harvest horns from live rhinos. There are, of course, private owners that already farm rhinos, and you can be assured that more will get into the business if a legal trade becomes a reality. Will we have taken a perfectly wild animal and turned it into something that suits us? Once you take the wild out of anything it might just as well go the way of *Meleagris gallopavo gallopavo*.

However, unless we learn the lessons of the past and continue taking appropriate action to conserve the remaining rhinos, there will be no point in calling for a legal trade in rhino horn. Both the state and private sector will need to demonstrate that they are serious about rhino protection and their long-term survival. Esmond Bradley Martin and Lucy Vigne argue that we can learn from 'India and Nepal about their rhino conservation success where rhino poaching has been dropping in

---

11 Various groups (PROA, AfRSG, RMG, etc.) are determined to know the numbers of rhinos in private hands, for very good reasons and should be supported, but how sure are we that we have the numbers of rhinos in South Africa that we think we do? Does the Kruger Park, for example, really have the number of white rhinos they say they have? Over 12 years from 1960, 330 white rhinos were relocated to the Kruger Park. A sustained growth rate of 6.75% would have had to be maintained, over and above deaths and sales, to reach the approximately 10,000 rhinos reported. It's possible, but how can we be sure?

recent years, and see which of their rhino conservation strategies would
be effective in Africa. Nepal and India are poor countries, but they have
put a high priority on effective rhino protection which is lacking in most
of the African rhino range states'. Many conservationists consider 'feet
on the ground' as the only solution to stop the poaching. In spite of the
military machine that Glen Tatham was running on his side of the rhino
war, however, he was unable to prevent the almost total obliteration
of Zimbabwe's rhinos. There is no doubt that 'feet on the ground' is
a fundamental component to dealing with the immediate short-term
poaching crisis, but this alone does not improve enforcement, especially
not on state parks and reserves. This requires committed political will,
which means increased spending. Conservation agency budgets across
the country have been reduced, so the necessary increase in spending
to ensure the survival of our rhinos means that other state departments
will have to sacrifice a portion of their budgets. The government and
the private owner will need to invest, and invest heavily, in order to
prove to the opponents of any form of trade that 'our house is in order'
and that they are serious about their investment. Both need to accept
that rhino conservation comes with some very heavy risks that need to
be financed.

We must, of course, remember Dr Ian Player's insistence that 'the
recovery of the white rhino was very much due to the "rancher /
hunter" who succeeded in placing a real value on the animal'. This is
true whether those of us who abhor shooting animals for pleasure like
it or not. The private rhino owner, however, has fewer options than the
state for the conservation of his rhinos, and they all cost huge amounts
of money. There is a growing body of opinion that if private owners
turn their backs on the rhino because of the costs and risks associated
with keeping the animals, the value of the species will plummet. In the
North West Province, the Limpopo Province and the Free State, private
owners with only a few rhinos have started to sell off their stock because
their care and conservation has become too expensive and onerous.
Fewer private owners means fewer live sales and less hunting, which
in turn devalues existing rhino stocks. There are already signs of that
beginning to appear. Those who rely on the sales of live rhino, such

as SANParks, Ezemvelo KZN Wildlife and private rhino owners, may well be facing a very sobering scenario – far fewer buyers.

Whether a legal trade in rhino products is established or not, whether ranchers abandon the conservation of rhinos or continue their struggle, there will always be state reserves and private sanctuaries where the bottom line is about protecting the rhino rather than using the animal as a commodity. Poaching will probably always exist. We need to remind ourselves that rhinos are not immortal and they die just like everything else. Perhaps the rhino specialists should reconsider rhino population expansion as a principal objective. Perhaps they should have fewer rhinos in smaller sanctuaries where they can be properly protected. I don't believe they will go along with this option, but they should be prepared to look more closely at the species' end destination.

That one of the world's most magnificent creatures is reduced, once again, to endless argument is an indictment of our inability to prevent its extinction. What will history say of us if we allow it to happen?

What is vital, is that unless those who continue to call for a legal trade and those who oppose trade from within and without CITES – the NGOs; private rhino owners; the state agencies, including the national parks; the legal system, especially the prosecutors; the SAPS crime unit; economists; both the AfRSG and the AsRSG; the consumers; TRAFFIC, who are critical to any discussion; and especially the Department of Water and Environmental Affairs, without whom no progress will emerge – collectively sit down and thoroughly and robustly debate all the view points, the debates and arguments will most likely continue ad nauseam and rhinos will die as each new resolution is passed.

The key is that all rhino keepers need to rationally deliberate on the issues, from one platform and then make informed decisions and take decisive, bold action.

Are we all, however, capable of setting aside our differences and forging a mutually acceptable and sustainable solution?

So, which way the rhino?

Maps and Graphics

Black Rhino Historical Distribution Map

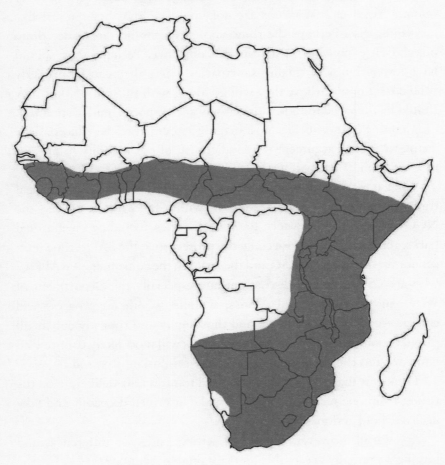

White Rhino Historical Distribution Map

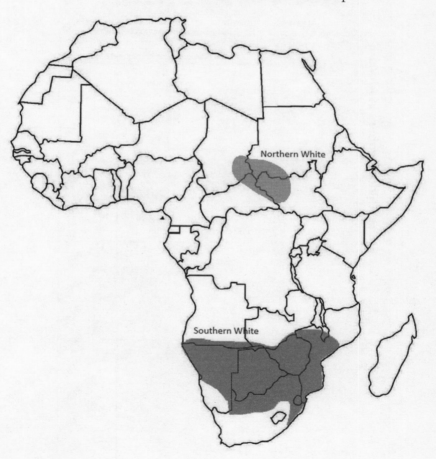

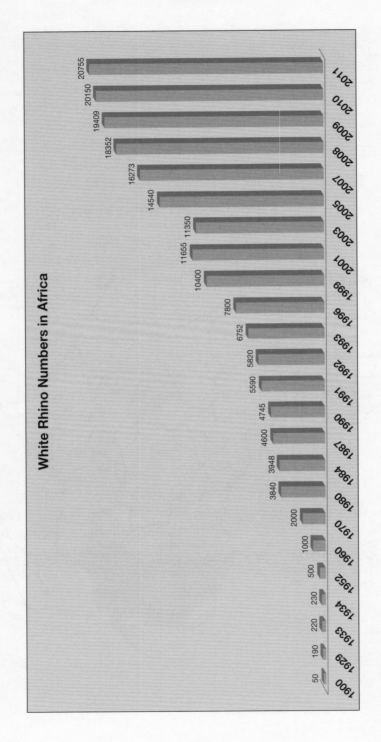

White Rhino Numbers in Africa

Year	Number
1900	50
1929	190
1933	220
1934	230
1952	500
1960	1000
1970	2000
1980	3840
1984	3948
1987	4600
1990	4745
1991	5590
1992	5820
1993	6752
1996	7800
1999	10400
2001	11655
2003	11350
2005	14540
2007	16273
2008	18352
2009	19409
2010	20150
2011	20755

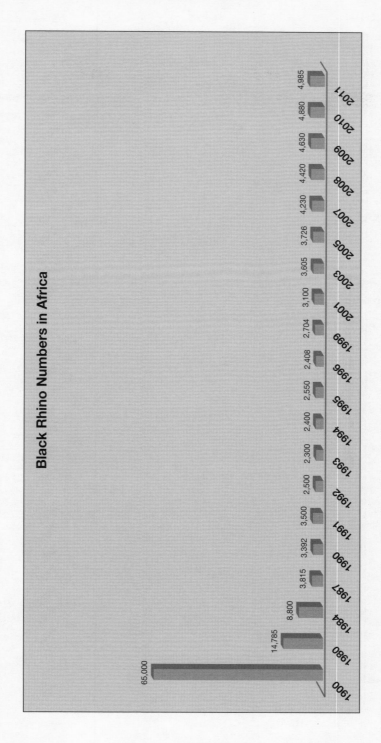

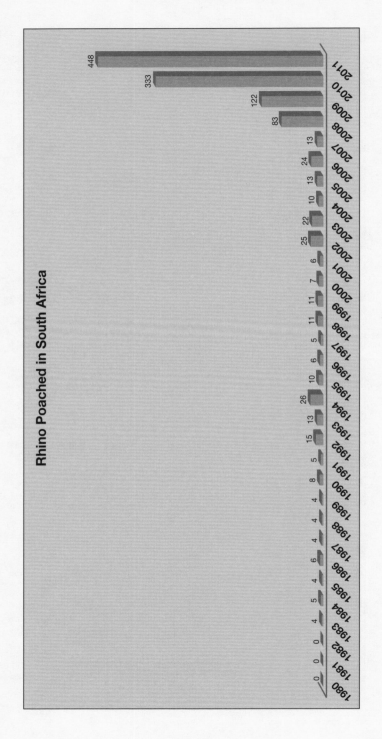

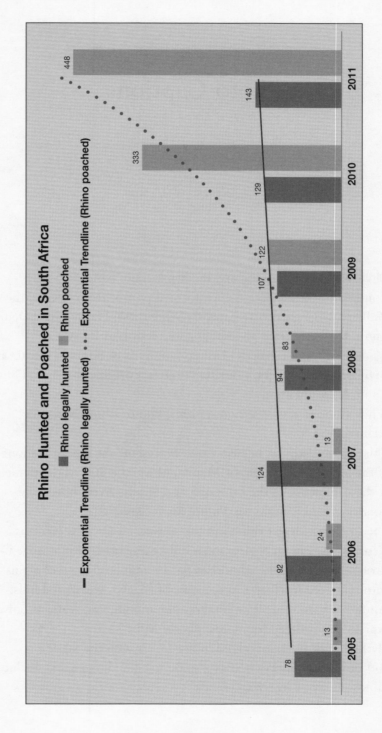

Rhino Hunted and Poached in South Africa

Photo Captions

1. Clive Walker feeding Bwana, the black rhino hand-raised by Conita, in his enclosure, which formed part of Doornleegte, the Walkers' large garden at Lapalala Wilderness. Photo: Nigel Denis.
2. Anton Walker during an annual game census at Lapalala Wilderness. Anton has clocked up hundreds of hours in the air as a navigator and counter in his function as a wildlife manager. Photo: Rhino Museum archives.
3. White rhino (*Ceratotherium simum*). Photo: Rhino Museum archives.
4. This gold-foiled, 'fat bellied' rhino represents the past splendour of the long lost kingdom of Mapungubwe, the 800 AD settlement at the confluence of the Limpopo and Shashe rivers bordering Botswana and Zimbabwe. Photo: Sian Tiley-Nel.
5. The so called 'desert rhino', of the subspecies *Diceros bicornis bicornis*, lives in an environment unlike any other rhino range in Africa. The landscape comprises flat to undulating gravel plains with scattered inselbergs and chains of rugged, weathered hills. The rainfall here is 30–100 millimetres per annum, and water is only available in isolated fountains. Photo: Mike Hearn.
6. Blythe Loutit in Damaraland in the 1970s with the lid of a 200-litre drum improvised as a snare to catch large game, including rhinos. Photo: Clive Walker.

7. The rugged landscape of Damaraland, Namibia. Photo: Clive Walker.

8. Clive Walker arrives at a remote airfield near the border of Namibia and Angola in 1977 to join the University of Pretoria's desert research project, which was to reveal the serious decline of both rhinos and elephants in the Kaokoveld. Photo: Koos Bothma.

9. The legendary Garth Owen-Smith, flanked by Dr John Ledger, then director of the Endangered Wildlife Trust, on the right, and David Shepherd, world-renowned UK-based wildlife artist, on the left. They are talking to a local headman in Damaraland about the auxiliary game guard programme. Photo: Clive Walker.

10. About 6,000 years old, this rock engraving of a black rhino in Damaraland, Namibia, bears testimony to the existence of these animals in this harsh environment. Photo: Clive Walker.

11. Clive Walker in 1982 after a long, hot, dusty drive in search of rhinos, elephants and giraffes in Damaraland. Photo: Koos Bothma.

12. Clive Walker suitably kitted out for a day-long search for rhinos and elephants atop the back of an open truck in the Kaokoveld. Photo: Koos Bothma.

13. Titos Moatshe feeding Bwana in 1997. Black rhinos become tame very quickly when in captivity, but resort to type almost immediately after their release back into the wild. Photo: Clive Walker.

14. The founders of the Rhino & Elephant Foundation, from left to right: Peter Hitchins, Dr Anthony Hall-Martin and Clive Walker, in 1987. Photo: Dick Wolfe.

15. Rozanne Savory, executive officer of the Rhino & Elephant Foundation, sitting among the skulls of rhinos poached in the 1970s and 1980s at Wereldsend in Damaraland. Photo: Clive Walker.

16. Peter Hitchins takes a nap on the rhino-flattened *Euphorbia damarana* after a long aerial survey. The black rhino is known to lie up on the ample stems of this desert plant during the heat of the day. Photo: Clive Walker.

17. This 1959 photograph by Ian Player shows his two companions looking back into the Umfolozi Game Reserve wilderness while on horse patrol. Together with the Hlhuhluwe Game Reserve, this was the last stronghold of both the white and the black rhino in South Africa at the turn of the 19th century. Photo: Rhino Museum archives.

18. Another photograph from 1959 shows Ian Player, back to camera, and scouts and rangers of the Natal Parks Board endeavouring to free a white rhino trapped in a mud wallow. Photo: Rhino Museum archives.

19–24. A combined capture operation by the crack team from the Kruger National Park and staff of the KwaZulu Bureau of Natural Resources. Ten black rhinos from Ndumo Game Reserve were relocated to the Kruger for safe keeping in 1989. The animals were eventually returned to the Tembe National Elephant Park. Photos: Clive Walker.

19. Hugo van Niekerk, chief pilot of the South African National Parks Board, takes off into the rising dawn in a Bell Jet Ranger. Photo: Clive Walker.

20. Dr Kobus Raath and Dr Vossie de Vos make final preparations to partially rouse a black rhino bull. Ropes are already in position around the animal's blindfolded head and one hind leg. Photo: Clive Walker.

21. Local helpers and rangers man the ropes with the vets, guiding the rhino on the path to the waiting container, which will hold the animal during its long journey to the Kruger Park. Photo: Clive Walker.

22. The vets hang on and do their best to ensure the animal does not fall over. Photo: Clive Walker.

23. From left to right: Drs Kobus Raath, Vossie de Vos and Danie Joubert, all of the Kruger National Park, approach the loading crate. Photo: Clive Walker.

24. The rhino, now safely in the container, is hoisted aboard the transport vehicle. Photo: Clive Walker.

25. The bludgeoned skull of the four-year-old calf found by Lloyd

Wilmot and Herman Potgieter on their aerial survey was recovered by members of the Anti-Poaching Unit (APU) of the Department of Wildlife of Botswana at Savute in 1988. Photo: Clive Walker.

26. The last two black rhinos seen in Chobe National Park in Botswana, in 1988. The cow and her calf were shortly thereafter killed by poachers. Photo: Herman Potgieter.

27. The scouts at Lapalala Wilderness assist in the recovery of an immobilised white rhino before translocation to a safe environment in 1996. Photo: Clive Walker.

28. A sad reminder of Botswana's once plentiful black rhinos. This superb San rock painting of a black rhino cow and calf is to be found at Tsodilo Hills on the western side of the Okavango Delta. Photo: Clive Walker.

29. The recovered horns of a black rhino, a pair of elephant tusks, a traditional axe and the ammunition clips of an AK-47 after a successful APU contact with poachers in the last rhino war in Zimbabwe. Photo: Glen Tatham.

30. Members of an APU examine the carcass of a white rhino poached in Hwange National Park, Zimbabwe during the last rhino war. Photo: Glen Tatham.

31. This rhino died of natural causes in the Vaalbos National Park, thus necessitating the removal of both horns. Photo: REF archive.

32. The dehorning of a white rhino in Hwange National Park, Zimbabwe, in 1992. Sadly rhinos were still poached for the base of the horn. Photo: Mike Kock (REF archive).

33. Dr Anthony Hall-Martin in the rhino skull store in Tsavo National Park, Kenya, in 1980. The skulls came from the hundreds of rhinos that were killed by poachers and the severe drought in the 1970s. Photo: Clive Walker.

34. A Yemeni man proudly displays his beautifully crafted *jambia*, a traditional dagger that is an important status symbol in Yemen and certain other Gulf states. The most prized and valuable are those with rhino horn handles. The use of rhino horn has fortunately diminished and been replaced by buffalo horn or hard

wood. Photo: Esmond Bradley Martin and Lucy Vigne.

35. A pair of black rhino horns on display in a medicine shop in Taiwan in the early 1990s. This is a very rare sight today, given the price of rhino horn. Photo: Bruce Evans (Rhino Museum archives).

36. A rare photograph of an even rarer pair of Sumatran rhino horns displayed in a medicine shop in Taiwan before the crackdown on trade in the early 1990s. Photo: Bruce Evans (Rhino Museum archives).

37. A captured Zambian poacher is questioned by members of the Zimbabwean National Parks APU during the last rhino war. Photo: Glen Tatham (REF archive).

38. A superb specimen of the black rhino subspecies *Diceros bicornis bicornis* in the Nairobi National Park, Kenya, in 1994. Photo: Clive Walker.

39. For the state and private owner the security of rhino horn, whether from natural mortality or recovery from poachers, is a nightmare. Permits, bar coding and DNA testing are part of the considerable security measures required. From the private rhino owner's perspective it's a major liability and presently contributes nothing to protecting his living rhino. Photo: Rhino Museum archives.

40. Lucky to be alive. A blood-splattered Clive Ravenhill, former manager of Lapalala Wilderness after a momentous encounter with a black rhino. Clive counted himself more than fortunate to get off with no more than a severe mauling. Photo: Clive Walker.

41. From the back of an elephant one is afforded the most marvellous views of the greater one-horned rhinoceros – creatures of an ancient past. Photo: Clive Walker.

42. Charles Norman's rhino just before she charged headlong into the tree he was sheltering behind. The Kruger Park officials are mesmerised atop the rhino transporter, wondering what will happen next. Photo: Charles Norman.

43. Colour transparency of an original pen-and-watercolour painting of a black rhino by Clive Walker, 1997.

44. Clive Walker in his studio at Lapalala Wilderness in 2000 alongside two of his paintings: one of a black rhino bull and the other of a white rhino bull. Photo: Graeme Wilson.

45. Anton Walker and his assistants guide a blind-folded white rhino bull towards the crate that will hold him during his relocation in 1997. It looks very simple, but it requires steady nerves, vets who know what they are doing, and highly experienced field men. Photo: Rhino Museum archives.

46. Clive Walker's favourite Asian elephant for rhino spotting, Shamshahar, in Chitwan National Park in 1984. The animal was very steady during any rhino encounter, but less so with any whiff of a tiger. Photo: Clive Walker.

47. Karen Trendler with Bwana, her most famous orphan, at her rehabilitation centre near Pretoria in 1993. The rhino calf was raised to adulthood at Lapalala Wilderness by Conita Walker. Photo: Clive Walker.

48. Conita Walker: wife to Clive, mother to Anton, and foster mother to three black rhinos, a white rhino and a hippo – not your everyday pets. Conita hand-raised a female black rhino, Moeng, who was the third rhino gunned down by poachers at the start of the new rhino war in 2008. Photo: Clive Walker.

49. A legally hunted white rhino taken on licence in 1987 by an American sportsman. Ian Player has stated that it was the legal hunting of the white rhino that placed a real value on the animal and contributed to the species' survival. Photo: Rhino Museum archives.

50. A contented black rhino browses on freshly cut natural bush in a holding pen in 1998. Note the distinctive prehensile lip and the precaution taken in the tipping of the horn prior to release into the wild in order to minimise any injury to any other rhino it might encounter. Photo: Clive Walker.

51. Note the one-horned rhino's distinctive armour-plated appearance as a cow and her calf enter a pool of water. Photo: Clive Walker.

52. Introducing black rhinos to a private property comes with a hefty price tag, apart from the cost of the animal. Secure holding pens

must be constructed prior to the animal's arrival, with specially constructed steel sliding doors. Photo: Clive Walker.

53. A white rhino observes a group of trailists standing in the dry riverbed of the White Umfolozi in the Umfolozi Game Reserve. This tour was led by Jim Feely of the Wilderness Leadership School. Photo: Bob Cleaves.

54. Game scouts of the Natal Parks Board in the 1960s and 1970s stand at ease with their .303 rifles and spears. These were dedicated and committed men who were led by some of the finest field men ever to come out of Africa. Photo: Peter Hitchins.

55. Early attempts at radio telemetry with black rhinos in Hluhluwe Game Reserve in the late 1960s. The devices were implanted into the posterior horn, but the constant rubbing of the horn often damaged the transmitters and aerials. Here Peter Hitchins prepares to place the transmitter into the horn before sealing it off. Photo: Rodney Borland.

56. Dr George Hughes, former CEO of the Natal Parks Board, congratulates Dale Parker of Lapalala Wilderness on the acquisition of a second batch of black rhinos at a Natal Parks Board auction. Clive Walker is seated between the two men. Photo: Mike Matthewman (*Natal Witness*).

Acknowledgements

THE AUTHORS WISH TO ACKNOWLEDGE the people who have made a contribution to the creation of this book. We are most grateful to each and every one for their time and input. If there are any omissions or errors, the fault is ours alone.

Firstly, our thanks to Dr Ian Player and all those from the Natal Parks Board who led the task of rescuing the white rhino. We acknowledge Ian's personal role in both conservation and education awareness. Thanks to the late Nick Steele for his unceasing dedication to conservation. Thanks to Peter Hitchins and Anthony Hall-Martin for revealing the world of the black rhino to us and the many journeys we shared on behalf of both rhinos and elephants. A special word of thanks to Jim Feely, my mentor and guide. A fond thank you to the past board members and staff of the Endangered Wildlife Trust and the Rhino & Elephant Foundation during my tenure, and to Jane Zimmerman, Rose Smith, Heather Cowie, Rozanne Savory and the late Petra Mengel, without whom I would not have achieved what I did or been able to write this book. To the generous and concerned public who have supported the cause of rhino conservation over so many years, and continue to do so, we say thank you. You are numbered among the 'rhino keepers'.

We owe a debt of gratitude to Dale 'Rapula' Parker for believing in me through the years and making an immense contribution to the conservation of black and white rhinos in South Africa.

For support and sustenance in so many ways, we are grateful to Dave and Jane Beattie, Mike and Cheryl-Lee Pretorius, Renning Walker and Warren Adams.

To Duncan Parker and Mike Gregor, thank you both for keeping the spirit of the black rhino alive in the Waterberg, Limpopo.

To the dedicated men and women who are out there daily in the heat, the rain, the cold and the wind, monitoring, protecting and 'keeping' Africa's rhinos, despite the high risk, we commend you.

Although there has been a lot of irresponsible media attention, we would like to acknowledge the positive role played by the media in rhino conservation. These are the people who have highlighted the various issues and have brought them to the attention of a wide audience: Julienne du Toit, James Clarke, Melanie Gosling, Chloe Rolfes, Anton Ferreira, Danie van der Walt, Tony Carnie, Don Knowler, Will Bernard, Sally Antrobus, John Yeld, De Wet Potgieter, David Holt-Biddle, Don Pinnock, Anita Allen, Jennifer Crwys-Williams, Jenny Griesel, Barney Simon, Martin Bester, Sue Derwent, Sarah Borchert, Dr John Ledger, Fiona Macleod, Lynette van Hoven and Johan van der Walt.

We are extremely grateful to the following for their correspondence and personal discussions during the compilation of material for this book, and their permission to use their statements, quotes and comments: Dr Esmond Bradley Martin for permission to quote from *Run Rhino Run* and his invaluable input, Lucy Vigne, Anthony Baber, Andre Burger, Tony Conway, Dr David Cumes, Cathy Dean, Ms Sue Downey, Vanessa du Plessis, Dr Herman Els, Dr Susie Ellis, Michael Eustace, Dr Kelly Enright, Dr Richard Emslie, who was particularly helpful and generous in sharing information, Ms Yolan Friedman, Antoinette Ferreira, Dr John Hanks, Dr George Hughes, Peter Hitchins, Dr Michael Knight, Li Lotriet, Dr John Ledger, Lucky Mavrandonis, Shaun McCartney, Elise Daffue, Andrew Muir, Dr Sven Ouzman, Dr Ian Player, Pelham Jones, University of Natal Press / Killie Campbell Africana Library, Dr Kees Rookmarker, Melanie Shepherd, Iziko South African Museum, Sian Tiley-Nel, Michael 't Sas-Rolfes, Richard Wadley and Susie Watts.

Acknowledgements

The opportunity to communicate with such a wealth of opinions from across the spectrum of rhino conservation has been a special privilege and has made the compilation of our material most gratifying, and we thank each for their contribution.

This book could not have been written without the support and encouragement of both Conita and Rene Walker who sustained both Anton and myself and put up with our endless rhino discussions.

Finally we wish to thank Mike Martin and Carol Broomhall of Jacana Media. It has been a privilege to work with Jacana, and especially with Carol who first conceived the idea of this book and has nurtured it every step of the way.

It has been a real pleasure working with Pete van der Woude, our editor. We thank him for his patience and input, which has been most valuable.

Kindly note that the authors do not necessarily agree with the sentiments expressed by individuals throughout this book.

Bibliography

Adams, A. 1861. 'Beetling at the Cape and in Java'. *Zoologist*, 19.

Allsen, T. T. 2001. *Culture and Conquest in Mongol Eurasia*.
    Cambridge: Cambridge University Press.

Andersson, C. J. 1987. *Lake Ngami*. Cape Town: Struik Publishers.

Andersson, J. G. 1934. *Children of the Yellow Earth: Studies in
    Prehistoric China*. London: Kegan Paul, Trench, Trübner & Co.

Baines, T. 1968. *The Gold Regions of South Eastern Africa*.
    Bulawayo: Books of Rhodesia.

Baldwin, W. C. 1967. *African Hunting and Adventure*. Cape Town:
    Struik Publishers.

Bauer, W. 1976. *China and the Search for Happiness: Recurring
    Themes in Four Thousand Years of Chinese Cultural History*. New
    York: Seabury Press.

Beeckman, D. 1718. 'A voyage to and from the island of Borneo, in
    the East Indies'. *Philosophical Transactions of the Royal Society of
    London*, 3–6.

Bishop, C. W. 1933. 'Rhinoceros and wild ox in Ancient China'. *The
    China Journal*, 18.

Bond, C. 1978, 'Heave-ho! Puff! Push!' *African Wildlife*.

Borcherds, P. B. 1802. Letter to his father, Rev. Meent Borcherds.
    Van Riebeeck Society Publication Works, 2 (10). Cape Town: Van

Riebeeck Society.

Bradlow, E. & Bradlow, F. (eds) 1979. *William Somerville's Narrative of His Journeys to the Eastern Cape Frontier and to Lattakoe 1799–1802*. Cape Town: Van Riebeeck Society.

Brander, M. 1988. *The Big Game Hunters*. London: The Sportsmans Press.

Bredell, H. C. & Grobler P. G. W. 1986. *The Memoirs of Paul Kruger*. Johannesburg: Scripta Africana.

Bruemmer, F. 1991. 'Unicorn of the sea'. *Canadian Geographic*, 111 (5).

Bull, B. 1988. *Safari: A Chronicle of Adventure*. London: Viking.

But, P., Lung, L. & Tam, K. 1991. 'Ethnopharmacology of rhinoceros horn II: antipyretic effects of prescriptions containing rhinoceros horn or water buffalo horn'. *Journal of Ethnopharmacology*, 33.

Buttrey, T. V. 2007. 'Domitian, the rhinoceros, and the date of Martial's Liber de Spectaculis'. *Journal of Roman Studies*, 97.

Buys, D. 1997. 'Rhino watch'. *Rhino & Elephant Foundation Journal*, 6.

Canard, M. 1988. *IbnFadlan: Voyage chez les Bulgares de la Volga*. Paris: La Bibliothequearabe Sindbad.

Cattrick, A. 1959. *Spoor of Blood*. Cape Town: Howard Timmins.

Chang, K. 1980. *Shang Civilization*. New Haven: Yale University Press.

Chauvet, J. M. 1996. *Chauvet Cave: The Discovery of the World's Oldest Paintings*. London: Thames & Hudson.

Clarke, J. 1988. 'Hunting whittles down SA rhino herd'. *The Star*, 2 May.

Clements, B. 1988. 'Black rhino crisis'. *The Game Ranger Newsletter*. Game Rangers Association of Africa.

Dala-Clayton, B. & Child, B. 2003. 'Lessons from Luangwa'. International Institute for Environment and Development, *Wildlife and Development Series*, 13.

Darwin, C. 1859. *On the Origin of Species*. London: John Murray.

De Alessi, M. 2000. 'Private conservation and black rhinos in Zimbabwe, Savé Valley and Bubiana conservancies'. Harare: Centre for Private Conservation.

Delegorgue, A. 1997. *Travels in Southern Africa, Vol. II*. Natal: Killie Campbell Africana Library / University of Natal Press.

De Watteville, V. 1935. *Speak to the Earth*. London: Methuen & Co.

Dubs, H. 1955. *The History of the Former Han Dynasty, by Ban Gu*. Baltimore: Waverly Press.

Du Plessis, S. F. 1969. 'The past and present geographical distribution of the Perissodactyla and Artiodactyla in southern Africa'. MSc thesis, University of Pretoria.

Du Toit, J. 1993. 'It's a matter of principle'. *Saturday Star*, 11 September.

Eastwood, E. & Eastwood, C. 2006. *Capturing the Spoor: An Exploration of Southern African Rock Art*. Cape Town: David Philip.

Edwards, M. 2000. 'Indus: clues to an ancient civilization'. *National Geographic*, 197.

Eldredge, N. 1998. *Life in the Balance: Humanity and the Biodiversity Crisis*. New Jersey: Princeton University Press.

Ellis, B. 1994. 'Game conservation in Zululand 1824–1947: changing perspectives'. *Natalia*, 23/24.

Emslie, R. 2011. '*Diceros bicornis* ssp. *longipes*'. IUCN Red List of Threatened Species. <http://www.iucnredlist.org/apps/redlist/details/39319/0>.

Emslie, R. & Brooks, M. 1999. *African Rhino: Status Survey and Conservation Plan*. Gland, Switzerland: IUCN.

Enright, K. 2008. *Rhinoceros*. London: Reakton Books.

Feely, J. M. 1974. *Background to the Natural History of Zululand*. Wilderness Leadership School. Durban: Bellair.

Fortelius, M. 1983. 'The morphology and paleobiological significance of the horns of *Coelodonta antiquitatis* (Mammalia: Rhinocerotidae)'. *Journal of Vertebrate Paleontology*, 3 (2).

Fortelius, M. & Kappelman, J. 1993. 'The largest land mammal ever imagined'. *Zoological Journal of the Linnaean Society*, 107.

Gerstaecker, F. 1853. 'Rhinoceros hunting in Java'. *Reynolds's Miscellany of Romance, General Literature, Science, and Art*, 10.

Gibb, H. A. R., Kramers, J. H., Lévi-Provençal, E., Schacht, J., Lewis, B. & Ch. Pellat. 1960. *Encyclopaedia of Islam*. 2nd ed. Vol. I, A–B. Leiden: Brill.

Groves, C. P. & Leslie, D. M. 2011. '*Rhinoceros sondaicus*'. American Society of Mammalogists, *Mammalian Species*, 43.

Gurung, K. K. 1983. *Heart of the Jungle*. London: Andre Deutsch.

Hall-Martin, A., Walker, C. & Bothma, J du P. 1988. *Kaokoveld: The Last Wilderness*. Johannesburg: Southern Books.

Hariyadi, A., Priambudi, A., Setiawan, R., Daryan, D., Yayus, A. & Purnama, H. 2011. 'Estimating the population structure of Javan rhinos (*Rhinoceros sondaicus*) in Ujung Kulon National Park using the mark recapture method based on video and camera trap identification'. *Pachyderm*, 49.

Harris, W. Cornwallis 1986. *Portraits of the Game and Wild Animals of Southern Africa*. Alberton, South Africa: GALAGO.

Hieronymus, T. L. & Witmer, L. M. 2004. 'Rhinoceros horn attachment: anatomy and histology of a dermally influenced bone rugosity'. *Journal of Morphology*, 260.

Hieronymus, T. L., Witmer, L. M. & Ridgely, R. C. 2006. 'Structure of white rhinoceros (*Ceratotherium simum*) horn investigated by x-ray computed tomography and histology with implications for growth and external form'. *Journal of Morphology*, 267.

Hitchins, P. 1975. 'The black rhinoceros in South Africa'. *EWT Newsletter*, 2.

Hitchins, P. 2002. 'Historical notes on the Khama Rhino Sanctuary, Botswana'. Unpublished.

Holman, D. 1969. *Inside Safari Hunting*. London: W. H. Allen & Co.

Hunter, J. A. 1952. *Hunter*. London: Hamish Hamilton.

Janssen, L. 1647. *The Diary of Leendert Janssen*. The Hague
  Archives.
Joubert, E. 1996. *On the Clover Trail*. Windhoek: Gamsberg
  Macmillan.

Lacombat, F. 2005. 'The evolution of the rhinoceros'. Save the
  Rhinos: EAZA Rhino Campaign 2005/6 info pack. London: Save
  the Rhinos.
Laufer, B. 1913. 'Arabic and Chinese trade in walrus and narwhal
  ivory'. *T'oung Pao*, 14.
Laurie, W. A. 1978. 'The ecology and behaviour of the greater one-
  horned rhinoceros'. PhD thesis, Selwyn College, University of
  Cambridge.
Leader-Williams, N. 1992. 'The world trade in rhino horn: a review'.
  A TRAFFIC network report.
Leader-Williams, N. & Albon, S. D. 1988. 'Allocation of resources
  for conservation'. *Nature*, 336.
Leakey, R. & Lewin, R. 1995. *The Sixth Extinction*. New York:
  Doubleday.
Lefeuvre, J. 1990. 'Rhinoceros and wild buffaloes north of the Yellow
  River at the end of the Shang Dynasty. *Monumenta Serica*, 39.
Lopes, T., Chermack, T., Demers, D., Kari, M., Kasshanna, B. &
  Payne, T. 2009. *Human Extinction Scenario Frameworks*. Denver:
  University of Colorado.
Lynch, L., Robinson, V. & Anderson, C. 1973. 'A scanning electron
  microscope study of the morphology of rhinoceros horn'.
  Australian Journal of Biological Science, 26.

Maguire, J. 1998. *Makapansgat: A Guide to the Palaeontological
  and Archaeological Sites of the Makapansgat Valley*. Pretoria:
  Transvaal Museum.
Marais, E. 1972. *The Road to Waterberg and Other Essays*. Pretoria:
  Human & Rousseau.
Marina, C. 1991. *Kenya: World Travel Guide*. London: Bartholomew.

Martin, E. B. 1983. *Rhino Exploitation: The Trade in Rhino Products in India, Indonesia, Malaysia, Burma, Japan & South Korea*. Preface by Talbot, L. M. Hong Kong: WWF.

Martin, E. B. 1985. 'Rhinos and daggers: a major conservation problem'. *Oryx*, 19 (4).

Martin, E. B. & Martin, C. B. 1982. *Run Rhino Run*. London: Chatto & Windus.

Martin, E. B. & Vigne, L. 1992. 'Zimbabwe's rhinos under threat'. *SWARA*, 15.

Martin, E. B. & Vigne, L. 1997. 'An historical perspective of the Yemeni rhino horn trade'. *Pachyderm*, 23.

Milledge, S. 2007. 'Rhino-related crimes in Africa: an overview of poaching, seizure and stockpile data for the period 2000–2005'. CoP14 Information Document: CoP14 Inf. 41, CITES Secretariat, The Hague.

Miller, J. 1969. *The Spice Trade of the Roman Empire, 29 BC to AD 641*. Oxford: Clarendon Press.

Milliken, T., Emslie, R. & Talukdar, B. 2009. 'African and Asian rhinoceroses: status, conservation and trade'. CoP15 Document: CoP15 Doc. 45.1 Annex, CITES Secretariat, Geneva, Switzerland.

Mountain, A. 1990. *Paradise Under Pressure*. Johannesburg: Southern Books.

Newman, K. 2002. *Birds of Southern Africa*. Cape Town: Struik Publishers.

Norton, P. & Associates. Undated. 'Mapungubwe National Park and World Heritage Site'. South Africa: Department of Environmental Affairs and Tourism.

Olver, C. 2010. 'Can't park a problem'. *Sunday Times*, 25 November.

Parker, J. T. 2010. *Chinese Unicorn*. <http://www.chinese-unicorn.com/qilin/book>.

Pienaar, D., Hall-Martin, A. & Hitchins, P. 1991. 'Horn growth rates of free-ranging white and black rhinoceros'. *Koedoe*, 34.

Pitman, D. 1991. *Rhinos: Past, Present and Future?* Harare: Roblaw Publishers.

Platter, E. 1990. 'Going all the way for a black rhino'. *Style*, September.

Player, I. 1972. *The White Rhino Saga*. London: Collins.

Player, I. 2011. 'Rhino's plaintive cry should reach all our hearts'. *Business Day*, 3 August.

Prothero, D. R. 1991. 'Fifty million years of rhinoceros evolution'. In Ryder, O. A. (ed) *Proceedings of the International Rhino Conference*. San Diego: San Diego Zoological Society.

Rachlow, J. L. & Berger, J. 1997. 'Conservation implications of patterns of horn regeneration in dehorned white rhinos'. *Conservation Biology*, 11.

Raup, D. & Sepkoski, J. 1986. 'Periodic extinction of families and genera'. *Science*, 231.

Raven-Hart, R. 1967. *Before Van Riebeeck: Callers at South Africa from 1488 to 1652*. Cape Town: Struik Publishers.

Rookmaaker, L. C. 1981. 'Early rhinoceros systematics'. *Papers from the Conference to Celebrate the Centenary of the British Museum (Natural History)*. London: Society for the Bibliography of Natural History.

Rookmaaker, L. C. 2002. 'The quest for Roualeyn Gordon Cumming's rhinoceros horns'. *Archives of Natural History*, 29.

Rookmaaker, L. C. 2003. 'Why the name of the white rhinoceros is not appropriate'. *Pachyderm*, 34.

Rookmaaker, L. C. 2004. 'The slow recognition of the African rhinoceros from Hondius to Campher'. *Nijmegen Studies in Development and Cultural Change*, 44.

Rookmaaker, L. C. 2005. 'Review of the European perception of the African rhinoceros'. *Journal of Zoology*, 265.

Rookmaaker, L. C., Nelson, B. & Dorrington, D. 2005. 'The royal hunt of tiger and rhinoceros in the Nepalese terai in 1911'. *Pachyderm*, 38.

Ryder, M. L. 1962. 'Structure of rhinoceros horn'. *Nature*, 193.

Scholfield, A. F. 1958. *On the Characteristics of Animals*. English translation of Claudius Aelian. London: Harvard University Press.

Selous, F. C. 1908. *African Nature: Notes and Reminiscences*. London: Macmillan.

Shepard, O. 1982. *The Lore of the Unicorn*. New York: Avenel Books.

Skead, C. J. 1980. *The Historical Mammal Incidence in the Cape Province*. Cape Town: Department of Nature and Environmental Conservation of the Provincial Administration of the Cape of Good Hope.

Soame, J. 1957. 'The Chinese rhinoceros and Chinese carvings in rhinoceros horn'. *Transactions of the Oriental Ceramic Society 1954–1955*, 29.

Swanepoel, G. 1996. 'The illegal trade in rhino horn as an example of an endangered species'. Paper presented at the Third International Criminological Congress hosted by IDASA and CRIMSA at UNISA, South Africa.

't Sas-Rolfes, M. 2012. 'The rhino poaching crisis: a market analysis'. Privately published.

Tiley, S. 2004. *Mapungubwe*. Cape Town: Sunbird Publishing.

Van Strien, N. J. 1986. 'The Sumatran rhinoceros, *Dicerorhinus sumatrensis*, in the Gunung Leuser National Park, Sumatra, Indonesia: its distribution, ecology and conservation'. *Mammalia Depicta*, 12.

Van Strien, N. J. 2005. 'Javan rhinoceros'. Save the Rhinos: EAZA Rhino Campaign 2005/6 info pack. London: Save the Rhinos.

Van Strien, N. J. 2005. 'Sumatran rhinoceros'. Save the Rhinos: EAZA Rhino Campaign 2005/6 info pack. London: Save the Rhinos.

Van Strien, N. J. & Rookmaaker, L. C. 2010. 'The impact of the Krakatoa eruption in 1883 on the population of *Rhinoceros sondaicus* in Ujung Kulon, with details of rhino observations from 1857 to 1949'. *Journal of Threatened Taxa*, 2.

Vigne, L. & Martin, E. B. 1989. 'Taiwan: the greatest threat to the survival of Africa's rhinos'. *Pachyderm*, 11.

Vincent, J. & Geddes Page, J. 1983. *Back from the Brink: The White Rhino Story*. Pietermaritzburg: Natal Parks Board.

Walker, C. 1992. 'Botswana aerial census'. *Rhino & Elephant Journal*, 7.

Walker, C. 1996. *Signs of the Wild*. Cape Town: Struik Publishers.

Walker, C. & Bothma, J du P. 2005. *Soul of the Waterberg*. Johannesburg: Waterberg Publishers & African Sky Publishing.

Walker, C. & Potgieter, H. 1989. *Okavango from the Air*. Cape Town: Struik Publishers.

Yanyan, D. & Qian, J. 2008. 'Proposal on protecting and sustainable use of rhinoceros' [in Chinese]. Institute of Scientific & Technical Information of China, *Resource Development & Market*, 24. In 'Wrathful rhino'. *You*, 6 October 1988.

Zafir, A., Di Payne, J., Mohamed, A., Lau, C. F., Sharma, D. S. K., Amirtharaj, R. A., Williams, C., Nathan, S., Ramono, W. S. & Clements, G. R. 2011. 'Now or never: what will it take to save the Sumatran rhinoceros, *Dicerorhinus sumatrensis*, from extinction?' *Oryx*, 45.

Zhufan, X. & Xiaokai, H. (eds) 1984. *Dictionary of Traditional Chinese Medicine*. Hong Kong: The Commercial Press.